The Iconic Dr. Johnson

Biography of an Image

Stefan Scheuermann

"The Iconic Dr. Johnson: Biography of an Image," by Stefan Scheuermann. ISBN 978-1-62137-911-9 (softcover).

Published 2016 by Virtualbookworm.com Publishing Inc., P.O. Box 9949, College Station, TX , 77842, US.

Table of Contents

Introduction

LITERATURE ILLUMINATES those universal threads that are sewn through the lives of all people, reminding us of our connectedness with the whole of our species. Unfortunately, generations of cultural and linguistic evolution have separated current readers from the full meaning and impact of the great English literature of our past. We may read these texts, but without an understanding of the cultural references, intended by the authors to intensify the impact of their narratives, great English literature from the previous centuries has lost much of its illuminative power. Yet, these books are still popular today, even with a weak understanding of the cultural references within. This is a testament to the power they must have had over their original readers, and a hint at the power they may yet have over current readers. In an attempted remedy, this book sketches the details of one cultural phenomenon riddled throughout the English literature and the discourse of English society from the 18th into the 20th century, Dr. Samuel Johnson.

Samuel Johnson was an 18th century author, poet, biographer, essayist, and lexicographer. He reached the height of his living fame after the publication of his *Dictionary of the English Language* in 1755. His image in the mind of the English public grew to iconic status before his death in 1784. After his death, his public persona exploded into a social phenomenon, increased and perpetuated by the literary figures who adored him and enshrined his image in their own publications. This is not a biography of Samuel Johnson. There has been magnificent and historical work on that front. There is little of significance that I could add to that august body. This is the story of Dr. Johnson's image. It tells the tale of the readers and writers of English literature, and how they have created, embraced, rejected, gilded, tarnished, and eventually destroyed the popular image of the most iconic figure

1

in English literature from the late 18th century into the 20th century.

This book is intended to serve two purposes. The first is purely academic. It is to map the image of Dr. Johnson through the centuries, as it evolves, mutates, and drastically affects the path of English literature. It is an exercise in English literary historical theory. Johnson's image is explored and mapped simply because it should be. Any cultural phenomenon with such a wide and deep reach into life and literature deserves to be plotted and documented. Accomplishing this required the exploration of several interdisciplinary avenues. The book begins with an historical study of England's middle-class upward momentum, an environment only inside of which could a figure like Samuel Johnson have attained such an iconic social and literary status. To illuminate the exact contours of that iconic figure, the research employs multiple genres of literature, from Johnson's own literary and moral canon, as derived from his published writing, through the critical commentary on his work and the biographical dissections of his life, to the many references to Johnson utilized for literary effect by novelists who both described and prescribed Johnson's public image in the wielding of their art.

It is this last genre that supplies the second purpose of this book. Johnson's name and image are prolifically employed by Victorian novelists, generally for the establishment of character. The references are dropped with an understanding and assumption of the image of Johnson in the minds of the readers at the time of publication. These great Victorian novels are still popular today. But the many references to Johnson, which often play a crucial role in the establishment of character or in the development of plot, are not understood by current readers, readers in a society and literary atmosphere where Samuel Johnson's name comparatively carries little weight or meaning. But it would not be enough to understand Samuel Johnson. A biographical study of Johnson would not provide current readers with the full meaning of these Johnson references, neither would a literary study of Johnson's publications. For that reason, this book only notes the biographical details relevant to, or in the establishment of, Johnson's public image. It is necessary to understand Johnson as he was perceived by the writers who employed his public persona to their literary ends. The factual Johnson is well dissected, in a great many vivid biographies. His literary achievements have been run through thousands of scholarly criticisms. None of these tell the current reading public who he was to these writers who referenced him or what those references meant to their contemporary readers. This project intends to document the birth, adolescence, prime, decline, and death of Johnson's public image, pinpointing the momentary perception of the icon during each of several distinct phases of its reign, returning the potency of the authors' initial intent to the many classic works of literature that reference Johnson and presenting current readers of those works an experience much nearer that of the original readers than could possibly be had without a clear and multi-angled understanding of the Johnson references within.

I developed this idea while reading Thomas Hardy's *Far From the Madding Crowd*. Presented with a Johnson reference on page one, rather than skimming over it as a lost and passé reference, I recalled other Johnson references that had gone unexplained in my reading and set myself to explore the phenomenon. Entirely unaware of the massive and often tumultuous ocean of Johnsonian-ism upon which I had just embarked, I began digging through Victorian literature for references to Samuel Johnson. Two peculiarities about the references I found stood tallest, especially in light of Johnson's relative obscurity today. The first was the sheer volume of Johnson references. This project grew quickly as the story of Johnson's image expanded with my research. The second peculiarity was the casual nature with which Johnson references are dropped by Victorian authors. No explanation was made to clarify the references or to explain the authors' intent. The references were written with an understanding that the authors' vision of Johnson was universally shared by the readership. I realized that a socio-literary figure would have to be tremendously iconic for so many different authors, spread throughout so many decades, to write under that same assumption.

As I began to place my finger on the Victorian-Johnsonian pulse, the scenes and imagery meant to be relayed and intensified by references to Johnson began to appear to me in greater number and profounder weight, a weight which I imagine was growing nearer to the intent of the authors who wrote them. I thought about the current readers, perusing these volumes with, at best, a weak notion of the nature of Johnson's image at the time. At this point, my goals for the project shifted from the purely academic mapping of a literary phenomenon, toward a more service-oriented obligation to pump some warm, youthful blood back into the veins of some of the English language's most revered writing. I took note of the fact that most of the cinematic representations of these classic narratives (cresting and waning in propagation and popularity) entirely dismissed all references to Johnson, even in the cases when Johnson's image is an omnipresent facet of the original narrative. Some screen adaptations left one or two uses of Johnson's name but diminished the role of the Johnson image, presumably based on the assumption that the current viewers would fail to catch the Johnsonian ball when it was thrown to them. I acutely felt the tragedy of the current readership's loss of intimacy with their favorite authors. Of course, there are many other lost or misunderstood components of the Victorian Literary Era, like all past eras, causing a dilution of the original intentions of the authors of the period. This book will not return all of the lost components. But it will attempt to intensify the flavor inherent in the original references to Dr. Johnson. For many of the narratives, the Johnson image is so dominant over the other components that its return should bring current readers refreshingly near the intensity of the original flavor.

I entered the research with a single reference to Johnson, and hope that a handful more might provide a complete enough circumspection of the matter to triangulate the nature of Johnson's image during a couple of the more prolific years of its literary usage. Years of sifting through texts, some tremendously famous and others quite obscure, yielded in small portions shards of a massive mural. Some of the shards were larger than others, but none significant enough to give a revealing clue to the nature of the entire image. With few exceptions, the contribution of each individual shard did little to enhance the whole. Eventually enough pieces were in place to see roughly where the pieces were taking me.

During the height of its iconic fame, the name of Samuel Johnson was the most recognizable name in the Anglophonic world. Johnson's plummet into obscurity has made impotent hundreds of powerful literary references that made full employment of that recognition. The great beauty of these classic works should return to the current reading public, who both deserve and desperately crave intimacy with this literature. A reintroduction is needed. An intimacy must be rekindled. Great writers like Elizabeth Gaskell, Charlotte Bronte, William Thackeray, Benjamin Disraeli, and Charles Dickens can once again nestle beside their adoring readers, snuggling under the same blanket, beside the same fireplace, and sip a warm drink with the same tender intimacy as they did with the readers of their own time.

Chapter 1

Fertilizing the Soil that Grew and Flowered Johnsonian-ism

THE JOHNSON SOCIAL PHENOMENON grew and flourished in a soil fertilized by centuries of historical events. Before embracing the life of the phenomenon, the historical soil in which it grew must first be evaluated. Both during his lifetime and in the centuries beyond, Johnson was a middle-class hero. It was Johnson's position in the middle-class, and his ability to rise to the very heights of social acclaim, that fueled his iconic rise. A man too poor to remain in college died as a literary giant, whose notice was an honor for any member of society. Johnson's intimate social circle became London's most coveted company. His fame was the flower of a long developing middle-class growth and upward momentum in England, one that began with absolute segregation between the nobility and the working classes and continued to eventually elevate the son of a poor bookseller to the zenith of social and scholarly eminence, enshrining in the hearts of a nation the most awkwardly unlikely hero to saturate a language's literature. That ever-upward moving middle-class momentum began in the wake of the plague, hit its apex in the Glorious Revolution, blossomed during the Augustan Age, and reached full maturity during the Victorian literary era. Johnson's development into an icon can be traced directly along that path. It is a continuation of the same story. For that reason, this book begins with the initial growth and movement of the middle-class, the events that nurtured its growth, and the historical contributors to its speed and force, focusing primarily on the events that would either kill the momentum or send it sailing perpetually forward in time, the events surrounding the Glorious Revolution in 1688.

England's Glorious Revolution was built of three primary revolutionary materials. The foundation was commerce and the commercial opportunities for the social advancement of the revolutionaries. The support structure was politics. The revolution of 1688 and the subsequent struggles to cement its accomplishments were the apex of the struggle between monarchal absolutism and constitutionalism. The final material, the religious aspect, served mostly as a façade for the structure of the revolution; giving it a palatable hue for the contemporary support of the revolution while also serving as an excuse by the winning liberal Whigs for the continued reverence of the revolution through the following centuries. The façade became the identifying characteristic, not the foundation or support. Ultimately, the religious aspect of the Glorious Revolution is only the lingering sentiments of an earlier struggle of an earlier age, which was used as propaganda and a distraction from the real merits of the revolution. Religion lies far from the true heart of the revolution and can therefore be almost entirely excluded from study focused on the foundation of the revolution, the immediate commercial implications, and the larger battle of political philosophies. The commercial opportunities for the social advancement of the middle-class and the associated political entanglements are the true story of the Glorious Revolution, a story that began with the birth and improvement of that class' commercial prospects in the wake of the plague outbreak of 1348 and continued to its ultimate victory in the bourgeoisie dominated Augustan Age. Johnson's advancements to the pinnacle of social acclaim and the rise of his long lingering iconic image are quite natural and expected results of the historic occurrences that preceded them.

If an event, or series of events, is to be credited with fathering the strong and influential middle-class from which Johnson arose, it must be the outbreak of plague, particularly the 1348 outbreak, even though London's 1665 outbreak had the more direct effect on the Glorious Revolution. Although London first saw the plague in the year 664, then again in 1258 [1], it was the infamous 1348-49 outbreak that set the wheels in motion for the rise of a powerful and affluent middle-class. The century prior to the 1348 outbreak witnessed a tremendous population boom in Europe. This contributed to the spread of the plague through urban over-crowding and created an economic infrastructure accustomed to a massive labor class. It was this class that suffered the greatest losses in 1348-49 [2]. In less than a year, the labor force was drastically diminished. The shell of the standing economic infrastructure could not easily adjust to a fraction of its previous work force. Those laborers who survived found themselves in an unfamiliar position of demand, with unprecedented control of work conditions and pay. For the first time, the labor class had negotiating power with their employers [3]. As the labor population recovered and again diminished with subsequent outbreaks, the lord to labor relationship evolved into one of mutual need. The labor class had a muscle to flex. This loud commercial voice translated to a loud political voice.

The changes in the acceptance of science and the promotion of inter-related fields, such as art and philosophy, associated with the Renaissance, rode into Europe on the back of devastation. Certainly a project like *Johnson's Dictionary*, with its scientific categorization of language, can look back and credit the events of 1348 and their results as a cardinal and imperative prerequisite of its existence. The tremendous loss of life, from the plague, created new economic realities which filtered throughout all aspects of society. The all-encompassing wave of modernization began with some rotting food in the post-plague fields of Europe. When looking at the massive casualties from the plague and comparing them beside the economic make-up of medieval Europe, it is understood that the majority of the deaths were in the proletariat, the lower, wage-earning class. With the majority of the work force dead, surviving laborers found themselves with substantial bargaining power. Serfs demanded plots of land as payment for their services. Their demands were granted, for without their work, the land owning elite would have no income [3]. This created an entire new class of property owners, not as established or affluent as the pre-plague nobility, but a class of people who would soon wield significant political and economic power.

The economic shake-up did not stop at the rural manor. Urban wages rose by as much as 100 percent in the decades immediately following the plague [4]. The hand of industrialization was forced by the lack of sufficient agricultural production. Local economies began to rely more on the manufacturing of trade goods. Although agricultural production decreased significantly from pre-plague outputs, the population decrease was more severe. Per capita agricultural production actually increased in the 1350's [4]. This event lowered produce prices and drove the proletariat into the urban centers. Suddenly, the socio-economic system had some wiggle room. The previously implacable economic and social stratum became more fluid, and people seized their new opportunities to break through the ceiling of their economic class and create a wealthy middle-class [3]. Even the urban laborers used their higher wages against the drastic drop in land prices. Out of the ashes of the plague rose a new class of citizens, the bourgeoisie. Everything became about the one commodity least available to the pre-plague masses, land. As Karl Marx would later put it when speaking of England's Glorious Revolution, "They inaugurated the new era by practicing on a colossal scale the theft of state land" [5]. Marx spoke of land being given away, cheaply sold, and even annexed for private use. He went on to say, "The bourgeois capitalists favored the operation with the view to promoting free trade in land" [5]. The events of 1688 were the most significant milestone toward the destination of a journey begun by the serfs and laborers in the neglected, rotting, labor-deficient fields in the wake of the plague of 1348.

This new middle-class had room for plenty of inhabitants. Families with centuries of serfdom behind them rushed this new expanse, each in the steps of the previous, all the way down to the lowest in society. As each slice of society moved upward, abandoning their previous position, those beneath seized that position. Virtually all of lower society improved their social position. The upper classes, with their heads against the social ceiling could go no higher. It would be unrealistic to say that they declined much in position. But their proportionate position to those beneath them was drastically altered. The decline of serfdom had begun and the rise of a wealthy peasant class bubbled to the surface alongside the new bourgeois land owners[3]. These new classes had no precedent of identity or expectations. It did not take long for them to create one. Wanting to distance themselves from the stigma of their impoverished past, they altered their behavior, beliefs, in fact, their very process of thought.

As the demographic of pre-plague serfs entered the sphere of the affluent, they also entered the sphere of the literate. Having not entirely shaken the culture of their serfdom past, they brought it with them into their new sphere, creating a brand new set of literate sensibilities. Published literature had to adjust to the desires and expectations of a new reading demographic. Evidence of the expanded literati comes in the form of the long poems of the 15th century. Poems such as John Lydgate's *Troy Book*, a 1420 work of over 30,000 lines, and Henry Lovelich's 1450 poem, *Merlin*, with over 27,000 lines, were far too long to be intended for the recitation of minstrels [6]. These poems were written to be read by a rapidly expanding literate public. Not only was the length of poetry affected. The subjects of literature bore the sensibilities and interest of a slice of society just a couple generations out of serfdom. Unlike the rigid sensual imitations of Antiquity, or the mystical and moral dictates of the medieval sermon, these new long poems covered topics fanciful and imaginative, such as the Arthurian legends, topics of oral tradition dragged with them from the traditions of the new bourgeoisie's illiterate grandparents. But this alone would not have been enough to lift a character like Johnson to the heights of literary acclaim. It would not have promoted him to the personification of what is quintessentially British.

Remnants of Ancient Roman greatness lingered all over Western Europe, in both architecture and literature. In their quest to create and secure a new identity, the bourgeoisie likened themselves to the land owners of Ancient Rome. They embraced the literature, and subsequently, the poetry, science and philosophy therein. This was eventually reflected in the title of an era of society and literature dominated by them. This new class' hunger for an admirable identity drove a new acceptance of and common access to classical knowledge and ideals, contrasting them severely to the superstitious pagan/Christians who shot in the dark for explanations and cures for the very same plague that elevated them to their new positions.

The study of Classical philosophy, particularly Athenian philosophy, shined a new light on the established political order, rendering unpalatable the limited control the previous systems of government allowed the new classes. Having soared so high, so quickly, their focus was up, and that is where they intended to keep moving. They grasped political power and they did so with force. It was their strangle hold on the economy and the purse strings of the upper classes that permitted their firm political stance. In the 1350's and following decades, unprecedented labor strikes occurred. Simply crushing the labor uprisings, in accordance with tradition, would have had a devastating effect on the economy. There was no mass of unemployed laborers to take their places. Political reforms were the last, desperate efforts of the ruling classes to maintain peace under the demands of the rising new classes [7]. These reforms invited the middle-class even higher into the previous sphere of the elite. Political influence allowed the broad spread of their adopted Classical Greco-Roman culture. Literacy continued to spread with the popularity, influence, and growth of the new classes. Literary figures became the property of these classes. They arose but never reached the gilded and deified status that the figure of Johnson would reach because the stability of the new classes was not yet fully secured and they were not yet so fully steeped in literary tradition to place a literary figure from their own ranks to the most enviable heights of social influence.

A brief mention of the religious aspect of these changes must be made, not as it relates to theological belief but as it relates to political self-determination. The Catholic Church clung to Dark Age social precedents. The new bourgeoisie and political urban

12

labor class were not to live under the boot of any tyrant, whether that tyrant was an oppressive system of serfdom, an abusive upper-class, an absolutist monarch, or a pope who wished to reach the glove of religion into every aspect of society and life. The backlash against Catholicism began as a political stance and was only translated to a theological issue for the support of those disconnected with the political issues or unable to understand them. And just as population increases began to threaten a return to any semblance of pre-plague conditions and superstitious blind devotion to church, another outbreak would ensure the continuation of the new political and economic order [8]. Small circles of Dark Age ignorance reared its head during those outbreaks, as it still does during times of doubt and despair. But the creation of the new socio-economic classes could not be undone and progress has followed perpetually in their wake. In the generation before the Glorious Revolution, plague was united with the other result of urban crowding to put the final pieces in play for middle-class revolution.

The years of 1665 & 1666 dealt Londoners a one-two punch of plague and fire. The 1665 plague outbreak devastated the city. The year recorded a confirmed 55,797 deaths from a city population of 459,000, or about 12.2 percent. Estimates through 1666 are between 70,000 and 100,000 [1]. In his famous diary, Samuel Pepys records the losses of individuals he knew. On July 31, he wrote the deaths of "Proctor, the vintner of the Miter, in Woodstreet, and his son." On August 8, it was "poor Will that used to sell us ale, his wife and three children dead" [9]. Pepys recorded many more deaths in his diary, most of which were businessmen with whom he had acquaintance. As London recovered and commercial norms returned, the positions of Pepys' dead associates had to be filled. They would not be filled from above. They were filled by those ambitious members of the lower classes. Middle-class commercial positions, previously held by a more complacent, stagnant, established breed of middle-class businessmen, who had long been firmly wedged into their social position by the inflexible layers of social strata above them, were assumed by a population on the rise. Their

13

upward momentum did not cease when they settled into their new positions. They wanted to rub elbows with the aristocrats and were able to do so as middle-class commerce brought the negotiation rooms into middle-class settings. Taverns, ale houses, and coffee houses became the primary locations for the striking of commercial deals [1]. To survive economically, aristocrats had to seek these arenas of business and deal eye-to-eye with business partners whose recent ancestors had worked their lands as faceless serfs, virtual property of the estate. They were willing to do so because of the immense economic benefit the commercial revolution had to offer anyone willing to play its game, by its rules. The economic expansion of England circled around its primary port and the middle-class urban locations of social confluence. The gentry and the laborers hobnobbed, for the economic benefit of both, in ways unseen at court. This previously unprecedented interaction between classes serves as foreshadowing toward Johnson's attendance at Oxford and his eventual affiliation with English society's most notable names. The identity of England had become commercial in nature and was forged in the streets of London, not the palaces of the King or the estates of the rural aristocracy. The English greatness associated with the economic boom was a middle-class greatness and the middle-class knew it. Although there was a mutual symbiosis, the merchants were hosting this party and the aristocracy had to present all of the cordial niceties and delicacies of a visiting guest. Plague cleared a path for the rise and perpetual advancement of a labor class who had been faceless commodities of the wealthy in the High Middle Ages. They became quite wealthy themselves and a necessary part of the economic security of the established commercial classes. The destruction from fire kept money flowing downward.

The fire of 1666 destroyed 13,200 houses, 87 parish churches, and damaged or destroyed almost every structure within the city gates. An estimated 70,000 people were made homeless by the fire [1]. Many suffered exposure the following winter. The urgency to rebuild was prodigious; not just to house the homeless, but to recover the infrastructure of commerce in what was approaching

Amsterdam as the world's grandest trade port. Who would rebuild the city? Who stood to gain from the massive project? It was not those who paid for the reconstruction. It was those who were paid for the skilled and unskilled labor, a force significantly diminished by a plague outbreak that had ended the same year. The combined disasters gave incredible opportunity to the surviving working-class to advance itself commercially. Momentum is a key consideration when looking at the rising middle-class and its reluctance to slow its advancement. There was little time for stagnation. The commercial revolution was moving quickly and quality of life changes were noticeable on a yearly basis, not a generational basis. The thought of sharing the fate of the subjects of Louis XIV and those under papal control bore a rancid aroma to the bourgeois noses that were pointed upward and accustomed to sweeter smells and loftier prospects.

In 1670, Anne, the wife of James, Duke of York, converted to Catholicism. The conversion was kept secret. By 1673, James' inclination toward conversion hit the public ear. In 1676, the Pope acknowledged James' conversion, setting off a long parliamentary struggle to remove James from the line of royal succession [5]. Again, the tone of these events was political, not theological. The concerns of those opposed to a return to a Catholic England were political and commercial concerns. The last place the advancing new classes wanted to look was backward. James' conversion and position as heir to his brother Charles II forced the bourgeois eyes over their shoulders, harkening them to a time they would prefer to leave in the past. Fortunately for them, they had climbed high enough to be in a position to prevent their fears from actualizing. The sound of civil war cannons were still ringing in their ears. The bitterness from hearing Charles I's defiance, as he asked by what authority did the Parliamentarians hold him on trial, reemerged. The Restoration was a quick fix to a desperate situation. It was also a step backward. The prospect of a Roman King and life under the perceived tyrannical papal thumb must have given the newly affluent middle-class a sense of walls closing around them. The animal was free and terrified of the prospect of returning to the cage. One century later, Johnson's rejection and defiance of aristocratic literary patronage and the subsequent liberation of his industry owe their very spirit to this middle-class refusal to be pushed backward. Charles II's dissolution of Parliament was all of the evidence needed to justify their fear of the cage. Parliamentary power had increased by force. But the law still granted the king the right to dissolve Parliament and call for new elections [5]. A perpetually reassembling Parliament could never get its feet beneath it to wield the influence it had worked hard to procure. The bourgeois political wheels were still spinning but spinning in place with the risk of sliding backward. The highly celebrated Restoration probably began to seem like a rash and poorly thought response to the "dictatorship of the proletariat" under Cromwell. The English bourgeoisie began to look for a third option. But stability was needed while that option was explored. Another civil war would set England in a perpetual cycle, to the benefit of none involved. A moderate response was in order, the success of which would set "moderation" as the cornerstone of British qualities.

On April 27, 1679, debates in the Commons about the preservation of the king turned focus toward James, as MPs unanimously viewed James' Catholicism and position as heir to the throne as an invitation to more Popish plots on Charles' life [5]. They had not forgotten the attempts on the life of the highly revered, and by this time deified, Queen Elizabeth. Charles refused to allow changes to succession but agreed to terms allowing certain executive powers to pass to Parliament during the reign of a Catholic king. This was a highly satisfactory concession. Since a Catholic King's theology was of absolutely no relevance and the continental influence over the king and his policies was primary, the concession shifting power to Parliament, where it could not be handed over to the Pope or Louis XIV, probably prevented another civil war. Support was not unanimous. Parliament was divided in its response to the king's offer. Some were ready to draw up papers on the king's recommendations. Others continued efforts to prohibit a popish successor and suggested Mary Stuart, the Princess of Orange, for succession [5]. The third option was coming to light and being made brighter with every snub of parliamentary power by the Crown.

On May 21, a bill excluding James from succession passed the Commons. This flexing of parliamentary muscle was enough to alarm the king to prorogue Parliament again. The new Parliament was to meet on October 7. Under pressure from James, Charles prorogued Parliament for another eighty days. The organization of public processions against James, plus petitions presented personally to the king to set elections for a new Parliament, only led Charles to announce another postponement, this time until November 1680. The pressure continued and Charles announced on August 26 that Parliament would reconvene in October. A new Exclusion Bill was introduced on November 4. Parliament had high hopes of the king's support because they attached a generous executive budget to the bill. This new bill suggested that, for the purposes of succession, James should be considered dead, passing the throne to the heir in the case of James' death, his daughter Mary. At this point, eight years before William landed in England, a bill for the reign of William and Mary already came through the Commons. Charles refused it but suggested that James take the throne and Mary rule during James' reign. This was not good enough for Parliament. They did not trust the arrangement considering Charles' previous advocacy for his brother. They wanted an exclusion bill [5].

Parliament had another reason not to trust any deal proposed by Charles. Charles had amassed a significant standing army. Parliament had to wonder why. Discontent with the king's lack of cooperation with Parliament, and his clear lack of scruples in proroguing the body, must have given both King and Parliament flashbacks to the Civil War. Charles II was prepared as his father never was. The king's standing army could have crushed any force Parliament could have conjured, especially considering how seldom Parliament was sitting in counsel. Concern also abounded about Charles' liaisons with his cousin Louis XIV and what plans the two may have been cooking to bring England to a style of absolute monarchal rule like that of Louis' France [10]. Under such rule, Parliament, with its bourgeoisie base, precariously perched on the edge of modernity, would be stomped back into the Middle-Ages and that heritage they had long struggled to erase. Parliament's survival instinct for their cherished political self-determination kicked in strongly. This political issue was a bourgeoisie concern, echoing only in that particular layer of society. In either course, the established aristocracy had little to lose or gain. Similar was the case with the poor. The bourgeoisie had everything to lose. Their very identity and existence as a layer in the economic and political system was at stake. There was no place for an active, affluent, and politically influential middle-class in a Louis-style absolutism.

With so much at stake, factional tension between liberal Whig party and conservative royalist Tories climaxed. Whigs drew propaganda connections between James and Mary Tudor. Tories compared Whigs to the Puritans who killed Charles I [5]. Neither held hopes of swaying the other side. These campaigns had their sights on public sensibilities. Although Popish concerns were not atop bourgeois fears, the public Popish frenzy kept Whigs in control of Parliament [10]. The instability of the time was brought into sharp relief by the insurrection of the Duke of Monmouth. James Scott, Duke of Monmouth, the eldest illegitimate son of Charles II, landed two ships of poorly equipped rebels at Lyme on June 11, 1684. The ill-fated insurrection had no chance of securing the throne and resulted in the Duke's beheading [5]. Still, the incident left Parliament in fear of the instability of the government, of invasion, and speculation as to their own fates should one of these insurrections succeed. The moderate order, reason, and steady flow of the status quo, required for the continued affluence of the middle class, was seriously threatened by any threat of war, like Monmouth's insurrection. Matters had to be taken into their own hands to create a stability that would receive popular support with the right propaganda promotion, secure them the powers of political self-determination, and sever the frightening connection between their own monarch and the royal absolutist, Louis XIV. It had to be done in a way that would not offend the popular desire for dynastic congruency. The bourgeois commercial connection with the Dutch coincided neatly with a Stuart marriage to a Dutch prince to satisfy these needs. Although Samuel Johnson, as a self-proclaimed, devout Tory, came to consider the events of the Glorious Revolution a "necessary evil", the proverbial eggshells that the bourgeois Whigs were forced to walk upon during the turmoil preceding 1688 established the exact sort of English sensibilities that promoted Johnson's stardom.

On February 6, 1685, Charles II died. The death seemed universally mourned for a few reasons. First, Charles had committed support of the Church of England toward the end of his life. Second, he maintained support of his brother James. This appealed to the other side of the political and religious controversies. Most importantly, he ruled for twenty-five relatively stable years in the wake of a devastating civil war and a brutal military dictatorship [10]. The English people wanted stability over every other concern. Charles had an easy manner with common appeal. James, on the other hand, was highly controversial. No doubt, the English mourning was as much an uneasy anticipation of the inevitable instability to come as it was a heart-felt loss of a fellow Englishman. The Whig hopes of passing an exclusion bill was valiantly and successfully fought by the Tories. James would take the throne. Whig political capital was diminished after a failed plot to assassinate Charles and James in 1683 [10]. Political faction fighting was at its worse and there was simply no telling how the country would react to the accession of James. Charles' death pulled the floor out from under the English and they had no idea what they would fall into. The Whigs determined to control the answer to that question. The revolution of 1688 was a continuation of a series of events initiated and perpetuated by the Whigs, beginning with the attempts at a legal exclusion bill, from 1679-1681, to the support of Monmouth's failed insurrection in 1685, to the appeal to William in 1688. The national apprehension to the accession of James was short-lived. The majority of the nation welcomed James [10]. Monmouth's poorly equipped rebellion relied on a popular uprising in his defense; an uprising that simply did not happen. This is why the revolution of 1688 cannot be considered a popular, internal revolution, though it is portrayed that way to posterity. The Whig attempt at a popular revolution failed with Monmouth.

Although many moderate Whigs stood behind James, the failed Whig attempt on Charles' and James' lives in 1683 did little to associate the Whig agenda with political placidity in the eyes of the moderate English public. Those eyes were not bent on turmoil and revolution. As the dean of Ripon, Thomas Cartwright, recalled one year after James took the throne, "the ark of God was not shaken as many feared it would have been at the death of our late gracious sovereign Lord, Charles the second" [10, p. 94]. If the Whigs were going to have their revolution, they would have to leave the English people out of it. The people were in no mood for civil war or revolution. The Whigs must have been surprised by the overwhelming support of James' accession, considering the religious and political atmosphere in Charles' last years. James was enthusiastically embraced. He and his supporters enjoyed the resounding support of the parliamentary electorate in the elections following James' accession [10]. He handily defeated the man who had been his most popular opponent to the crown. The fears of instability and turmoil were mitigated. In the summer of 1685, religious rebellion of no significant threat showed James' opponents to be fanatics. In a moderate society, this bought James even more political capital.

The Whigs had to make their move and hope to sell it to the public once it was all done. They had to promote their own sentiments to the public as conservative sentiments, not radical ones. James' absolutism was no greater than that of his Stuart predecessors. Yet the revolution was sold to posterity as a conservative movement. The bourgeois House of Commons secured unprecedented parliamentary control with their bill of rights and constitution presented to William and Mary. Theirs was the more radical movement. There was no return to conventionalism as the revolution was presented by the victors.

With the public desire for stable moderation and their support of James, how did the revolution gain the broad support it needed?

James' tight and public affiliation with France frightened the English public and Parliament. The religious similarities only served as supporting evidence to the political similarities. It was France's brand of despotic, monarchal absolutism. James' court, in line with the court of Louis XIV, believed that neither the people nor Parliament had the right to challenge, or even petition against, the king's policies [10]. Thomas Babington Macaulay describes James' policies as "tyranny which approached to insanity" [10]. It was not so much the policies, but the inflexible application of the policies that threatened the cherished bourgeois self-determination. Even the Tories, who supported the integrity of monarchal control, stood up against James' brand of absolutism. Having alienated his traditional support, James turned to moderate Whigs. To that group, the Dutch style of middle-class-tradesmen political dominance far better served their interests than the French style of monarchal absolutism. In the taking of political sides, it was either the Dutch way or the French way. Moderate Whigs would never choose James' French style.

By the summer of 1688, James had lost all of his political capital. Many English sailed against him with William. Many, including officers, fled his ranks to join William once he landed in England [5]. Macaulay's account of the revolution pays particular emphasis to James' policies but still over-stresses the role of religion in his downfall, writing of the "one great design on which the king's whole soul was bent", referring to the restoration of Roman Catholicism as the English national religion [10, p. 119]. It was the king's policies, not any dubious scheme to control the religious fate of the country. There is no evidence that James ever intended to return England to Catholicism [5]. For his harshly despotic and conspicuously French policies, the country had turned against James in just a few years. The Whig attempts at insurrection that had failed during the height of James' popular acclaim now had a chance at success. No other group had demonstrated the audacity to turn to violent means to their desired political ends. The revolution of 1688, like all other attempts, would have to be initiated by the Whigs. They invited and promoted another champion to their cause, this time, far better prepared than Monmouth. In a landing not far from Monmouth's landing, William landed by invitation of Whig tradesmen, commercially intimate with the Dutch and desperately opposed to the French [5].

The nature of the invitation and of William's marriage to a Stuart princess clouds attempts to define the Glorious Revolution with the same cut and dry terms as other revolutions. There are many facets to the Glorious Revolution which distinguish it from other revolutions, in fact, from what is commonly held as the definitive qualities of a revolution. Among these are the political views and positions of the revolutionaries. In general, revolutionaries are not in positions of political power. They seek political freedom through the revolution. The revolutionaries of 1688 were established politicians already in positions of political influence. With this in mind, toppling James II in 1688-89 is more comparable to the assignation of Julius Caesar by his own senate than the popular rebellions of the French and Russian revolutions. Also, revolutionaries generally rise from the political extremes. In the Glorious Revolution, they were the moderates, a fact that still garners English pride in the revolution [10]. The parliamentarians involved wanted neither a perpetuation of the old system nor the instability of popular revolution and dramatic change. The revolution was a rejection of political extremism and a desperate act to settle and center the political pendulum that had been violently swaying back and forth since the initial tensions of the civil war. The Puritan Revolution pulled the pendulum far from the side of Charles I, and the Restoration yanked it so sharply and decisively back. The fear of a second civil war and a perpetual swinging of the political pendulum were haunting the minds of the sitting moderate Members of Parliament and commercial shareholders. The Commonwealth forced such drastic social intolerances. Charles II and James went out their way to rub French social standards (like debauched theatrical productions) in the faces of the Puritans. Had either side taken a gradual and moderate balance between Puritanism and the preferred continental sensibilities of the Stuarts, the ruling MPs would not have found themselves in the precarious no-man's-land between the extremes. Instead, they needed to expel the extremes with a shove from the middle, yet another difference between 1688 and the revolutions that push one extreme from the far opposite side.

Researching the results of the revolution gets complicated, taking note of the fact that many of the notable results of the revolution occurred before the conflict truly ended. It would be like if the American Constitutional Convention of 1787 had met in 1776 and Americans lived under the ultimate results of their revolution before it was actually won. On the other hand, many of the results of the revolution were not realized until the House of Hanover sat on the throne. Research into the course of the Glorious Revolution should not only include the French supported Jacobite Uprisings but also the wars with Louis XIV, the economic rewards of the victory against Louis, the final stamp that cemented bourgeois political dominance and declared an ultimate winner of the revolution. When it is viewed as a commercial revolution first, a political revolution second, only sprinkled with a dusting of religion, the broader view of the European balance of power and trade into the following century comes into the portrait of the Glorious Revolution. Not until a winner in the battle for commercial supremacy and political ideology is declared can the revolution truly be said to have finished. It finished just as Samuel Johnson's moderate and stable traditionalism came into public light, just as the winners needed to secure one of their own on a social throne, a literary throne, a throne that would be undisputed by the old order, out of danger from counter-revolution.

There are two distinct lenses through which the revolution should be viewed, especially when looking ahead to an evaluation of Samuel Johnson and the iconic rise of his public image, each casting a distinct hue on the subject. The first is as an internal revolution, initiated, carried out, and benefitting internal factions. The second is as an invasion by a foreign power. Whig historians did what they could to ensure the average English schoolboy did not don that second lens. The first lens is an arguable case with much evidence. A wider view reveals that the two lenses are not mutually exclusive. The internal faction and the foreign invaders shared a common interest, both for the development of England and for the English role in the larger Europe, politically and economically. Considerations on the local level must be balanced with a wider, global angle. In the second half of the seventeenth century, there were two polar beacons of governmental philosophy, France and the Dutch Republic. The Glorious Revolution was a profound move in a chess match between France and the Dutch Republic, between absolutism and democracy, between a continent that had lived under the shadow of Louis XIV for half of a century and its democratic destiny. Under the Sun King, France had a tiny middle-class, exacerbated by the persecution and forced immigration of the French Huguenots, the bulk of the French merchant middle-class. In the three British kingdoms and the Dutch Republic, the middle-class was powerful, wealthy, and expanding. In 1688, Amsterdam was the wealthiest and most important trade center and banking market in Europe [12]. Their culture was controlled by, and reflective of, the tastes of wealthy merchants, not of the royalty, as was the case in the rest of Europe. As evidence, the Dutch art of the time, that of Rembrandt and Vermeer, depicts the daily lives of the merchant class, ordinary people, not the lavish extravagance of royalty [12]. It was a merchant middle-class culture, with trade, opportunity, and increasing affluence as the sacred symbols. Popular culture and media were reaching farther into the depths of the social strata than in other European countries. The revolution of 1688 should be viewed as the continued efforts of that class, their English counterparts, England's liberal Whig MPs, William & Mary, and Anne, with key input from John Churchill and Charles Montagu.

The revolution was internal in that the English bourgeoisie had a simple choice before them. On one hand stood their ruling monarch, James, with his loyalty to Louis, his constant dissolving of Parliament, both feet firmly planted in the High Middle Ages.

On the other stood the Dutch Republic, a thriving economic power controlled by and enriching the merchant middle-class. They chose the Dutch example, which could only be brought about by a Dutch invasion. The trade wars that England lost against the Dutch in 1664-67 and again in 1672-74 might tend one to believe that William's invasion would have occurred with or without the cordial invitation of the English liberal faction [12]. They also served to increase the confidence of the MPs involved, after the lopped-sided failure of the Monmouth insurrection.

It is easy to see England's 1688 as just another step in the ongoing Dutch feud with France. The events of 1688 spawned the Grand Alliance against Louis XIV in the Nine Years War and the War of Spanish Succession that followed. The conflict was coming and sides had to be taken. Under James, England and its intimate neighbors clearly stood with Louis. The Dutch needed England on its side and the English merchant middle-class needed to be on the side whose victory would secure their interests. William's invasion was a winning scenario for both the Dutch and the liberal merchant Whigs. The Tories would consistently resist war with France. The checks and balances of a factious, partisan, parliamentary government, so frustrating to the Whigs who supported the war efforts, proved to be the primary ingredient in the ultimate victory over Louis XIV.

Regardless of the internal factors, William's landing and march across southern England in the Fall of 1688 was an invasion of foreign troops against a reigning sovereign and his army. The fact that many of James' key officers, including his commander, the vicar of Sedgemoor, John Churchill, fled his ranks and joined William adds strength to the notion of an internal revolution [11]. Churchill would eventually become one of the main figures in securing the legacy of the revolution through his continental victories over the French army. James commanded a larger army than the one William brought with him. The loss of such key officers tainted his palate for battle; perhaps with the image of his father's fate still fresh in mind. England's pathetic showing in the trade wars against the Dutch must have also weighed heavily. James' army dissolved and he fled to France [5].

With William's background, it is unlikely he would have tried to run his new kingdom in the fashion of James or Louis. Nevertheless, the MPs who invited the invasion presented William with a list of monarchal limitations before he assumed the throne. These were followed by a bill of rights [5]. Mary's Stuart relation fogs the question of just how revolutionary the Glorious Revolution really was. Had the Exclusion Bills succeeded and Charles II's intentions of a William & Mary regency during James' reign come to pass, the same results would have occurred without the landing of a Dutch army. As it was, the Dutch army did land and their presence was acutely felt. At William & Mary's joint coronation, in April of 1689, and for the following two years, Dutch troops garrisoned London [11]. The Dutch language was heard throughout the gathering places of the city, much as German was heard in Paris in the summer of 1940. The uniforms of an army England had so recently fought in the trade wars, marching up and down London, must have given a feeling to Londoners very much like an occupation by a foreign power, even with their own Stuart daughter as a co-monarch. With an awareness of global concerns, the English seemed to readily accept the 'alliance' with the Dutch and their agenda. The English people also aligned themselves culturally with the Dutch, opening the doors for cultural heroes like Dr. Johnson and his sort of middle-class artists. The very character of England had soundly taken a stance and declared its position in the greater European picture of the times.

There was an intricate web of wars, revolutions, and alliances in Europe in the late seventeenth century. A strong Sweden was wreaking havoc on Northern and Central Europe. Peter the Great seized control of Russia in 1689. The Ottoman Empire seized Vienna, later liberated by the Polish. The Peace of Westphalia weakened the Holy Roman Empire's grip on its German states [12]. Amid all of this turmoil, one ominous figure stood supreme. Louis XIV's ambitions had the European balance of power in great peril. In 1688, against this threat, rose the Grand Alliance, consisting of the Dutch republic, the British kingdoms, Spain, Portugal, and the Holy Roman Empire [12]. It was a Dutch led coalition with England acting much more like a Dutch protectorate than an equal partner in the coalition. The 1688 arrival of the British in the coalition was crucial to the success of the alliance and eventually to the shaping of the entire Western World. This was not immediately apparent. Unlike Louis, who could fund wars immediately with taxes taken directly from his peasants, the British treasury was controlled by Parliament, who was not quick to jump into Continental affairs. The crown of England may have been Dutch, but the constitution and bill of rights agreed to by William largely left English policy in English hands. Those hands had chosen to wear Dutch gloves. Their pride was their navy, not army. 1688 proved the army and its officers politically unreliable. Many civil servants were Jacobites. All of these factors added to the British reluctance to dive head first into Continental war. In the long run, this proved to be the winning ingredient. Louis eventually tapped his peasants dry, bankrupting his war efforts. In opposition, the British struck deals with their merchant class to fund war. In essence, they privatized their military. While Louis' war efforts impoverished his subjects, the British war efforts enriched the British people [12].

In the beginning of the Nine Years War, the British kingdoms focused mainly on their navy. This was an attempt to stay out of the quagmire of continental land battles but ultimately set the table for a British dominance of the seas, to be enjoyed for two centuries. On the ground, the Grand Alliance was losing. Louis took many key posts on the Dutch border. With William on the English throne, Dutch concerns were intimately English concerns and vice versa. James' personal connection with Louis made the French conflict with England personal. In the summer of 1689, Louis backed James' attempt to retake his crown with an invasion of Ireland [12]. French victories at the Dutch border prompted William to send Churchill, by this point the Earl of Marlborough, to defend the Dutch border [11].While the French offered little tangible support in James' Irish rebellion, the persecuted and dispossessed Irish Catholics swarmed to James' banner. The ragtag group of Catholic Irish peasants managed to push the Protestants as far north as Londonderry. Thousands of Protestant Ulster residents died of disease and starvation. In July, William's army arrived in relief. In the summer of 1689, the two men with a claim on the English crown met on the battlefield at the Battle of the Boyne [12]. In this battle, William suffered an injury by cannonball but stayed with the battle until his overwhelming victory [11]. After his retreat, James never again stepped foot on any of his former lands. The victory saved the efforts of the revolution from military reversal. More profoundly, the victory allowed William to shift his military focus to France, which was always his concern and always his ambition.

William managed to keep the Alliance together long enough to wear out Louis. More poignantly, he wore out Louis' resources. English resources and moderation of war spending eventually placed William in a superior position. This is where the brilliant maneuverings of Montagu, as Chancellor of the Exchequer, secured the English ability to wage war while giving birth to a modern bureaucracy, and where the revolution attaches directly to the birth of the modern Western economy and why England's Glorious Revolution must be understood to understand the development of Western culture, politics, and economy. In the 1690s, while Louis drained the limited wealth of his peasants, Montagu convinced the affluent English merchant class to give loans to the government. This had broad and profound effects. Montagu took the allowance of Parliament, not nearly enough to support a war, and dedicated it to paying the interest on the loans, set at fourteen percent. The principal had no guarantee. But the interest would be paid for the life of the loan. The return for investors was unlike any investment opportunity of the time. Montagu created war bonds and a perpetuating national debt. This had another effect that secured the aims of 1688. With Parliament in charge of government money and a perpetuating national debt, parliament had to meet on an annual basis. A continually sitting parliament solidified another stone laid in 1688. In 1694, Montagu established the Bank of England. The bank also lent money to the government. It received private investors and deposits and served as a federal reserve for the regulation of national money. Montagu even established a national lottery to raise war money [12]. The result was a true *Tale of Two Cities*. Louis bled his subjects dry to fund military campaigns. Under William, the English were enriched by the war efforts. The English were preparing their county for the rise from poverty and obscurity of a figure like Johnson, who would unite the extremities of society in the heart of a substantial and secure middle-class. The French were strangling the growth of any such icon, further isolating the extremities of society from one another on opposite ends of increasing middle-class void.

The depleted Louis asked for peace in 1697 and had to submit to a treaty leaning heavily in favor of the Alliance. After four months of negotiations, the Treaty of Ryswick reversed many of Louis' long lasting endeavors. He gave back land that he had been acquiring in war since 1678. In a powerful stroke of validation for the 1688 revolution, he recognized William and his heirs as the rightful leaders of the three British kingdoms, promising not to directly or indirectly assist any attempts to challenge William's claim on the crown, temporarily ending his support of James and his heirs [5]. He entangled himself in an agreement to portion out the wealthy and expansive Spanish Empire upon the death of its weak leader, King Carlos Segundo. This last clause of the treaty was made moot with the surprise deathbed bequest of King Carlos in 1700. He left his entire empire to Louis' grandson, Philippe, Duke of Anjou [12]. Suddenly, Louis' ambitions breathed new life with the War of Spanish Succession. The Nine Years War had been bloody. As both a spark of the war and a result of the war, the Glorious Revolution's intimate involvement negates the old argument that it was a bloodless revolution. More war and blood would soon follow in a conflict that cannot be separated from the Glorious Revolution.

William was aware of the precarious nature of the peace established with the Treaty of Ryswick. In his December 3, 1697 speech to Parliament, he addressed his concerns, rationalizing his desire for a large standing army. Standing peacetime armies harkened Parliament back to the days of James II and royal absolutism. Although William asked Parliament for a standing army of 35,000, he was only granted 10,000. The tax burden on the English was great enough just paying off the wartime debt. Maintaining such a large army would simply cost too much [5]. William was right. A couple of deaths, Carlos' and James' led Louis to disregard the promises made in the Treaty of Ryswick. The English parliament still would not budge as long as the terms of the Treaty of Ryswick remained intact and the crowns of France and Spain sat on different heads. They should have known that Louis would seize the opportunity handed to him with Carlos' bequest. Although Philippe, now Philip V of Spain, was king, Louis treated Spain as his own [12]. He took control of fortresses in the Spanish Netherlands, to the obvious apprehension of the Dutch. Simply accepting Carlos' last minute will violated the Treaty of Ryswick. Upon hearing of the will, William called for war. The Tory parliament that was sitting in 1700 was reluctant to support war, as was their *modus operandi*. They needed a stronger push from Louis, which they got in November 1701 when James II made a deathbed request of his old friend Louis. James asked Louis to recognize his son, Prince James as King James III of England and Ireland and James VIII of Scotland. Although unable to support another war, Louis agreed, reversing his validation of the Glorious Revolution with the Treaty of Ryswick [12]. Still, the Tory parliament did not waiver. It was not until Louis enacted a trade embargo against England on behalf of both France and Spain. It was clear. No matter who held the title of King of Spain, the border between France and Spain was erased. Louis was emperor over the French and Spanish Empires, which included parts of Flanders and Italy. Most profoundly, Catholic Europe was united under Louis [11]. This was enough for Parliament to grant William a virtual *carte blanche* in protecting the liberties and interests of Europe. William reconvened the Grand Alliance with the exception of Bavaria, which allied itself with Louis [12].

Unfortunately, William would not see the fruits of his laborious diplomatic efforts in reassembling the Alliance. On vacation in February 1702, at Hampden Court Palace, William suffered a deadly accident. While hunting in Richmond Park, his horse tripped on a mole hill. William broke his collarbone. The injury caused pneumonia and William died in March 1702. For years afterwards, Jacobites would declare toasts to "the little gentleman in a black velvet waistcoat", in honor of the mole that took William III off of the English throne [11, p.203]. Queen Anne inherited a nation at war. She providentially appointed Churchill to the head of her land troops.

It is in this new war that Churchill secured his legacy as one of the saviors of the Glorious Revolution and the continuation of England's middle-class momentum. At stake was the very existence of constitutionalism in Europe. It truly was a world war, fought in North America, where it was called 'Queen Anne's War', in the Caribbean, and of course, in Europe. In 1704, with mostly German troops, Churchill separated Bavaria from France, eliminating Louis' only ally, and broke through the heart of the French forces at the Battle of Blenheim. Churchill killed or captured 30,000 French and Bavarian troops. Eighteen generals surrendered [12]. Europe had no recent memory of such a defeat of French forces. Louis' image of invincibility was shattered. England was established as a major European power. The victory prompted major Whig victories in Parliament in 1705 and 1708. In line with tradition, those Whig parliaments voted to support Churchill's continental campaigns. The financial support made possible a series of great victories for Churchill over France. It is not a far stretch of the imagination to conclude that these victories influenced the Act of Union in 1707. The Treaty of Utrecht in 1713 set the final pieces in play for the ultimate victory of the 1688 revolution. The Whigs who supported the war were expecting the sort of huge land settlements usually due in such a decisive victory. They were blindly disappointed. What England got in the treaty were small but strategically and commercially crucial pieces of land in Gibraltar, the Caribbean, and Canada. These ports gave England complete and undisputed control of Western trade. Equally lucrative was the *asiento*, the right to deal in slaves to the Spanish New World. And more symbolic than logistic, Louis recognized the new Hanoverian dynasty as the rulers of the united British kingdoms [12]. Britain was at the dawn of global dominance not seen since Augustus' Rome.

The stage was set for the Triangle Trade. The English merchant middle-class ruled England and England ruled the new global market. The miracle of seventeenth century Dutch free commerce found a more permanent and secure home in the British Isles. The gradual rise of the bourgeoisie, which began with the plague of 1348, clearing them a path upward, finally reached its zenith. The fateful decision to embrace the Dutch model, at the treasonous rejection of a sitting monarch, in 1688, finally reached its ultimate rewards. The Glorious Revolution was a success and the extent of that success was wider and grander than any of the original plotters of the revolution probably dared imagine. London was the center of the world. It rivaled Rome at its most glorious. The British were keenly aware of this comparison. The following generations of the eighteenth century came to refer to themselves as 'Augustans', likening themselves to the imperial glory of Rome under the emperor Augustus. The Glorious Revolution took much of the credit [13]. The economic affluence of the moderate middle-class brought their Classical Mediterranean ideals and identity to the forefront of English society. Moderation, a rejection of the emotion of political extremism, came to personify the British character. Literature of the age dissected human nature from a lofty perch, above the chaotic swirling of daily life, building a bridge between the literary traditions of Antiquity and the new literature of England, a bridge over Medieval and Renaissance literature. Philosophy, art, wit, and manner developed only as it can in a safe, powerful, and affluent society. In line with their Dutch predecessors, Britain developed increased religious tolerance in this age. Queen Anne was the last British monarch to veto an act of parliament [14]. Absolutism was on its last leg.

Like the Dutch of earlier generations, middle-class tastes and attitudes dominated English society. Everyday commerce was well represented by the social icons elevated by the influential middle-class. The stage was set for the rise of middle-class iconic social heroes, like Samuel Johnson, who wrote in his 1759 *Rasselas*, chapter twenty-eight,

> While courts are disturbed with intestine competitions, and ambassadours are negotiating in foreign countries, the smith still plies his anvil and the husbandman drives his plow forward; the necessaries of life are required and obtained, and successive business of the seasons continues to make its wonted revolutions[15].

The British found their Rembrandt and Vermeer in the common sense, moderate scribbling and conversation of the most iconic social figure from the end of the 18th century into the beginning of the 20th, Dr. Samuel Johnson. He and his circle of friends transcended the realm of literary figures. They became social icons whose conversational modes and witty banter were more influential in establishing their public appeal than any piece of their published work. Even as the waters of the revolutionary Romantic Era subsided, and the public tastes longed for the moderate common sense of the Glorious Revolution and the Augustan Age, there stood the image of Johnson, as iconic as ever, a symbol of wit, wisdom, conventionalism, and socio-political stability. He was the quintessential representative of the ideals of the Glorious Revolution and the lingering symbol of the victory of its devotees, a breed of people spawned in the wake of the plague whose snowballing momentum eventually wiped out European absolutism on its way to economic, political, and cultural supremacy. The Johnson Canon, as discerned through Johnson's published works, could not have taken root in a different type of social soil. The message of Johnson's canon, and the awkward, middle-class sage who delivered it, caught the wind of a powerful historical squall, timed perfectly for their advancement to the pinnacle of social eminence.

Chapter 2

The Johnson Canon: Distinguishing the Contributors to the Johnson Image

THE IMAGE OF JOHNSON, through the centuries, comes from four primary sources. The first source is Johnson's own writing. With his typical Johnsonian bluntness, Johnson laid forth his thinly veiled social and moral canon in his essays, poetry, stories, letters, and even the definitions in his *Dictionary*. Speaking as clearly as his tongue-in-cheek, quasi-sarcastic definitions are the quotations he uses in validation of his definitions. Often, the sources of the quotations supply ample evidence toward his ideals and moral code. The second source of Johnson's public image is the public discourse. Johnson was often the talk of town, being credited with quotations which, while perhaps highly Johnsonian, are unlikely to have ever been uttered by Johnson. The public discourse was both descriptive and prescriptive of Johnson's image. The third source is the literary references to Johnson, employed liberally in the centuries after his death, particularly in the Victorian Age. The references in fiction, like the public discourse, serve both to document the image of Johnson at the time of their publication and to affect Johnson's image in the minds of the readers. The fourth source of Johnson's image is James Boswell's famous biography, *The Life of Johnson*. Although Johnson enjoyed great public acclaim during his life, Boswell's biography enshrined the icon and handed the public a gilded idol that could be carried around or stored on a shelf. Like any gilded representation, Boswell's Johnson falls well short of an identical reproduction of the original. However, there is no doubt that Boswell's biography solidified an iconic status for Johnson's image. A comparison of the biography against the published works of Johnson and the reports of others who documented aspects of Johnson's life, like Hester Piozzi, exposes inconsistencies and brings into question the accuracy of Boswell's Johnson. Regardless of how accurately descriptive Boswell's biography is, it is undoubtedly prescriptive of the public image of its subject. However inaccurate it may be in reflecting the true Samuel Johnson, it is a precise description of the Johnsonian image that is the subject of this book, because it played such a crucial role in giving birth to the image. In the study of Johnson's image through the centuries, and the many references to Johnson used to construct that image, it is important to understand the source, or sources, of the reference. In other words, a reference to Johnson derived primarily from Johnson's canon, from Johnson's own published writing, will bear a distinctly different attitude than one derived from Boswell's *Life of Johnson* or one that comes from the common talk about Johnson. As the references to him piled up over time, they too became a key source of Johnson's image and must be considered when trying to identify the source of the Johnson image used in a reference. This chapter will evaluate some of Dr. Johnson's more impactful publications under the light of current understandings of the writer and as they relate to the evolution of the Johnsonian public persona. The next chapter will present Boswell's contribution to the construction of the icon.

Johnson expert, Bertrand Bronson writes,

> A great writer is defined not only by his own works but also by what posterity makes of him. What he has meant to the generations between his own and ours is an essential part of what he comes to mean to us. [1]

Bronson writes of an ideal that springs up to replace the mortal author and adds, "…it is in this ever changing surrogate, not the original, that we inevitably form our judgments" [1]. He claims that this tainted judging perpetuates the evolution of the author's public image. There is no English author with whom this is more prevalent than Samuel Johnson. As the evolved persona was reflected in popular literature, each published alteration added a layer to the Johnsonian character, painting the lenses through which each subsequent generation viewed the body of Johnson's published work and the character of the man, and each slightly altering the definition of the term "Johnsonian". Johnson's character, or the public perception of it, became more notorious than his writings. This too is unique to Dr. Johnson. Thomas Babington Macaulay wrote in his Johnson biography, "The memory of other authors is kept alive by their works. But the memory of Johnson keeps many of his works alive" [2]. This is an historian's perspective, one that looks more closely at the man as an historical figure and less at his writings. The biographies of Macaulay and of Thomas Carlyle contribute to a trend that transcended Johnson's image from literary to socio-political. The literary light shined less on Johnson's writing than did the socio-political light in the evaluations and criticism of his work. It is important to view Johnson's writing under each of those lights separately, then again under them both, in order to grasp the relationship between the published work and public persona.

Since Johnson died in 1784 and Boswell's biography was published in 1791, the isolation of contributions to the Johnson image must begin by drawing the distinctions between "Johnson's Johnson" and "Boswell's Johnson". Neither may be terrifically near the actual character of Samuel Johnson, but both contribute profoundly to his image in society. Since this book is about that image and not the man behind it, these two sources are both truthful, even in their contradictions. They are truthful depictions of the image of Johnson and must be considered relevant despite the factual inaccuracies. Broken down and isolated, the differences between the two sources will bring clarity to the many other contributors to the Johnson image that are built on one or both of these two sources. In the literary and social ages that followed the death of Samuel Johnson, many ideals, virtues, character traits, and socio-political agendas have been titled "Johnsonian" and have been vindicated by an affiliation with Johnson's broadly accepted morality. In many cases, various touted Johnsonian ideals have contradicted one another. A line of truth connects each of these to the Johnson Canon, as derived from the writings from the author's own hand.

Johnson was primarily a moralist, whose moral messages remained fairly consistent through his entire literary career. How then does his legacy encompass such a varied spectrum of beliefs? As is common in the interpretation of much literature, pieces are employed to the neglect of the whole. The Johnson Canon covers three major moral beliefs of Dr. Johnson's: 1. Poverty and obscurity offer shelter from the vices of vanity that haunt and hound the wealthy and renowned. 2. As a general rule in society, literary genius goes mostly unrecognized and underappreciated. 3. Vice and sloth can be handled and manipulated through the development of virtuous habits. These three moral messages saturate Johnson's body of published works, from his poetry and essays to his fiction and personal correspondence, each quite personal to Johnson and fitting neatly together into a single mural, not intended to be isolated for the advancement of a single cause and not intended to fit neatly into the expectations of their perspective genres.

Poverty and obscurity offer shelter from the vices of vanity that haunt and hound the wealthy and renowned. This was the moral message of *Vanity of Human Wishes: The Tenth Satire of Juvenal as Imitated by Samuel Johnson* (1749). Johnson probably saw parallels between Juvenal's *X* and his contemporary Britain. People who read *Vanity* as a satire modeled after Juvenal and less as an attempt to show the perpetual universality of human folly by drawing such tight parallels between Juvenal's *X* and Johnson's poem miss the author's intent. Johnson was a humanist. He was not merely imitating Juvenal. He was using a writing of Antiquity to show how little human nature has changed and how little the results of human folly have changed since Ancient Rome. *Vanity* is considered satire for being modeled after satire. A much more personal emotion is attached to *Vanity*, bringing into question the satirical nature of the poem. Although *Vanity* begins with objective, Augustan catchphrases like "observation" and "survey mankind", the view of the characters switches back and forth from the bird's eye observation to the intimate thoughts and emotions from within the characters' perspective. *Vanity*, like other inaccurately categorized works of

Johnson's, is a moral sermon, intended for direct humanistic application.

Vanity's "Tragic Quartet", as Kniskern put it, falls in part from their own folly, the same sort of folly satirized in the great satires of the Augustan Age [3]. They also fall by the hands of misfortune and outside influences. In the case of Wolsey, greed and power-lust turn allies to enemies. The humility of obscurity gives way to blind ambition and the stubbornness of greed. As Johnson writes in the beginning of *Vanity*, "How rarely reason guides the stubborn choice" [4]. Johnson notes on many occasions that affluence changes desires and expectations. He studied and admired John Locke, as is evident in the 1,674 quotations from Locke that he puts in the first volume of his *Dictionary*. In "Of Modes of Pleasure and Pain," Locke defines desire as the "uneasiness a man finds in himself upon the absence of anything whose present enjoyment carries the idea of delight with it" [5]. Locke continues, describing the "uneasiness" that drives desire as the "chief, if not only, spur to human industry and action" [5]. Johnson cites this quotation in his *Dictionary* under his definition of "spur". He echoes the same idea in his essay, *The Adventurer No. 67* (The Benefits of Human Society), writing that "all the wants of man may be immediately supplied; Idleness can scarcely form a wish which she may not gratify by the toils of others" [6]. He supports Locke's notion that desire is related to uneasiness, continuing, "Happiness is enjoyed only in proportion as it is known; and such is the state or folly of man that it is known only by the experience of its contrary" [6]. In other words, Johnson writes that the "spur" that motivates actions toward happiness is the "uneasiness" of having experienced its contrary. In other words, it is the taste of affluence that sours the milk of poverty. Without that taste, poverty would not carry the same bitterness. When the spear of possible promotion penetrates the bubble of blissfully ignorant poverty, desire is born and the irritating "spur" pricks the flesh. The greed that took down the Tragic Quartet also brought ruin to the subject of Johnson's 1744 biography, *An Account of the Life of Mr. Richard Savage*.

Savage reads far more like a narrative fiction than a chronicle of events from the life of the subject. Just as Johnson could not dryly document the definitions of words in his *Dictionary* without adding personal opinion and witty, sometimes moral commentary, he could not write a biography without similar injections of his own character and morality. With this, a reading of Johnson's biographies, including *Savage*, is as much a study of Johnson as it is of the subjects of the biographies. Knowledge of particulars from Johnson's own life betrays an intimate connection between his biographical narratives and his own experiences, presented in the same personally embittered manner as his other tragic writings and with the omniscient bias of a narrator in a fictional novel. The first three paragraphs serve as a prologue to lay forth the moral points Johnson intends to demonstrate with the narrative, far more consistent with moral fiction than with biography. Johnson presents his vision of tragic truths before mentioning Savage's name. These truths are reflected in *The Vanity of Human Wishes*, published five years later. Johnson also describes the other characters in Savage's life as a novelist would build them. Savage's mother is clearly established as the antagonist, not simply a person of influence, with as biased of a description as Dickens gives to the loathsome Mr. Squeers, or more fittingly, as Charlotte Bronte gives to Jane Eyre's Aunt Reed. Unlike Jane Eyre, who made no presumption on what should have been owed to her; Savage's discovery of his connection with nobility altered his expectation of life, raising his tastes and their associated vices from their simple beginnings. Savage commits a folly similar to that of Thomas Hardy's Jack Durbyfield, in *Tess of the D'Ubervilles*. Had Jack never come to know of his claim to aristocracy, he and his family would likely have continued their charming, however impoverished, pastoral existence. The taste of affluence altered Jack's desires and expectations, guiding the narrative of this charming country family into one of the Victorian Age's darkest tragedies [7]. In *Savage*, Johnson's prologue speaks clearly of the perils of wealth and of the vices that follow and of the violence of a rapid descent from a lofty social station. The moral reasoning behind Savage's descent is presented to the reader in a manner more consistent with a moral essay or a sermon than biography. Johnson writes, "But the danger of this pleasing intoxication must not be concealed; nor indeed can anyone, after having observed the life of Savage, need to be cautioned against it" [6]. This line is proof that Johnson expects his readers to learn from the moral message of *Savage*. More like a parable from the Bible than any current biography, Johnson uses the story of Savage's life to teach and to warn with the expectation of altering the moral canon, and therefore the behavior, of his readers.

Readers of Johnson cannot help but notice the thematic connections between poverty, as understood by Johnson, and the tragedy of unrecognized talent. That common lack of recognition is the next part of the Johnson Canon. In *Savage*, Johnson writes that affluence and power "flatter the mind with expectation of felicity which they cannot give" [6]. He next remarks that "intellectual greatness should produce better effects" [6]. But he reminds his readers that "The heroes of literary as well as civil history have been very often no less remarkable for what they have suffered than for what they have achieved" [6]. This notion of the tragic sufferings of the extraordinarily talented runs both wide and deep in Johnson's writing. Johnson echoes this theme in the preface to his *Dictionary*. He writes of "those who toil at the lower employments of life" as being "exposed to censure without hope of praise" [6] and continues that "success would have been without applause, and diligence without reward" [6]. Johnson's own bitterly regretted frustrations about leaving Oxford, the lack of support he received in the promotion of his *Dictionary*, and the perpetual expectation that his genius should have been able to purchase him some peace all contributed to this potent portion of the Johnson Canon. His dealings with Lord Chesterfield, capped by his infamous letter in 1755, contribute to the importance of this very Johnsonian notion of neglected talent. Johnson's reaction to Chesterfield's attempts to stake a claim of patronage with the *Dictionary* was a culmination of decades of frustration on this issue. This, and other concurrent experiences and beliefs of Johnson's, found its way into his *Dictionary*, both in the definitions and in Johnson's choice of literary excerpts included with the definitions.

There are two faces of the iconic Johnsonian persona that remained consistent through the evolution of Johnson's public image into the twentieth century. The first is the famed Socratic symposiums of his intimate circle. The second is the *Dictionary*. These two contributors to the Johnsonian socio-literary phenomenon dominate the literary references to Dr. Johnson. The *Dictionary* became the most important facet of the Johnsonian persona. References to it are seen throughout Victorian fiction, betraying a reverence for the *Dictionary* and its author that cannot be fully understood without researching the impact that it had on the writing profession. When Thackeray writes of Becky Sharp's insolent treatment of the *Dictionary* given to her by Miss Pinkerton in the beginning of Chapter One of *Vanity Fair*, it serves to establish Sharp's character right away [8]. Thackeray felt that the best way to establish her villainy is to have her defile his profession's most sacred symbol. Similar evidence of the *Dictionary*'s claim on literary affections is found throughout the 19th century.

To fully grasp the power Thackeray and his contemporaries intended when casually dropping a reference to the *Dictionary*, the many social and literary implications associated with the *Dictionary* in the minds of British readers need consideration. The *Dictionary* ties together many aspects of the iconic Johnsonian figure in the Victorian Age and beyond, aspects which touch all levels of society. Though the English were the leaders of European scientific, military, and political advancement in the middle of the 18th century, they found themselves behind the Continent in many matters of culture [9]. In 1755, the English language was intricate, expanding, and a source of great pride for literate English people, but it had no comprehensive dictionary [9]. Since 1612, Italy had boasted its *Vocabulario degli Accademici della Crusca,* and France had *Le Dictionnaire de l'Academie* in 1687 [9]. Samuel Johnson accomplished what Pope, Addison, Swift, Defoe, even Shakespeare did not. While, those writers published their language in beautiful, expressive, and witty form, Johnson defined and documented it, giving validity, on a global scale, to its intricacies and many peculiarities. If they had been chemists instead of linguists, English authors before Johnson would have been like medieval alchemists, toying and creating with a substance not fully identified or commonly understood. The result of their work was half talent and half luck. Johnson identified and categorized the nature and function of each of those "chemicals," dragging English usage, in conversation and literature, from the realm of pure art, mysterious and intangible, into the realm of categorized science. Just as the identification and categorization of chemicals took alchemy from magic to science, so Dr. Johnson's *Dictionary* provided the same service for the English literary world. In a sense, Johnson added the English language to Britain's mass of exported commodities. He did so with the wit and humor to connect him with his fellow Augustans, yet with an opinionated sarcasm, striking a chord of connection with a disgruntled, gritty, and increasingly vocal working-class. He personalized his definitions just as he did the toils of his satirical characters in *London* and *Vanity*. Writers in the Victorian Age display their sense of indebtedness to this accomplishment through the homage they paid in their many references to the *Dictionary*. For patriotic imperialists, the *Dictionary* filled a void, remedying a source of shame to an empire in dominance over virtually every other subdivision of European society. The English were proud of their language and they were becoming more and more literate with the educational reforms of the 19th century.

In the *Preface to the Dictionary*, Johnson spills forth the same bitterness toward the toils of obscure talent as he does in his satirical verse, clearly harboring resentment for the lack of assistance received from his "patron", Lord Chesterfield. He writes of the fate of the lexicographer.

> Among these unhappy mortals is the writer of dictionaries; whom mankind have considered, not as the pupil, but the slave of science, the pionier of literature, doomed only to remove rubbish and clear

obstructions from the paths of Learning and Genius, who press forward to conquest and glory, without bestowing a smile on the humble drudge that facilitates their progress. Every other authour may aspire to praise; the lexicographer can only hope to escape reproach, and even this negative recompence has been yet granted to very few. [4]

Just as with his satires and biographies, Johnson seems unable or unwilling to remove his personal resentment and evidence of his struggles from his writing. In the third paragraph, Johnson explains the necessity of his *Dictionary* by telling what the English language has suffered without it. Johnson's humanistic morality receives a linguistic reflection. He claims that the language has "itself been hitherto neglected, suffered to spread, under the direction of chance, into wild exuberance, resigned to the tyranny of time and fashion, and exposed to the corruptions of ignorance, and caprices of innovation" [4]. It is easy to imagine these exact words used by Johnson in the description of a character in one of his biographies or satires, which were in turn description of one or more facets of his own life. He seems able to lay his perceived flaws in human nature and society easily over language, holding them both to the same moral code and pointing them toward a similar solution. He continues describing the tangled, unorganized state of the language, writing, "I found our speech copious without order, and energetick without rules: wherever I turned my view, there was perplexity to be disentangled, and confusion to be regulated" [4]. This sounds very similar to the mind of Savage.

Johnson enters into a history of linguistics followed by a history of the English language. He explains one of the reasons for linguistic mutation; writing, "We now observe those who cannot read to catch sounds imperfectly, and utter them negligently" [4]. He continues to justify his endeavor by citing specific examples of language misuse and misunderstanding that can be remedied by the standardization provided by a dictionary. He expresses his intentions of ending the wild, unguided evolution of the language, granting it a steady permanence. "Language is only the instrument of science, and words are but the signs of ideas: I wish, however, that the instrument might be less apt to decay, and that signs might be permanent, like the things which they denote" [4]. He presents more of the language's roots, followed by examples of words that have been used inconsistently by different writers. He wished to make uniform words "which by different writers have been differently formed, as <u>viscid</u>, and <u>viscidity</u>, <u>viscous</u>, and <u>viscosity</u>" [4]. This justification receives unintentional support in Charlotte Bronte's attempt to insult Dr. Johnson. In her 1857 biography, *Life of Charlotte Brontë,* Elizabeth Gaskell relays a tale of Brontë's harsh criticism of Dr. Johnson when Brontë claims that "Johnson hadn't a spark of cleverality in him." [10]. Of course, the word is "cleverness". This is the exact sort of inconsistent use of suffixes that Johnson explains with his example of "<u>viscid</u>, and <u>viscidity</u>, <u>viscous</u>, and <u>viscosity</u>". Ironically, 'cleverality' is not an accepted word in Brontë's time, thanks to *Johnson's Dictionary.* Its use in the insult of a lexicographer seems rather to promote his usefulness and solidify the justification Johnson gives for his project in the preface.

Ultimately, the *Dictionary* did much more for English literature than the benefits described by Johnson in his preface. The *Dictionary* served as inspiration to future generations of English writers who had remained hopelessly dependent on the patronage of the aristocracy, in a way not connected to the *Dictionary's* contents. They found a champion in Dr. Johnson due to his unpleasant dealings with the Earl of Chesterfield. A line in the sand is drawn. It is between the aristocracy and the artists, writers, and working class who had been in bondage to them for centuries. It is between the practice of patronage and the liberation of the profession of writing. At first, Lord Chesterfield appeared to be the ideal patron for Johnson's dictionary project. He had long been a supporter of the humanities and had a personal connection to Johnson, since Johnson's cousin and highly influential mentor, Cornelius Ford, had served as Lord Chesterfield's chaplain [11]. Johnson paid the delicacies typical in an author's courtship of a patron. He presented himself and his plan for the *Dictionary* to Lord Chesterfield with all of the cordiality required of the lowly in addressing the lofty. Johnson, however gifted, was obscure and needed the involvement of a name like Chesterfield to be given the credibility required in wooing the booksellers to purchase the *Dictionary*. Indeed, in August of 1747, Johnson dedicated the *Plan of a Dictionary of the English Language* to Lord Chesterfield. However, over the seven years of the *Dictionary's* construction, the only support Lord Chesterfield gave to Johnson was a few suggestions in improving the plan and a paltry £10 [11]. Still, Johnson pushed forward with his *Dictionary*. Upon finishing, he took a brave stance, denying Chesterfield's claims of patronage, a move that inspired an entire profession and raised him to the status of middle-class hero.

When the *Dictionary* was on the verge of publication, Lord Chesterfield wrote a couple of promotional essays, hoping to attach his name as patron to an achievement for which he clearly foresaw greatness. Johnson was furious at this affectation of involved patronage. Although accepting the ill-timed support might have served Johnson and his *Dictionary*, it was not in his nature to do so. As he expressed to former student, David Garrick, "I have sailed a long and painful voyage round the world of the English language; and does he now send out two cockboats to tow me into harbor?" [11]. So, on February 7, 1755, Johnson took a stand against Lord Chesterfield's purported patronage in a letter that would be credited with liberating authors from the need for aristocratic patrons and raising them to the level of merchants of their own commodity. The letter has become one of the most famous and infamous examples of epistolary expression, particularly as Johnson's distain and anger were expressed in such polite and reserved form. The entire letter bears the affectation of cordial civility and humble obedience to the established etiquette for addressing the great, all except for one passage. The passage reads,

> Is not a patron my lord, one who looks with unconcern on a man struggling for life in the water,

and, when he has reached ground, encumbers him with help? The notice which you have been pleased to take of my labours, had it been early, had been kind; but it has been delayed till I am indifferent, and cannot enjoy it: till I am solitary, and cannot impart it; till I am known, and do not want it. [11]

Johnson ends the letter with the expected formality, "My lord, your Lordship's Most humble, most obedient Servant, Samuel Johnson"[11]. One might think that Lord Chesterfield would be incensed by the sarcastic insolence of the letter. In a turn that most surely added to the letter's powerful influence, Lord Chesterfield was not offended but in fact impressed by the power of the language. He displayed the letter for visitors to read [12]. *A Dictionary of the English Language* had a profound effect on Johnson's growing and evolving public persona in British society by presenting all the facets of the Johnson Canon, thinly veiled in his sarcastic and sometimes bitter definitions, and entirely unveiled in his introduction, and by revealing Johnson's most admired authors. In some Victorian references, the *Dictionary* is given credit for people understanding each other, as if verbal expression was entirely incomprehensible before 1755. The *Dictionary* and the *Letter to Lord Chesterfield* alloyed into one tremendously iconic portion of the Johnsonian persona, surpassing in importance all other aspects of and contributors to Dr. Johnson's character or legend. Many of his moral essays were written while work on the *Dictionary* continued. Johnson's morality bled into the *Dictionary*. Just as with his biographies and satires, his *Dictionary* served as a moral sermon.

In Johnson's *Rasselas*, Imlac tells the Prince, "The business of the poet … is to examine, not the individual, but the species; to remark general properties and large appearances" [6]. Consistent with his own words, Johnson's moral essays followed the influence of Enlightenment philosophers, like John Locke, focusing on the generalities of society and the universalities of human nature and needs. Johnson wrote his moral essays to the universally familiar themes certain to strike a chord of recognition with all readers. Imlac continues, "He is to exhibit in his portrait of nature such prominent and striking features as to recall the original to every mind" [6]. Although Johnson exhibits the objective distance of Locke, he maintains a passionately intimate aspect that betrays the personal origins of his moral determinations. In other words, he writes of a wider vision of mankind, but writes it from within the vision, while personally experiencing the truths he relays, like a reporter in the field, with the sights, sounds, and smells of his story directly affecting his senses, as opposed to a report given from a news anchor's desk.

Johnson makes no attempt to hide his admiration for Locke's moralistic mode. Johnson's interest in Locke's moral philosophy is evident in the nature and number of the Locke references in the *Dictionary*. He includes over two hundred quotes from the two moral chapters of Locke's *The Essay Concerning Human Understanding*. The chapters are "Of Modes of Pleasure and Pain" and "Of Power". In essence, Johnson rebuilds Locke's moral arguments in many segments of his *Dictionary* [5]. In compiling the *Dictionary*, Johnson chose the texts he enjoyed, underlining the words to be defined and bracketing the segments used to illustrate the contextual employment of the words. For this reason, the *Dictionary* is a remarkable tool for determining Johnson's literary tastes and influences [5]. Once those influences are determined through study of the *Dictionary*, research into Johnson's moral essays is firmly grounded in an understanding of his moralistic influences. As Boswell writes in *Life of Johnson*, "… it should not pass unobserved, that he has quoted no authour whose writings had a tendency to hurt sound religion and morality" [13]. Although certainly serving a particular literary need, the *Dictionary* should be viewed among Johnson's moral writings, or at least as a catalog of Johnson's moral influences. His consistent reflections of his *Dictionary* citations throughout his moral writings complete the roadmap between Johnson's moral essays and his moralistic influences. Much of the morality that remained a part of the perpetuating Johnsonian image, as other facets of the icon evolved, remained because it is spelled clearly in the *Dictionary*, and the *Dictionary* remained such a sturdy foundation of a popular image that changed size, shape, and position as it traveled through the centuries.

Johnson defends Locke's generation of post-Glorious Revolution philosophers, recognizing the public need to place blame for the failed expectations of the revolution. Locke was in exile until 1688, returning with William and Mary and publishing Two Treatises of Civil Government, a work written during the Whig attempts to overthrow Charles II [14]. In his essay, *Idler No. 88*, Johnson describes the excited expectations for rapid advancements in all portions of society, but reminds the reader that change is slow and the expectations of the public in the wake of the Glorious Revolution were unrealistic. Johnson writes, "The truth is, that little had been done compared with what Fame had been suffered to promise" [4]. He vindicates Locke, citing the true achievements of a moralist, writing that at the end of life "He that has improved the Virtue or advanced the Happiness of one fellow-creature, ... ascertained a single moral Proposition, or added one useful experiment to natural Knowledge, may be contented with his own Performance" [4]. Both Locke and Johnson express their naturalist view of human motivations. Both believe that ultimately all human action is an instinctual reaction more than an intentional, pre-meditated action. In *Idler No. 22* (The Vultures' View of Man), Johnson takes it a step further, referring to man as having "only the appearance of animal life, being really vegetables with the power of motion" [6].

If Johnson's observations of human folly are from an Enlightenment philosopher's distant survey, his suggestions of remedy are from an intimate preacher's pulpit. It is from that pulpit that Johnson presents his readers with the third facet of the Johnson Canon. He writes copiously about the habitual nature of human actions. Walter Jackson Bate observes in Johnson's moral writing that "a recurring theme of Johnson's is the need to exploit habit rather than be made its victim" [15]. Johnson supports this throughout his conversation, correspondence, and published works, speaking consistently about the need to form positive habits. He writes of the vegetative nature of habitual man from Locke's lofty angle, and then looks the reader directly in the eye with the fire of a local preacher. Katherine C. Balderston's 1960 article "Dr. Johnson and William Law" compares the moral writings of Johnson with the sermons of Anglican cleric William Law (1686-1761). Balderston writes,

> Another broad area of agreement in the ideas of the two men, which eludes specific textual demonstration of influence, is their common concern for the power of habit, both for good and ill, in the economy of the moral life. The idea, as all readers of Johnson know, is omnipresent in his works. An outgrowth, however, of Law's belief that the power of habit may be utilized for good by making our bodies conform to "such habits of life as naturally produce habits in the soul" did, I believe, influence Johnson and help to explain those practices of his religious life which his contemporaries found so singular. [15]

Boswell and other Johnson biographers note Johnson's devotional adherence to habit. Unlike Law, Johnson does not often advocate for the positive power of good habits in his moral essays. Rather he warns of the dangers of bad habits, offering little advice other than to avoid them. This is not surprising from an author noted for tragic narratives. Law's notions of positive habitual morality were common among Anglican divines of the period. Among those known through references to have influenced Johnson were Richard Hooker, Jeremy Taylor, Henry Hammond, and John Tillotson. All advocated the power of habit in affecting good [15]. Johnson seems to support the clerics' ideas on habitual goodness, or "practical divinity", in *Idler No. 91*, where he claims that morality "is comprehended in practical divinity, and is perhaps better taught in English sermons than in any other books ancient and modern" [15]. Examples of this third facet of the Johnsonian image can be seen lingering into the Victorian Era. Characters like Elizabeth Gaskell's Deborah Jenkyns, in her novel *Cranford*, staunch Johnson devotees, are built upon virtuous habits.

The *Dictionary* is riddled with evidence that Johnson did extensive reading of Anglican homiletic literature. He cites Hooker 1,216 times and Taylor, Hammond, Tillotson, and South 292, 207, 380, and 1,092 times respectively [15]. In an attempt to sum up Johnson's notions of habit as influenced by the Anglican homily, Paul Alkon constructs a list of nine consistencies on the matter among the writings of Johnson's primary influences.

(1) repetition of any particular thought or action tends to make it habitual; (2) though such repetition may be difficult at first, it becomes less difficult with each iteration; (3) as any habit develops, it becomes not only less difficult but more pleasant; (4) habits may be either mental or physical, or both: that is, they may take root in, and affect, either the mind or the body as Tillotson puts it, "by virtue of a habit a man's mind or body becomes pliable and inclined to such kinds of actions as it is accustomed to"; (5) habits of thought may influence our conduct; (6) habitual behavior may influence the nature and direction of our thoughts; (7) as habits become more powerful we partially or completely lose our liberty to sup-press and break away from them: in Tillotson's phrase, strongly implanted habits may induce "a kind of necessity of acting accordingly"; (8) it is easiest to break away from a habit in its early stages of development; (9) firmly implanted habits may affect us so powerfully that they become a kind of second nature, and their effects must therefore be considered as important as those dispositions which all human beings naturally inherit by virtue of their common humanity. Acquired traits, in other words, may be as significant as inherited ones. [15]

Alkon's list becomes an outline of Johnson's precepts on the nature of habit and its effect on human morality, drawn from the same literature Johnson read and cites in his *Dictionary*, and reflects thoroughly in his moral essays. If a single theme must label Johnson's moral essays, that theme would be "habit".

The theme of habit is thoroughly covered in Johnson's three series of moral essays, *Rambler, Idler,* and *Adventurer.* Here are some examples of the theme of habit as it occurs in Johnson's

Rambler essays. In *Rambler No. 173*, Johnson declares that "Nothing is more despicable than the airiness and jocularity of a man bred to severe science, and solitary meditation" [16]. He blames "that gay negligence and vivacious levity" on having entered "late into the gay world with an unpliant attention and established habits" [16]. He continues in *Rambler No. 173*, "A man not early formed to habitual elegance, betrays, in like manner, the effects of his education, by an unnecessary anxiety of behavior"[16]. In *Rambler No. 174*, he writes, "Every man has some habitual contortion of body, or established mode of expression, which never fails to raise mirth if it be pointed out to notice" [16]. In *Rambler No. 177*, Johnson associates habit with surroundings and society, writing, "I soon found that the suppression of those habits with which I was vitiated, required association with men very different from this solemn race" [16]. In *Rambler No. 180*, he warns of the human susceptibility to habit when the eyes are too long from self-evaluation. "Many who compare the actions, and ascertain the characters of ancient heroes, let their own days glide away without examination, and suffer vicious habits to encroach upon their minds without resistance or detection" [16]. Whether or not Johnson's *Rambler* essays were widely and often read in the several generations following his death, Johnson's notions on habit, as disseminated in his moral essay, remained tightly stitched to the common perception of Dr. Johnson and an integral part of the social icon.

This theme continues in the *Adventurer* and *Idler* essays. In *Adventurer No. 108*, Johnson advocates the active perpetuation of good habit, or the active perpetual exclusion of bad habits, writing that, "habits grow stronger by indulgence; and reason loses her dignity, in proportion as she has oftener yielded to temptation: 'he that cannot live well today,' says Martial, 'will be less qualified to live well tomorrow'" [17]. He recommends a habitual consideration of death in *Adventurer No. 120*, when he writes, "Nothing confers so much ability to resist the temptations that perpetually surround us, as an habitual consideration of the shortness of life, and the uncertainty of those pleasures that solicit our pursuit" [17]. In *Adventurer No.126*, he returns to the connection between habit and surroundings, noting that "Some are unable to resist the temptations of importunity, or the impetuosity of their own passions incited by the force of present temptations" [17]. His solution is "to fly from enemies which they cannot conquer ... till they have formed strong habits of virtue, and weakened their passions by frequent victories" [17]. In *Idler No. 27*, Johnson writes of the near impossible difficulty of breaking hardened habits. "Custom is commonly too strong for the most resolute resolver, though furnished for the assault with all the weapons of philosophy" [17]. He concludes the thought with, "Those who have been able to conquer habit, are like those that are fabled to have returned from the realms of Pluto" [17].

The *Dictionary* creates a map of Johnson's preferred reading as well as his moral influences. His influences include a broad vision of society, as influenced by John Locke, and a more narrow and personal vision of the toils of the individual, as influenced by Anglican homiletic literature. This map guides the readers of Johnson's moral essays through the major themes, primarily that of the power of habit. It allows the reader to anticipate the points on the map before arriving at them, permitting and encouraging a more thorough reflection on the themes as they were intended by Johnson. He sums up his notions of the habitual nature of human behavior, and the associated perils, in one line from *Idler No. 27*.

> Those who are in the power of evil habits must conquer them as they can; and conquered they must be, or neither wisdom nor happiness can be attained; but those who are not yet subject to their influence may, by timely caution, preserve their freedom; they may effectually resolve to escape the tyrant, whom they will very vainly resolve to conquer [17].

It is in Johnson's periodical essays that his canon has the greatest potency. This is because his essays are used by critics to determine his moral code. Although his other genres of writing had the same intentions, they are held by critics to the standards of their genres, blinding them to their part in supporting

Johnson's canon. A study of Johnson's writing for the sake of criticism of form precludes a broad and unified understanding of Johnson's canon. No work of Johnson's suffered this mistake like *Rasselas*.

Rasselas has been viewed in criticism from two distinct angles. First, it is viewed as a novel, in which light it has received brutally harsh criticism. Second it is seen as a moral work. In this light it has been hailed as "probably the wisest" [18] book in English literature. The diverse visions of the book are a result of separating aspects of the book which are best to be kept united. The lauded moral message of *Rasselas* and the criticized mechanical structure of the chapters and character introductions are identical and fit each other flawlessly. To put the moral message within a more accepted novel structure would be like putting a dozen roses in a work boot, or wearing vases to work in the field. The structure supports Johnson's intended morality by presenting the message in a format more used to educate than entertain. The episodic structure reflects that of the majority of the Old Testament and its presentation in such a format primes the audience to receive the morality from a familiar vessel. The polarized critical visions of *Rasselas* parallel the polar use of the book in later literary references. By uniting the critical visions of *Rasselas*, one can also unite the literary references to it, revealing that the story ultimately possesses the universal human application that was a primary theme throughout Johnson's literary career.

As a novel, *Rasselas* has received severe criticism against the weakness of structure and the lack of dramatic flair in the characters. It is seen as an unsuccessful attempt to write an ordinary novel. The episodic nature of the book's structure and character involvement are seen by many critics as a cause of the diminishment of character impact, resulting in a lack of excitement [18]. Another popular complaint is that the story ends with no resolution, as if Johnson just put down his pen and stopped writing. Despite the complaints, both of these structural aspects are consistent with and supportive of the moral message within the narrative. They illicit the same feelings. The structure of the novel would have created the same unsettled feelings in the reader, even if the story was different. Likewise, the story would have created the same effect, albeit to a lesser degree, without a parallel structure. Johnson combined the two for maximum potency.

As Johnson rightly conveys, life is episodic. This is evident in great biographies, easily divided into sections of the subject's life. If this was not so, biographies would not contain chapters. There would be no point appropriate for the sort of break in action signified by the end of a chapter. In many cases, the episodes of life do not end with satisfactory resolution. The absence of a tidy, satisfying conclusion to a life episode does not make life less episodic. The quintessence of Johnson's literary philosophy was the survey of human nature, particularly the pains, duality, and yes, even the episodic nature of human existence. In each of Johnson's biographies, the distinct episodes of the lives of his subjects each carry a particular theme. Each would receive a different genre heading if made into individual books for resale, from 'Romance' to 'Horror', from 'Mystery/Thriller' to 'Family'. The character of the subjects is determined by what lessons are learned in each episode and carried forward into the next. So if literature is to reflect the observations of life, the *structure* of *Rasselas* reflects the truths of human life as much as the story's moralistic message. It serves as the perfectly matched frame for the portrait within. Just as an ornately gilded frame befits a Byzantine mosaic and not a Rembrandt, the structure of *Rasselas* befits the moral message. The standard structure of a novel, regardless of the opinions of literary critics, would have been an awkwardly incongruent frame for Johnson's story of the Prince of Abyssinia.

Each chapter portrays a single potential path to happiness for the prince. Johnson's intention is for his reader to attempt to recognize each path personally and consider what Rasselas learns from each, that the reader may draw the parallels and therefore guide behavior and decision making. The division of the chapters along such clear lines makes for a choppy narrative if the reader is expecting to be swept away in a fanciful fiction and float in suspended disbelief. If the reader views the story as a series of metaphoric essays, each chapter being an essay dedicated to a single point of view, the chapter structure contributes to, not detracts from, the author's intended impact of the book. Critical review of the book is so polarized because the moral philosophy is the only point of the narrative, rendering moot all criticism of a structure inconsistent with a novel and non-conducive to the fictional flow required to maintain the audience's suspended disbelief. Johnson intends for the audience to be snapped back to reality (the greatest fear of most novelists) so that the morals of the chapter may be applied. It is the unnecessary separation of the moral message and the structure that has perplexed the critics into assigning a duality that is simply not there. The moral essay is Johnson's preferred tool for the delivery of moral truths. *Rasselas* is a series of moral essays, stitched together by replacing the second person directives of a sermon with a third person representative. Perhaps if it had been released in chapter installments, intended to be read, pondered, and absorbed one moral lesson at a time, its structural criticism would not moderate the historical acclaim of the book. Praise of its applicable wisdom would not be weighed down by the harsh reviews of its structure.

Johnson's own literary criticism shows that *Rasselas* is consistent with *his* view of the form and purpose of superior literature, rather that revealing an accidental ineptness in the structuring of a novel. In a novel, the author's obligations to reality are only as they relate to maintaining suspended disbelief by excluding such extreme absurdities as would snap the chord of communion between the narrative and the reader's sphere of relatable experiences. The purpose is generally entertainment. If *Rasselas* would have been first published in this age, it would be situated in the bookstores somewhere between self-help and spirituality, not sitting alongside the vampire novels or magical fantasies of the fiction section. Sitting on a spirituality shelf, *Rasselas* would precisely fit critical expectations in both structure and story. A study of Johnson's influences in the writing of *Rasselas* offers some vindication for his chosen structural mode. Most critics who have sought Johnson's literary influences have credited Father Lobo's *Voyage to Abyssinia* (1622) and various Ethiopian literatures. Thomas Preston draws a convincing connection between *Rasselas* and the book of *Ecclesiastes* from the Bible (1969). *Ecclesiastes* begins and ends with "Vanities of vanities, all things are vanity" [19]. It is difficult to find any work of Johnson's not more or less summed up by that quotation from the bible. *Rasselas* has other connections to *Ecclesiastes*. In *Ecclesiastes,* Qoheleth's perfect garden he painstakingly builds for himself proves to be as unsatisfying as the Happy Valley is for the Prince in *Rasselas*. Qoheleth says, "Nothing that my eyes desired did I deny them, nor did I deprive myself of any joy" [19]. The inhabitants of the Happy Valley were "gratified with whatever the senses can enjoy" [6]. Neither character is able to find happiness amid the pleasures that surround them. Even Boswell makes the connection in *Life of Johnson,* when he quotes *Ecclesiastes* in his description of *Rasselas*. Boswell writes that Johnson's story "leads us through the most important scenes of human life, and shows us that this stage of our being is full of 'vanity and vexation of spirit'." [20]. *Ecclesiastes* is broken down in divisions of various vanities and critiques, in a manner quite similar to Johnson's breakdown of character encounters in *Rasselas*. There is no expectation of a novel's flow placed upon *Ecclesiastes*, so it is not criticized for inadequacies on that account. It is *Rasselas'* misrepresented genre of literature that has placed the faulty expectations, resulting in faulty criticism.

Depending upon the point of view, *Rasselas* can be considered conventional in its structural and thematic similarities to the Bible. It can also be considered unconventional, due to its break from the standard form of a novel. This segregated criticism and isolated vision of a single aspect of *Rasselas* was employed by authors of the Victorian Age in the establishment of characters. Polar ideals were represented by the book, based on which aspect was featured in the representation of the character or situation. Charlotte Brontë's 1847 *Jane Eyre* not only maintained a Rasselasian theme throughout the narrative, complete with escaped imprisonment and an eventual return, it referenced *Rasselas* by name in the title character's first encounter with the book's first great secondary character. The reference is made in subtle passing, rendering a current obscurity to the reference like so many Johnsonian references in Victorian literature. When Jane meets Helen Burns, Helen is reading a book that attracts Jane's attention. At this point, Jane is not the academic sophisticate she develops into by the time she encounters Mr. Rochester. Brontë writes, "From where I stood I could see the title. It was "Rasselas"; a name that struck me as strange, and consequently attractive" [21]. Helen offers to let Jane read the book. Jane finds the contents less alluring than its exotic title. This is a short encounter, one that might go unnoticed by a reader who has not already recognized the explicit parallels between the two narratives. In addition, the story of Jane Eyre has an episodic structure. Brontë's use of *Rasselas* and her Johnsonian connection throughout *Jane Eyre* are employed as anti-conventionalism rhetoric. There is a discontent in Jane, throughout the book, which is identical to that of Rasselas. Even when Jane gets to Thornfield Hall, happy as she is there, she is described as looking off to the horizon, in pensive, speculative contemplation. In *Jane Eyre,* a Johnsonian reference and running Johnsonian theme run in contradiction to status quo and content conventionalism. In just a few years, *Rasselas* is referenced, in another major novel, as the very banner of Augustan conventionalism.

Elizabeth Gaskell's 1853 *Cranford* also references *Rasselas* while maintaining a running, reflective Johnsonian theme. In Gaskell's book, the opposite of what occurs with Rasselas occurs with the narrator. She moves from a hectic industrial city to a rural town, untouched by the rapid changes of the era. In essence, she escapes from the world at large to the Happy Valley. Just as with the Brontë book, *Cranford* invokes the Rasselasian reference and thematic parallels early in the narrative. There will be much more on Gaskell's Johnson references in the chapter on the Victorians. In any account, the Gaskell use of *Rasselas*, just a few years after the Brontë reference, gave an entirely different impression of both Johnson and *Rasselas*. An enthusiast of Victorian literature today, unfamiliar with Johnson's work, might think these must be two different novels with the same peculiar name, their themes seemingly polar opposites of one another.

The writers who use *Rasselas* in their efforts to distinguish opposing characters with opposite traits miss Johnson's point entirely. One of the running themes throughout Johnson's entire body of work is the universality of the human experience. Just as critics of *Rasselas* separated the structural form and the moralistic message, resulting in their inability to allow one of those aspects to enhance the other, novelists who invoked Johnson's tale separated the running experiences of the character, Rasselas, from the lessons gained from an overall view of the many, admittedly disjointed, sections of the book, fail to see the lessons of the moments as they fit into the lesson of the whole. They too missed Johnson's intentions. The raising of *Rasselas* as the representative banner of opposite socio-political agendas is like both Republicans and Democrats violently debating an issue from the same side. A more thorough study of Johnson's primary themes, in his other works, grants a greater understanding of *Rasselas* and a greater ability to employ it in reflection, the way Johnson intended it to serve its readers. A better understanding of *Rasselas* is required to grasp the intentions of the writers who reference it in establishing themes in later novels, and to understand the deficiencies in those writers' one-sided understanding and use of the book. The contrast will provide a clear portrait of 'Dr. Johnson', as the iconic image in the minds of the Victorians. *Rasselas* has a claim on the title "probably the wisest" book in English Literature. It stands out as all the wiser when it is grasped and digested as a whole, without the continuing pattern of unnecessary separation of its themes, form, and connected aspects and used as a piece in the mosaic of Johnson's entire body of work to place a firm finger on the Johnson Canon. Step a bit farther out and it is easy to see how that mosaic serves as a piece in the larger mosaic of Johnson's public image over the centuries. Whether novelists who reference *Rasselas* suffer from the common critical misunderstanding of the relationship between moral and structure, *Rasselas* plays its undeniable role in the growth and development of the iconic social image of Dr. Johnson.

True to his Augustan designation, Johnson believed that literature should reflect life. He swayed from that formula with his expectation that it should also guide. For this reason, Johnson's literary criticism opens a second eye to a view of the Johnson Canon, giving a third dimension to the other evidence used to piece the canon together. Johnson's literary criticism reveals a bias in favor of real, rational reflections of experience. He was harsh toward pastoral and imaginative poetry. He thought that poetry should present a humanist, moral perspective, based on first hand observation and connected to the emotional response elicited by the observed situation [22]. He was critical of narratives based on the supernatural, because they taught no moral lesson that could be applied to human society. He was critical of abused clichés of fiction. Johnson had little good to write about any poetry or novel that strayed from his preferred formula of, as he writes in *Rambler No. 4*, "accurate observation of the living world" [6]. He had a strong opinion of virtue, morality, and behavioral obligations, and he believed the duty of literature was to address those aspects of the human experience for the designed purpose of improvement.

Rambler No. 37 addresses pastoral poetry and Johnson's notions of the inherent weaknesses of that mode in instilling moral lessons in the readers. Johnson relays in his many critical essays on pastoral poetry in *Rambler, Adventurer, An Essay on the Writings and Genius of Pope*, and the *Lives of the Poets*, even the reports of his conversations in Boswell's *Life of Johnson,* that the pastoral mode lacks authenticity, declaring it the poet's obligation to reflect personal experiences, not conjure fanciful imagery, no matter how beautifully envisioned or eloquently expressed they may be. He criticized the over-simplification of a complex world and the tendency of some poets to form their poetic vision more from imagination than reason and observation. Johnson suggests that rather than trying to create new pastoral poetry in lieu of reflecting direct observation, readers and writers should satisfy themselves with study of the pastoral poetry of

Antiquity. He recommends to enthusiasts of the form that a study of Virgil's pastorals would be better than contemporary attempts at "advancing principles which, having no foundation in the nature of things, are wholly to be rejected from a species of composition" [6]. In other words, if the pastoral poetry of Johnson's time could not contribute to the "species of composition", adding some value upon the literary bequests of Virgil, it is far better no attempt is made. Virgil's pastorals are successful because they are the observations of the poet, without imagination needed to fill in the blanks left by mere observation. Johnson applauds Virgil, while criticizing contemporary imitators, by standing in sharp relief of the invention required by his pastoral contemporaries and the authenticity of Vigil's poetic motives. Johnson writes that Virgil "employed his powers rather in improving than inventing" [6]. Johnson is not concerned with the lack of novelty in authentic observation, supplied in contemporary pastorals by contributions of imagination. He points out the lack of newness in Virgil's poetry but claims that he "must have endeavored to recompense the want of novelty with exactness" [6]. This is another facet of the Johnson Canon that lingered deeply into the life of the iconic image. Johnson studied Virgil's pastorals, leading him to the following definition of pastoral in his *Dictionary*: "a poem in which any action or passion is represented by its effects upon a country life" [23]. The revival of pastoral poetry was a part of a trend of neo-classicism that Johnson saw as unauthentic and unnecessary. He thought that any need for the Classical style should be filled by a study of the Classical poets, not by inventing new work in imitation of them, lending further support to the earlier argument that Johnson's *Vanity*, although titled as an imitation of Juvenal, was not an imitation of a poetic mode but a comparison of civilizations. In an evaluation of Johnson's essays on the pastoral, Richard Kelly writes, "He revolts against a narrow neoclassicism, and his thinking rests on rationalistic and empirical premises" [22]. To Johnson, pastoral poetry is offensive on two points. It is an imaginative, unauthentic recreation of a world never experienced or observed by the poets who use it. It distracts readers away from a study of the originals of the mode, the writings of

Antiquity that Johnson revered and believed should be studied, not loosely copied.

Rambler No. 4 addresses Johnson's ill opinion of fanciful fiction that has no bearing on the human experience and offers no guidance within the narrative that the reader may recognize and apply to real life situations. He begins *Rambler No. 4* applauding the familiar intimacy of the Augustan fiction and the good tastes of the Augustan reader in preferring moral literature to the wild and fanciful fiction of earlier generations. He writes that the "works of fiction with which the present generation seems more particularly delighted are such as exhibit life in its true state" [6]. It is easy to see reflections of this opinion in Johnson devotees. Jane Austen for example, while publishing during the Romantic Era, was a staunch Dr. Johnson devotee and writes squarely in the Augustan mode and presents the standards and morality of the Johnson Canon. Austen's work stands in stark contrast to the far more fanciful publications of her contemporaries. Her well documented admiration for Dr. Johnson parallels her mode of expression, fictional settings, moralistic themes, and her personal familiarity with the scenes of her novels. Johnson noticed a certain irresponsibility in literature whose themes are so far removed from common life that the reader can find no moral guidance from the experience of having read. Many of the writers of the subsequent literary eras, who were true Johnson devotees, focused on this facet of the Johnson Canon in the establishment of characters in their novels. Johnson writes harshly of authors who must "employ giants to snatch away a lady from the nuptial rites" or "knights to bring her back from captivity" [6]. Johnson believed that literature should place responsibility for self-improvement on the reader. His contention with detached and fanciful fiction was that the reader found within the characters "neither faults nor excellencies in common with himself" [6]. If the narrative does not set the characters near enough to the reader's own circumstances for parallels to be drawn, no moral benefit can come from the experience.

In Johnson's mind, literature was practical, with applicable lessons. He could not understand the notion of literature serving strictly as entertainment. He continues in *Rambler 4*, "Why this wild strain of imagination found reception so long in polite and learned ages, it is not easy to conceive" [6]. He found such writing to be silly non-sense. In this area, Johnson remained staunchly Augustan. The Augustan ideals of human observation with practical and universal parallels to common life held strong in his literary criticism. It is that strain of familiarity, that recognizable moment, from epic moments to the mundane, which served the reading population the way Johnson felt literature should. In Johnson's thought, it is the memory of these common moments that makes literature impactful. He explains in *Idler No. 44* that imaginative fiction should simply compound universal sense impressions into complex ideas laid upon fictional lives. He writes, "Judgment and ratiocination suppose something already known, and draw their decisions only from experience. Imagination selects ideas from the treasures of remembrance, and produces novelty only by varied combinations" [24].

Johnson believed that the lessons of fiction can be more penetrating than those issued from the preacher's pulpit. He writes in *Rambler 4* that the lessons of literature may be "made of greater use than the solemnities of professed morality" [6]. He writes of the reader's potential for self-improvement in studying the fictional hero "by observing his behavior and success to regulate their own practices" [6]. Johnson echoes the writer's responsibility to associate fictional circumstances with practical life, in a manner that may be employed for self betterment, in *Rasselas*, when Imlac gives advice to the poet. "He is to exhibit in his portraits of nature such prominent and striking features, as recall the original to every mind" [6] But are all aspects of the human experience to be portrayed in fiction's reflections of observation? Johnson did not think so. Certainly, moral lessons may be extracted from examples of folly as well as heroism, debauchery as well as prudence, and dubious as well as pure intentions. This is a predicament that artists face today. Should the artist exercise a sense of propriety or give the audience the most direct imitation? What degree of censorship conducts, through the art, the most profound morality? *Rambler 4* addresses the writer's quandary of what should be excluded from observation in the attempt to present the reader with the deepest moral impact.

Johnson supports the direct reflection of nature, writing, "It is justly considered the greatest excellency of art to imitate nature"[6]. He quickly qualifies his statement continuing, "it is necessary to distinguish those parts of nature which are most proper for imitation" [6]. He warns of the great care required in representing life, which is "so often discolored by passion, or deformed by wickedness" [6]. He advocates censorship through moral filters, rather than a purely faithful chronicle of observations. He defends his position, claiming "If the world be promiscuously described, I cannot see of what use it can be to read the account" [6]. He continues, warning that many writers attempt such a faithful reflection of nature and the duality of the human moralistic nature as to include equal portions of the admirable and the abhorrent. He theorizes that the reader of such narratives begins to relate so closely to the character that he may be too quickly inclined to forgive, or at least overlook, the more morally wretched behaviors in light of the too closely associated admirable ones. He warns that such writers "so mingle good and bad qualities in their principle personages that they are both equally conspicuous"[6]. Johnson displays a lack of trust in the reader's ability to separate and distinguish the good from the bad, and an understanding of the tendency to blend them all together as a whole of character traits worth imitating, thus stripping the narrative of all moral guidance. This is another lingering predicament for current readers. Bad characters are often given lovable traits. In either embracing or rejecting the morality of the character, the reader often embraces bad or rejects good. Johnson struggled with such moral ambiguity, intentionally presented to the readership by authors whose position as artists demand their moral leadership.

Johnson does not stop with the advocating of a degree of moral censorship. He supports additions to the direct observations of nature in gaining moral impact. He does not allow invention of qualities, rather selections from the collective traits and tendencies of "the mass of mankind", those traits which "most ought to be employed" [6]. He brings this into relief with a metaphor, reminding his readers that a diamond cannot be made, just as human traits in fiction should not be made. It can be polished by art. Again, his metaphor of polishing what is not worth viewing to make it admirable is in contradiction to the purest ideals of Augustan observation. It more closely parallels a preacher's interpretation of the lessons from the great biblical characters. The polishing and manipulation of human traits as an addition to fictional narratives does not create what does not exist. It simply reveals "that luster which before was buried among the common stones" [6].

In Johnson's literary criticism, two primary themes are detected throughout. One is in strict adherence to Augustan poetic ideals. It is the recording of the direct observations of the writer, free from fanciful invention and embellishment in the replacement of experience, free from loose, inexperienced imitation of a trendy neo-classical mode. On the other hand, Johnson did advocate a stray from such a strict, Augustan chronicle of observations. Ever the moralist and ever the humanist, he allows for the addition of traits not directly observed, as long as they are drawn from the universal pool of human tendencies. He also allows for the censorship of licentious folly in order to avoid moral confusion in the reader, with the fear that abhorrent traits in an admirable character would be embraced with the bundled whole of the character. Johnson's literary criticism, like his poetry, reveals a man standing alone, straddling two literary eras. He breaks from the strict Augustan chronicles of observation seen in his Augustan predecessors. But he demands authenticity, rejecting neo-classicism, or neo-anything for that matter, remaining highly critical of any addition that does not come from the common pool of observed human traits.

A narrow focus used in literary criticism, albeit quite effective for its own purposes, inhibits the necessarily broad vision of the Johnson Canon. Johnson was a moderate, and as a moderate, he had to maintain a position distant from the extremes, yet near enough to view them well. Any attempt to appoint a stagnant and polarized political position to Johnson and his canon misses Johnson's point entirely. Critics of Johnson's *Lives of the Poets* have sought to assign political partisanship, even Jacobite revolutionary rhetoric, to the biographies within. There are a few points in dispute of that claim. Johnson did little research in the construction of the biographies, taking his material from existing biographies, particularly in the biographies of Milton and Dryden. He felt his primary obligation to the project was to fix errors with the existing biographies while concentrating the material to the most relevant details. There was no invention in the truths relayed in the biographies. The biographies were consistent with the nature and form of biographies of his age. For more than a century after Johnson's death, as his image gained iconic social status, his name was used as the political banner for various groups and agendas. A look at Johnson's own literary convictions and the biographical trends of his day shows that *Lives of the Poets* should be viewed as literary, perhaps even ecclesiastical, but not political. Johnson includes, as he does with all of his published works, moral commentary with the hope of guiding the reader toward virtue. He extracts from his sources the details most poignantly directed at the same moral messages found universally throughout his writing.

Johnson's political comments on Milton and Dryden were a needed revision upon the comments of other biographers, making them more literary than political. But as with all of his works, including the *Dictionary*, his convictions on matters of virtue and piety are thinly veiled. Johnson wrote in a private memorandum, upon the completion of *Lives*, that he had hoped that his biographies had been written "in such a manner as may tend to the promotion of piety" [25]. Johnson's well documented opinions on the duties and merits of good literature support the notion that the seemingly politically charged comments in *Lives* arise more from Johnson's literary convictions than any political agenda. The fact that Johnson was a well known Tory seems to have tainted some criticism of his biographies. The known convictions of the author do not necessarily dictate the nature of the work. If a Catholic priest reads the *Lord's Prayer*, the reading should not be considered particularly Catholic just because of the affiliation of the reader. Likewise, knowledge of Johnson's Tory leanings alone should not be enough to paint all politically related comments in his writing with a Tory-ish hue.

The inclusion of the political aspects of the lives of his biographical subjects was no innovation of Johnson's. He inherited the realms of biography from the influence of earlier publications, like the *Biographia Britannica*, published in 1747 [25]. The biographers of *Biographia Britannica* who compiled the history of the family of Granville reported that they felt "obliged to state and examine some very curious and interesting facts in our civil history, which, to speak the truth, is the greatest service that performances of this nature can render to the republic of letters" [25]. It is known that *Biographia Britannica* was one of Johnson's influences. Volumes I-IV of *Lives* were published in 1779 and V-X in 1781. A letter Johnson wrote to Mrs. Thrale in September 1777 requested the loan of *Biographia Britannica*. The request was made again six weeks later [26]. A novice glance at the political turmoil in England between the English Civil War in 1642 and the end of the Jacobite Rebellions in 1745 reveals the impossibility of writing on the life of any prominent English figure without some mention of politics. Any social or cultural consideration must be laid upon the political landscape to truly evaluate the minuter contours. Every life was affected by the political upheaval of that time and every biography must reflect the connections if it is to remain true to the Augustan ideals of faithful observation. Not to write of the political entanglements of his subjects would have been more revolutionary of Johnson than to adhere to the biographical mode of his era by including the political truths in the lives of his subjects.

J.P. Hardy, editor of the 1971 *Johnson's Lives of the Poets: A Selection*, writes in his introduction, "The Lives are distinguished not so much by original research, as by the skill and relevance with which their author has reworked and compressed available material" [26]. Hardy writes of Johnson's debt to public sources and cites six different sources Johnson uses for the Milton biography alone [26]. The Milton and Dryden biographies borrowed the most because there were more published resources available on those two subjects. In *Lives*, *Pope* is the longest, with 130 pages. *Dryden* is right behind at 116 pages. *Savage* should not be included in comparisons of length for a couple of reasons. First, it was written decades earlier and not with the intention of inclusion in the not yet conceived *Lives*. Second, Johnson's friendship with Savage and his subsequently intimate and personal biography thrusts *Savage* into a different category than those biographies whose details Johnson had to retrieve from other biographical sources. If *Savage* is taken out, only one biography is more than half of *Dryden*. It is *Milton*, with its 77 pages. In addition to the general biographical sources like *Biographia Britannica*, Johnson relied on several publications dedicated strictly to the lives of writers. Some of the sources Hardy credits in the construction of *Milton* are

> Edward Phillips's Theatrum Poetarum (1675); William Winstanley's Lives of the Most Famous English Poets (1687); Gerald Lang-baine's Account of the English Dramatic Poets (I691); Giles Jacob's Poetical Register (1719-20); and the work ascribed to Theophilus Cibber, but in all probability compiled mostly by Robert Shiels, The Lives of the Poets. (I753) [26]

All but the last of these influences were published in the time between the civil war and the end of the Jacobite Rebellions. They would have been steeped in political entanglements.

In *Milton*, if Johnson does betray a biased leaning, it is in the criticism of Milton's religious affiliation, or lack of one. He writes nothing critical of Milton's faith or his virtue, but writes with harsh astonishment of wavering and enigmatic loyalty to particular denominations of faith. Johnson writes that, "His theological opinions are said to have been first Calvinistical, and afterwards, perhaps when he began to hate the Presbyterians, to have extended towards Arminianism" [4]. Johnson attributes this to a lack of conviction in his general character, rather than to any inner theological turmoil. Without directly declaring Milton's lack of conviction to be a character weakness, Johnson writes, "He had determined rather what to condemn than what to approve" [4]. He continues, writing that, "We know rather what he was not than what he was" [4]. Although it was entirely outside of Johnson's *Modus Operandi* to refrain from the injection of personal opinion, these injections were always moral and never political. Johnson's matter-of-fact chronicle turns into a sermon. He declares, "To be of no church is dangerous" [4]. He writes that Milton "grew old without any worship" [4]. Then, in a manner of subtle but distinct censure, he writes, "In the distribution of his hours, there was no hour of prayer, either solitary or with his household, omitting public prayers, he omitted all" [4]. Entirely concordant with his earlier works, Johnson takes a moral stance through the example of the hero of his story. Political moderation and religious consistency became key components of the revered image of Dr. Johnson.

The debate over Johnson's political intentions with *Milton* comes with the declaration that Milton's politics were "those of an acrimonious and surely republican" [4]. It is not difficult to see why, with a lesser understanding of Johnson's literary mode, the section on Milton's politics might be viewed as Tory propaganda. A closer look reveals that the criticism is not toward republicanism, but toward the faulty reasoning Milton gives in support of republicanism. It is distinctly Milton's reasoning that is attacked by Johnson. He writes that Milton gave no better defense of his stance than to claim that "a popular government was the most frugal" [4]. He attacks this position, writing that "It is surely very shallow policy that supposes money to be the chief good" [4]. This quotation is more congruent with Johnson's adversarial relationship with money than with any shameless political rhetoric. Republicanism received no rebuke from Johnson in this passage. The power of wealth and greed to decay happiness is one of Johnson's running themes throughout his career. It is the promotion of money as the presidential factor in determining government that received Johnson's stern disapprobation. Johnson hoped to promote piety in his biography. As an avid student Antiquity, he would have been aware of the

Roman tradition of "pietas". The term referred not only to a discharge of duty to God, but also a duty to those in superior relation [25]. It is on this account that Johnson took particular exception to Milton's lack of "pietas", on a moral basis, regardless of how the issue fit into the contemporary political factions of England.

What has been deemed a Tory stance against parliamentary government harkens those familiar with Johnson's work back to his most prevalent theme, human vanity. Johnson claims that Milton's vanity dispelled his sense of duty to those in superior relation. He writes that Milton's republicanism was "founded in an envious hatred of greatness" [6]. He writes in far more obvious censure than before, stating that, "He hated all whom he was required to obey" [6]. He lists the primary targets of Milton's vain envy as "monarchs in the state and prelates in the church" [6]. Johnson has embodied in Milton the corrosive power of vanity, as displayed in the 'Tragic Quartet' from *The Vanity of Human Wishes*, married with the caustic qualities of wealth and affluence, as shown in *Savage*. The recognition of these very familiar themes should peel suspicion away from any thought of *Lives* as a political treatise. *Milton* should not be viewed as Johnson's maiden voyage into political activism. It slides quite comfortably into the body of his moral writings, to which familiar position any criticism of it should be directed.

The key points of focus in determining the purely literary nature of Johnson's *Lives*, particularly his biography of Milton, are the common mode of the biographical influences available to Johnson and Johnson's own literary standards. *Lives* was written toward the end of a career that was consistent in themes and purposes. The theory of a politically motivated biography is inconsistent with the whole of Johnson's body of work and diminished further by a closer look at the theorized political comments in their congruency with the moral themes that run universally throughout Johnson's work. Just as it is more difficult to recognize in a crowd a person of less intimate familiarity than it is to recognize an old friend, a familiarity with Johnsonian themes that span his career is helpful in recognizing how *Milton* and Johnson's other biographies fit in the crowd of eighteenth century literature. The themes of vanity and virtue strike of chord of familiarity, settling the biographies snuggly among Johnson's other moral writings and away from any political supposition.

Evidence of Johnson's political moderation is clear in his biography, *Life of Pope*. Politics and religion, the standard polarizing ideologies, are subdued for the exaltation of more universally humanistic traits. Johnson's *Life of Pope* contains evidence that Johnson had reason to both admire and ridicule Pope. Johnson's praise of Pope dramatically outweighs his censure. Despite disagreements in matters of religion and politics, Johnson found his likeness in Pope, in many aspects of their extraordinary lives. In *Life of Pope,* he displays, in form and content, his admiration and intimate sense of connectedness with Pope. He dedicates a much larger volume to Pope than to most of the other poets in his *Lives of the Poets,* favors him with shining literary criticism, and draws lines of familiarity between himself and Pope, particularly in shared struggles, in matters of life from physical attributes to Johnson's lifelong theme of under-supported genius.

Johnson and Pope shared philosophies on human observation as opposed to heavenly focus and scholarly submersion. In *Rambler No. 180*, written in December of 1751, Johnson references Milton's *Paradise Lost*, following a famous theme of Pope's *Essay on Man.*

> The learned, however, might generally support their dignity with more success, if they suffered not themselves to be misled by the desire of superfluous attainments. Raphael, in return to Adam's inquiries into the courses of the stars, and the revolutions of heaven, counsels him to withdraw his mind from idle speculations, and employ his faculties upon nearer and more interesting objects, the survey of his own life, the subjection of his passions, the knowledge of duties which must daily be performed, and the detection of dangers which must daily be incurred. [17]

This follows Pope's couplet from *Essay on Man* precisely, which reads,

Know, then, thyself, presume not God to scan;

The proper study of mankind is man. [27]

In his 1986 article, Ian Donaldson draws a connection between part of Pope's *Essay on Criticism*, which Johnson pays particular praise in *Life of Pope*, and a line from *Vanity of Human Wishes*. *Vanity* reads,

Are these thy views? Proceed, illustrious youth,

And virtue guard thee to the throne of Truth. [4]

The couplet echoes the sentiments from "Essay on Criticism."

Fired at first sight with what the muse imparts,

In fearless youth we tempt the heights of arts

While from the bounded level of our mind

Short views we take nor see the lengths behind. [27]

In Vanity, Johnson's Wolsey submerges himself in his books, to the neglect of the world around him. Johnson offers advice in line with Pope's "Know then thyself" line.

Yet hope not life from grief or danger free,

Nor think the doom of man revers'd for thee:

Deign on the passing world to turn thine eyes,

And pause awhile from letters, to be wise [4].

Johnson connected intimately with Pope in their shared quest to "Let observation with extensive view survey mankind from China to Peru" [4].

There is a far more personal tale from Pope's life that Johnson tells in *Life of Pope*. It is in this tale that Johnson perceives the most intimate connection. Pope's encounter with the presumptuous Lord Halifax bears a striking resemblance to Johnson's encounter with Lord Chesterfield, ending in the infamous *Letter to Lord Chesterfield*. Pope also writes a letter, which Johnson relays in *Pope*. Aside from some minor details, Johnson is telling his own story. He tells with an obvious bias, resulting from an encounter of his own that he perceives as identical, the story of Pope's struggle with a wealthy patron.

It is seldom that the great or the wise expect that they are despised or cheated. Halifax, thinking this a lucky opportunity of securing immortality, made some advances of favor and some overtures of advantage to Pope, which he seems to have received with sullen coldness. All our knowledge of this transaction is derived from a single letter (Dec. 1, 1714), in which Pope says,

> I am obliged to you both for the favours you have done me, and those you intend me. I distrust neither your will nor your memory, when it is to do good; and if I ever become troublesome or solicitous, it must not be out of expectation, but out of gratitude. Your Lordship may cause me to live agreeably in the town or contentedly in the country, which is really all the difference I set between an easy fortune and a small one. It is indeed a high strain of generosity to think of making me easy all my life, only because I have been so happy as to divert you some few hours. But if I may have leave to add it is because you think me no enemy to my native country, there will appear a better reason; for I must of consequence be very much, (as I sincerely am) yours &c. [4]

Johnson writes that Halifax was not used to such "frigid gratitude"[4]. Like Johnson's encounter with Chesterfield, Pope "fed his own pride with the dignity of independence" [4].

73

Johnson expresses his coherence with Pope in the *Dictionary*, in his definition of the word 'coherence'. As C. H. Knoblauch points out, "In the Dictionary Johnson defines "coherence" as a "sticking together" of things, an interconnectedness or "dependency" apprehended as a pattern of relationships among separate entities, parts of entities, or bits of information" [28]. Not surprisingly, Johnson cites Pope's *Essay on Man* in the defense of his definition. Coherence is the very reason Johnson gives for compiling his *Dictionary*, as he explains in the *Preface to the Dictionary*. In *Preface*, he writes of the "various dialects of the same country" . He writes of the "derivatives" and "uncertainty" of English language usage [4]. The concerns Johnson relays in his preface are identical to those faults Pope attributes to the scribblers in *The Dunciad* [28]. Johnson shows "coherence" with Pope through the creation of the *Dictionary,* a project intended to give coherence to the use of the English language. The value of coherence is associated tightly with Johnson in Elizabeth Gaskell's *Cranford*, demonstrating its place among the contributors to the Johnson image. Pope's influence is not thickly veiled by Johnson. He and Pope shared a coherence of a different kind. Both had awkward physical peculiarities. Perhaps Johnson found some comfort in the literary company of a man whose aesthetic awkwardness matched his. Johnson writes of Pope's stunted stature and of his "tender and delicate" constitution, as well as the "weakness of his body" [4].

In 1780, when Johnson was researching for *Life of Pope*, he asked a bookseller named John Nichols to obtain for him a set of the Warburton edition of Pope's works. The *Dictionary* would have been mostly compiled before the Warburon edition was released. Johnson would have used the Twickenham Edition of *The Poems of Alexander Pope* for his references to Pope in the Dictionary. In the first edition of the *Dictionary*, under the letters A, K, and W, Johnson includes 363 passages from Pope. They include the translation of *The Odyssey*, with 76 citations, *Essay on Man* with 33, *Essay on Criticism* with 25, *The Rape of the Lock* with 25, the four Ethic Epistles with 22, the two versions of *The Dunciad* with 22, *The Memoirs of Scriblerus* with 10, and the translation of *The Iliad* with 9 [29]. Johnson was very particular in the choices of his citations. They can be used to determine much about Johnson's opinions of the authors he cites. Quotations from Pope account for 3.5 percent of all citations in the *Dictionary* [29]. In addition to volume, the definitions that the citations are used to support speak to Johnson's opinions of the writers he cites. Likewise, *Lives of the Poets* tells much from the size of the biographies and from their placement in the volumes. For example, *Dryden* and *Pope* are placed to begin the second and fourth volumes [30]. This serves to emphasize these two among the long list of poets covered. Johnson dedicated more time and pages to the poets he revered. Pope leads them all with 130 pages in the 1825 Oxford edition, compared to a single page for Pomfret [30]. *Milton* is much shorter than *Pope* or *Dryden*. Johnson's linguistic coherence with Pope, which he fails to recognize with Milton, is the reason for the smaller tribute. Johnson credits Milton with an accomplishment, in *Paradise Lost*, more prominent than anything written by Pope or Dryden, yet *Milton* is still significantly shorter. Despite Milton's contribution, Johnson felt his use of language cruder and less representative of the beauties of the language than what is seen in the writings of Pope and Dryden. Some explanation is offered in *Rambler No. 88*. Johnson writes that "Milton therefore seems to have somewhat mistaken the nature of our language, of which the chief defect is ruggedness and asperity, and has left our harsh cadences yet harsher" [30].

Johnson's sense of kinship and coherence with Pope is spelled directly and bluntly in *Life of Pope* and scattered perhaps more vaguely, but not obscurely, throughout much of Johnson's other work. In comes in the form of direct tribute, like in the citations of the *Dictionary*, and through indirect imitations of Pope's themes in Johnson's poetry and essays. In *Pope*, Johnson draws a distinct connection between his own experience with patronage and Pope's. Johnson's consistent theme of the under-recognized talent going it alone is reflected in *Pope*. Johnson writes that, "Pope, finding little advantage from external help, resolved thenceforth to direct himself" [4], reflective of Johnson's unwillingness to owe that to a patron "which Providence has enabled me to do for myself" [4]. The lines of connection, whether in bold and praising criticism or in the many subtle, perhaps sometimes accidental tributes throughout his career, are drawn by Johnson for easy study. *Life of Pope* is the punctuation at the end of a long admiration Johnson maintained for Pope.

Another important portion of Johnson's surviving body of written work, in which can be found vivid expressions of admiration, as well as other emotions, is his personal letters. Letters play a large role in reconstructing Johnson's image in the Romantic Era, as will be evident in Chapter 4 of this book. If the purpose of biography is not to chronicle the events of the life of a subject who is meant to be seen and not touched, identified but not understood, but rather to grant the reader an intimate comprehension of the multiple layers of the character of the subject, then Samuel Johnson's familiar letters serve the function of biography better than Boswell, Piozzi, and Bate combined. Personal letters fall somewhere between the polished presentation of published works and the intimately personal submissions in a dairy or journal. Unlike a diary, letters are meant to be read by the recipient, adding a degree of pretention not found in diaries. By the end of his life, Johnson knew that his letters were preserved as objects of fascination by a British society already enamored by the reputation of his discourse [31]. Devotees gathered around Johnson's circle, from his trips to church to his evenings at the tavern, to catch an earful of his famous conversations. In the last ten years of his life, Johnson's letters bore more meticulous composition, written with an understanding of their public appeal. Nevertheless, they serve the purposes of biography because of the broad spectrum of recipients, covering several categories of relations. Johnson alters his epistolary mode for specific targets and circumstances, exposing the many facets of his character.

Of Johnson's surviving letters, more than two-thirds were written in the last ten years of his life [31]. The letters written before Johnson's last decade were less treasured as literary curiosities and therefore less scrupulously collected and maintained. When compared beside his later letters, they demonstrate an evolution in Johnson's character. Boswell recognized the autobiographic nature of a collection of familiar letters. He included around 340 letters or excerpts of letters in the first and second volumes of his *Life of Johnson* [31]. Only recently have Johnson's letters found intimate acquaintance with the body of his published works in the study of Samuel Johnson. This is partially due to Johnson's opinion of what he called "the great epistolick art" [32]. In a letter to Boswell, on December 8, 1763, Johnson criticizes the typical pleasantries passed in the standard Augustan letter. Johnson describes the "topicks with which those letters are commonly filled" as "written only for the sake of writing I seldom shall think worth communication" [32]. Johnson often included such comments on letter writing as part of his attempt to justify the rareness and brevity of his letters to acquaintances who expected more. Boswell describes the exchange from his perspective in *Life of Johnson*. "I wrote to Johnson a plaintive and desponding letter, to which he paid no regard. Afterwards, when I had acquired a firmer tone of mind, I wrote him a second letter, explaining much anxiety to hear from him [32]. After Johnson's death, many of his letters were published in magazines. Boswell searched those letters while soliciting many of Johnson's acquaintances for any contributions they could add to his store of Johnson's letters.

Letter writing in the 18th century demanded the same sort of formal observances as polite conversation. Although Johnson observed those demands, he left his unique mark on the genre, just as he did with his published work. His phrasing was courtly and meticulously intentional. He believed that letters should only be written when there is something to communicate. He made exception to that rule, as a general principle and matter of convention. Johnson believed that a letter to a friend who is far away broke the rules of convention. He wrote in a letter to Giuseppi Baretti, dated Wednesday, June 10, 1761, that "A short letter to a distant friend is, in my opinion, an insult like that of a slight bow or cursory salutation" [32]. He reiterates this opinion in a letter to Sir Robert Chambers who was in Calcutta. He writes to

Sir Robert, "with so much land and sea between us, we ought to compensate the difficulty of correspondence with by the length of our letters" [33]. Johnson had a clear affinity for formal observances. Most of his letters provide evidence to that aspect of his character. The letters he wrote to his far away friends provide a different insight, as do his letters concerning dire, emotional circumstances. Some of Johnson's most devout disciples, like Jane Austen, employ "the great epistolick art" in the most important scenes of their narratives. Consider Mr. Darcy's letter to Elizabeth, Captain Wentworth's letter to Anne, or Isabella's letter to Catherine.

Johnson's epistolary mode could appear down-right Romantic, when the topic of discourse touched his heart. Letters to his mother were among those. While still eloquent, as is expected, his highly personal letters did not hide behind a strong structure of Augustan epistolary expectations. He writes to his mother on January 13, 1759, "The account which Miss gives me of your health pierces my heart. God comfort and preserve you, and save you, for the sake of Jesus Christ" [32]. Professions of pierced hearts harkens readers more to the letters of John Keats than to anything by Dryden or Pope. The self-doubt and contrition that lies thinly veiled in his poetry and essays comes out in force in this letter to his mother, where he continues, "Pray send me your blessing, and forgive all that I have done amiss to you" [32].

Those letters which are less personal not only stand on formalities, but consistently include quintessentially Johnsonian proverbs. In many cases, the letter begins with Johnsonian proverbs. To George Strahan in 1763, he begins, "To give pain ought always to be painful" [32]. Philosophical advice and moral sermon dominate the letters when Johnson's emotions are not particularly stirred by the circumstances of the correspondence. He writes to Mrs. Thrale in September, 1773, "The use of travelling is to regulate imagination by reality, and instead of thinking how things may be, to see them as they are" [33]. Many of Johnson's letters prove him to be as relentlessly attached to his primary moral canon in familiar letters as he is in his verse, essays, and fiction. On January 14, 1776, he writes to Boswell, beginning the letter, "Apologies are seldom of any use". He begins a March 21, 1770 letter to Richard Farmer with, "no man ought to keep wholly to himself any possession that may be useful to the publick" [32]. These philosophical lectures all read as if they could easily be plugged into *Vanity of Human Wishes*. Although they were all written to acquaintances, they bear a striking resemblance in tone to the moral lectures he addressed to the faceless readers of his published poetry and essays.

Johnson's emotional state and ardent connections are betrayed by the letters that replace the Augustan sermon with frankly stated affection and concern. He moves from a dry explanation of poor correspondence with Strahan in May of 1765, when he writes, "That I have answered neither of your letters you must not impute to any declension of good will, but merely to the want of something to say" [32] to a letter to Mrs. Thrale in August where his tone is closer to John Keats' letters to Fanny Brawne than to the epistolary mode of Pope which Johnson praises so profusely. He writes to Thrale, "If you have really so good an opinion of me as you express, it will not be necessary to inform you how unwillingly I miss the opportunity of coming to Brighthelmston in Mrs. Thrale's company" [32]. One can almost imagine a love struck Keats scribbling that line on the Isle of Wight. Johnson's responses to tragedy are as personal and as far from sermon as his expressions of affection. In June of 1766, he writes to William Jessup in gracious criticism of ceremonious writing in times of tender emotion. He opens, "If your letter had been less ceremonious it would not have pleased me less. I read poor Grierson's paper with a very tender remembrance both of his learning and his humour" [32]. Johnson did not hide the vulnerability of his humanity behind Augustan ceremony when the circumstance and the correspondent were both personal. He writes a tender confession to Mrs. Thrale on May 18, 1769.

> Now I know you want to be forgetting me, but I do not want to be forgotten, and would rather send you letters like Presto's than suffer myself to slip out of your memory. That I should forget you there is no danger, for I have time enough to think, both by night

and day, and he that has leisure for anything that is not present, always turns his mind to that which he likes best. [32]

In this passage, Johnson presents one of his proverbs as it connects very personally to him.

Even in his satiric verses, Johnson's tone is distinctly personal, as if the subjects strike a personal chord from his own experiences, far more than relaying a distant observation. His letters are a more diverse source into the real Johnson and their dissemination made them a contributor to the social icon. They often supply the satire seen in his poetry, but also include effusions directly from the heart. They express regret and sorrow far more intensely than his published works. Johnson's biographies expose two primary portions of his life. They reveal the personal Johnson, through the eyes of family and friends, and they also connect those who read them with the mode and canon of Johnson's poetry, biographies, and essays. His letters reveal these same aspects, but without conjecture or assumption. If taken in as a single narrative, Johnson's familiar letters become the most diverse and honest biography of the man. Even where his epistolary mode is more intentionally fashioned, with the understanding of their public appeal, his letters serve as evidence to the Samuel Johnson they portray. When the similarities between Johnson's published writing and his personal letters comes into light, and the two are used in support of each other, a far more accurate autobiography is presented in Johnson's own words. Without the survival and dissemination of Johnson's letters, the iconic Johnsonian image would have been far more influenced by biographies like Boswell's, yielding a product more Boswellian than Johnsonian.

The expansive volumes of Johnson's literary achievements cover several varieties of literary forms and modes. Throughout it all, an ecclesiastical morality is handed to the reader in no subtle form. This Johnsonian morality has a canon with three major points. Johnson ever endeavors to convince his readers, through fiction and essays, through poetry and even the definitions and citations of his *Dictionary*, of the truth of the Johnson Canon. 1. Poverty and obscurity offer shelter from the vices of vanity that haunt and hound the wealthy and renowned. 2. As a general rule in society, literary genius goes mostly unrecognized and underappreciated. 3. Vice and sloth can be handled and manipulated through the development of virtuous habits. These three threads are sometimes interwoven and sometimes stand as clear individuals. But when the reader of Johnson observes the whole of his work, it is clearly noticed that all three combine equally on the patchwork quilt of Johnson's work to boldly exclaim Johnson's morality and the Johnson Canon. From there, alternating views of the whole or portions can be compared beside the references to Johnson and the uses of his image for literary purposes or socio-political vindication by the following generations to determine the relationship between the Johnson Canon and the perpetuating and diversifying Johnsonian persona.

Chapter 3
Boswell and the Art of Hero-Building

SAMUEL JOHNSON'S CONVERSATIONAL MODE and the elite circle of literati who experienced it became one of the dominant features of Johnson's enshrined legacy during the following literary ages. Although many biographies present details from Johnson's life, none place its readers within Johnson's intimate, Socratic circle of disciples like Boswell's *Life of Johnson*. Since it is Boswell who gives the public this ever important aspect of the Johnsonian image, it is Boswell who creates the largest portion of the Dr. Johnson that lingered in the English mind, on the English tongue, and within the English pages of literature during the life of Johnson's iconic fame. Many have criticized Boswell, noting that *Life of Johnson* fails to stand up to the current scholarly demands of the genre. Boswell's *Life* should not stand in comparison beside other biographies, nor held to the standards of their discipline, because it belongs to a different genre of literature. Regardless of the accuracy of Boswell's recorded words of Johnson, and regardless of how near Boswell's Johnson is to the true Samuel Johnson, the Dr. Johnson portrayed by Boswell is the Dr. Johnson of the common English discourse because it was Boswell's biography that defined its subject in the public eye. For the purposes of this study, identifying and mapping Johnson's public image, Boswell's *Life of Johnson* is completely accurate, because the quotations and anecdotes within became the image of Dr. Johnson, regardless of their historically factual inaccuracies. Even if the tales within are entirely fictional, they are reflective of the Johnsonian image at the time and they cement that image for posterity.

Boswell's *Life* gives a voyeuristic, almost paparazzi exposé of the intimate banter of a literary giant, with an equally paparazzi agenda and almost violent twisting of facts. What Socrates offered his disciples in matters of nature and science, Johnson offered in language. And Boswell was Johnson's Plato. It was Johnson's conversation, his casual talk, which became the stuff of legend, due almost entirely to its portrayal in Boswell's *Life*. Although still considered a biography, Boswell does not follow the current dictates of the genre. The primary purpose of Boswell's *Life* is to expose on a grand stage the conversational genius that could only be experienced by a coveted few. No post-mortem research could provide a biographer with the conversational details captured by Boswell during his friendship with Johnson. Boswell writes in his introduction, "What I consider as the peculiar value of the following work, is, the quantity it contains of Johnson's conversation" [1]. Boswell not only understood the "value" to English society of his documented Johnson conversations, he realized the "peculiar" nature of his presentation of Johnson's character through those conversations. Few had occasion to take note of Johnson's leisure conversational moments as did Boswell, particularly during the time of Johnson's life when his company and witty banter were most coveted. Before Boswell's *Life*, the familiar letter was the only ready documentation of the intimate conversations of the great [2]. But it is hard to determine sharpness of wit in a letter. In many cases, the absence of spontaneity in a hand written letter shrouds the familiar letter with a suspicion of calculated pretention. But instant, vocal responses, like those recorded in *Life*, stamp the spontaneous wit with a seal of authenticity.

Aside from being the desire of the public, Johnson's conversational mode was worth documenting because of its peculiarity. He violated all conventions of Augustan polite conversation [2]. So peculiar was his expression that even Boswell needed time to acclimate, as he writes in his introduction to *Life*.

> Let me here apologize for the imperfect manner in
> which I am obliged to exhibit Johnson's conversation
> at this period. In the early part of my acquaintance

with him, I was so wrapt in admiration of his extraordinary colloquial talents, and so little accustomed to his peculiar mode of expression, that I found it extremely difficult to recollect and record his conversation with its genuine vigour and vivacity. In progress of time, when my mind was, as it were, strongly impregnated with the Johnsonian other, I could, with much more facility and exactness, carry in my memory and commit to paper the exuberant variety of his wisdom and wit. [1]

It was that "peculiar mode of expression" that launched Johnson's iconic social image and made his company so coveted during his lifetime. But it was Boswell who bequeathed it to posterity. If held beside other biographies and to the standard guidelines of the genre, Boswell's cannot hold its place. If viewed as a preservative of the priceless treasure of Johnson's conversation, and seen in the light of the tremendous Johnsonian phenomenon of the following century, *Life of Johnson* must be revered as one of the most impactful biographies of any age. Other Johnson biographies may be more true, that is, more faithful to the facts of Johnson's life. But it is Boswell's Johnson that the world came to know. Boswell's Johnson defined the term 'Johnsonian' for generations to come. More than reflecting the living Johnson, Boswell created the posthumous Johnson, a task not utterly reliant upon accuracy. Other biographies tell what happened in the subject's life. The reader must determine from these facts who the subject is by drawing conclusions from the pile of presented facts. Boswell tells who his subject is. He hands his reader a gilded icon, pre-assembled and ready for worship.

Without Boswell, Johnson may have slipped quickly into obscurity, or at least not approached the heights of his nineteenth century fame. Although other contributors to the Johnson image have been profound, they are attached to Boswell's Johnson. Those contributors needed something solid to stick to. Without Boswell's biography, they may have slid into obscurity. *Life of Johnson* differs from the biographies of other literary figures in that the published works of the subject are of minor emphasis.

The point of *Life* is not to promote the writings of Johnson, rather the personality. Only a portion of a subject's character can be determined by studying his polished published works. Character is revealed in daily life, and no biographer captures the daily nuances of the mundane moments of the subject's life like Boswell. Subsequent English literature demonstrates this with the many references to Johnson's conversation and the revered and coveted nature of his inner circle as presented by Boswell.

Boswell writes in his introduction of "the quantity it contains of Johnson's conversation". But as far back as 1831, the source of all of this conversation was brought into question, when John Wilson Croker wrote in the preface to his edition of Boswell's *Life* that Boswell only deals with 180 days of interaction between him and Johnson [3]. Croker continues, calculating that the addition of the 96 days spent together in the 1773 tour of Scotland, the total 276 days accounts for one one-hundredth of Johnson's life, but occupies the majority of Boswell's *Life* and *Tour* [3]. Such criticism would have merit if held against other biographies. The point of Boswell's *Life* is not to compile a massive mound of facts about Johnson's life, or explain his character by an expose of forgotten childhood circumstances. It is to construct an icon, playing primarily on what Boswell knew to be the most iconic feature of Johnson's lingering image, his conversational mode. With Croker's criticism in mind, how is it that Boswell's accounts of Johnson, particularly Johnson's conversation, should come to form the definitive Johnsonian persona for posterity when Boswell's accounts cover so little of Johnson's life? This is a question concerning biographical purists, but not sociologists or literary historians. Boswell's biography did form the Johnsonian image, regardless of the degree of accuracy or the portion of Johnson's life covered. The term 'Johnsonian' came to represent the public image of Johnson, Boswell's image, comprehensively, despite the inaccuracies and flaws discovered and censured by later biographers. Among his many criticisms of Boswell, Croker complains of the mundane nature of many of Boswell's inclusions. In his critique of Croker's publication, Macaulay uses

Johnson's own words, as recorded by Boswell in one of those mundane moments, writing,

> Mr. Croker's performance is on par with those of a
> certain leg of mutton on which Dr. Johnson dined,
> while traveling from London to Oxford, and which
> he, with characteristic energy, pronounced to be "as
> bad as bad can be; ill fed, ill killed, ill kept, and ill
> dressed. [4]

Macaulay continues his attack, writing that "Nothing in the work has astonished us so much as the ignorance and carelessness of Mr. Croker" [4]. Despite Macaulay's hash words, critics of Boswell continue to fall into the same trap, holding *Life* to the accepted standards of biography and attacking each variance from those standards. It is important to keep in mind that Macaulay was primarily an historian. His ability to breach the strict borders of literature, into the realm of the social sciences, gives him a wider perspective on Boswell's work. It is that perspective that leads to the following assessment: "Homer is not more decidedly the first of heroic poets, Shakespeare is not more decidedly the first of dramatists, Demosthenes is not more decidedly the first of orators, than Boswell is the first of biographers" [4]. As a social scientist, Macaulay's take on Boswell's biography is more relevant to the study of Johnson's image than Croker's. From Macaulay's particular, historical perspective, he recognized that Boswell's *Life* transcends the confines of biography, and should therefore be exempt from the sort of criticism published by Croker and many other literary critics since. The credit that Macaulay pays to Boswell is vindicated by the extent of the literary world's employment of Johnson's image. Macaulay's life from 1800 to 1859 exposed him to a portion of the historical impact of Johnson's public persona.

An understanding of the immense breadth of the Johnsonian social phenomenon forces consideration of its origins. The source and nature of the phenomenon revolved primarily around Johnson's conversational mode and his intimate circle. The public's knowledge of those aspects of Johnson, whether accurate or not, came from Boswell. Boswell's biography profoundly affected English society, and in doing so, affected the subsequent literature that reflected English society. Johnson became a major theme in English literature, in both the essay and the novel, with hundreds of references to the Boswellian version of his character. Boswell's *Life* is literature and must therefore remain a faithful subject of literary standards, subject to the same criticism as the members of its genre. But its involvement in the creation of a social phenomenon much bigger than literature forces an expansion of its consideration beyond a mere biography. It must be viewed through the lenses of the social sciences as well as through literary lenses. This broader perspective renders moot many of the criticisms that have inhibited a more general reverence for the work. Macaulay's historical perspective allowed him to credit the work with the historical and social weight it truly carries. Readers of Boswell's work should adopt Macaulay's trans-discipline perspective, rereading the work after consideration of its broad, multi-discipline circumference and perhaps reading it after reading this book. An understanding of Boswell's role in the genesis of a tremendous social and literary phenomenon shines a warmer and certainly more reverent light upon *Life of Johnson*. This approach will alleviate the frustrations in encountering the many aspects of Boswell's work that violate the strict standards of the genre of literature that has labeled it with a degree of inaccuracy for over two hundred years.

Chapter 4
Johnson's Relationship to Romanticism

BEFORE TRYING TO LOCATE and identify the popular image of Dr. Johnson in the Romantic Period, it is important to identify his relationship to the period and subsequently, the period's relationship to him. He is commonly held and often depicted as the last literary sentry of rational, moderate, Augustan defense before the overwhelming wave of emotional, radical Romanticism. A comparison between Johnson's very personal poetic tone and that of the earlier, more cerebral and emotionally detached Augustans, particularly in his satires, will reveal undeniable Romantic leanings. Although satire was a favored poetic mode of the Augustans, and Johnson followed suit, Johnson's satires steered the genre toward Romantic sensibilities, leaving a distinctly different experience on the palate of the reader, a relatable experience, a sympathetic experience, and most importantly, an instructional experience. Johnson's conversations, as captured by James Boswell and Hester Piozzi, also reveal a more personal attachment to human suffering, a favored theme of the Romantics. Pope and Dryden were humanists, dedicating the bulk of their work to the observation and documentation of humanity. Johnson was also a humanist, but his observations spawned within him, or at least revealed, a humanitarian, in the manner of Byron and Shelley. Pope observed, pondered, and documented. Johnson observed pondered, felt, and documented, often with a tone of personal frustration with what he felt. Johnson permitted the infiltration of feeling into his writing, in strict violation of the precepts of Augustan Literature. Although Johnson did not write about nature, like many Romantics such as Blake and Wordsworth, and in fact sternly criticized pastoral poetry, his poetry had the personal and emotional tenderness of a Romantic, not the detached, stoic observations that defined the Augustan mode. He was not an Augustan soldier, defeated by Romanticism. He was more of an usher, guiding the English readership into a drastic and inevitable mutation toward individualism and personal emotion in popular literature.

Contrasting Johnson with his fellow Augustans clarifies this distinction. The seventeenth century and the birth of neoclassicism brought an official end to the Renaissance and Medieval critical precepts. Members of the Augustan school cling to the precepts of Classicism with greater loyalty than the Ancients they imitated. John Dryden's 1668 *Essay of Dramatic Poesy* provides the most comprehensive single example of the attitudes of Neo-Classicism [1]. Just as Thomas Hobbes guides the transition between the Renaissance and the Augustans by redirecting the critical eye to the precepts of the Ancients while maintaining the coating of virtuous pursuit handed down by Thomas Aquinas, as he demonstrates in his 1650 *Answer to Davenant's Preface to Gondibert*, writing "by imitating human life in delightful and measured lines, to avert men from vice and incline them to virtuous and honorable actions" [1], Dryden stood just on the Augustan side of the gateway between literary eras, hammering and forging whatever passed through into the rigid forms of Augustan decorum. Dryden loosens the binds of tradition for artists from the rigidity of Antiquity, but still insists on standards that would prevent the indecorous and fanciful ramblings of unchecked imaginings and is done so from the same lofty imperial perch as the Romans he adored. Dryden's essay begins with a tale of war. While incidental to the primary topics of the essay, the beginning demonstrates the dawn of the imperial-minded Augustan Age, an age of English writers whose country's military dominance over the world held before them a reflection of Roman greatness, binding the two cultures across the centuries. He writes of a naval battle against the Dutch and describes "the two most mighty and best appointed fleets which any age had ever seen" [1]. He recounts the many lookers-on who followed the sounds of the cannons, looking for an opportunity to profit from an account of the battle. The narrator wishes the victory. But as Dryden puts it, "he could scarce have wished the victory at the price he knew he must pay for it, in being subject to the reading and hearing of so many ill verses as he was sure would be made upon it" [1]. He refers to his literary ambulance chasers as "eternal rhymers, who watch a battle with more diligence than the ravens and birds of prey" [1]. Such behavior is vulgar to Dryden and beneath the decency of quality authors. Dryden continues extensively to outline the traits of bad poets, stating in unambiguous terms that "ill poets should be as well silenced as seditious preachers" [1]. Even satire, which at this time was beginning its rise to the dominant mode of English literature, is restricted by Dryden to the confines of decorum, chastising the broad and malicious attacks for which satire had become a weapon.

Dryden draws his contemporaries back to the humanistic and sensory imitation of the Ancients. He accuses some of having "debauched the true old poetry", adding that "nature, which is the soul of it, is not in any of your writings" [1]. Dryden refers to human nature, not the sort of natural consideration of the Romantic poets, like Blake and Wordsworth. For the Romantics and beyond, "nature" meant the non-human, not polluted by human civilizations, works of the living planet, such as trees, animals, lakes, and rivers. Their "nature" is more like what the Augustans and earlier ages refer to as "pastoral". For Dryden, "nature" refers to human inclinations and conditions, as it was meant by Aristotle and later by Horace. Dryden holds all literature to the same standard, adding later that a play ought to be "a just and lively image of human nature, representing its passions and humors, and the changes of fortune to which it is subject, for the delight and instruction of mankind" [1].

There are a few key words and phrases in this last quotation that speak clearly of Dryden's literary precepts and also serve as a map into the coming Augustan Age. Dryden writes of a "just" image. This refers back to Aristotle and the notion of reflecting the sharpest possible image when imitating nature. The phrase, "changes of fortune", foretells a popular theme in Augustan literature, that of the hero's constantly rising and falling fortunes, and how the hero deals with changes. This theme is more of a magnifying glass than a mirror. The changes of fortune in the lives of Augustan literary heroes are an exaggerated reflection of nature, taking the characters to the most extreme highs and lows. The last key word in the quote is "instruction". The Augustans peeled away from Plato's detached images, having maintained a thin coating of Middle-Age morality. Lessons must accompany Augustan narratives. The reader must come out of the experience with new tools to govern their own behavior. This is a crucial ingredient in Augustan literature, increasing in prevalence as the age progressed, and peaking with the last great Augustan, Dr. Samuel Johnson. Dryden would have approved of the moral instruction in Johnson's work, but would have severely criticized the sympathetic attachment and blatantly shared frustrations that binds Johnson to his characters with an intimacy that Dryden would likely have considered inappropriate.

The best way to accentuate Johnson as the variable in the transition between the Augustans and the Romantics is to contrast his satires against those more congruent with the Augustan mode. Despite the similarities between Pope's essays and Johnson's *The Vanity of Human Wishes*, a clear distinction in the authors' personal, emotional intimacy with their work is easily noticed. In *Vanity,* as in most of Johnson's work, there is an emotionally involved intimacy, straying far from the Augustan satiric poetic mode of Pope and Dryden, as is apparent in the following passage.

Now fears in dire vicissitude invade,

The rustling brake alarms, and quiv'ring shade. [2]

This does smack of the satiric observation of human folly, but it also recalls the reader to personal experiences, the universality of which he displays in his intimate expression of a human inclination with a universal impact, conjuring universal emotions. The humanist in Johnson lays this passage before his readers with that very intention. Satire dissects human nature from an unemotional distance. Such is not the tone of *Vanity*. Calling it satire because it uses a famous satire to prove a passionate point is a gross over-simplification of a complex work by a complex author. Satire puts matters of sadness into ridiculous, comical form. The intent is to make the readers laugh at themselves before seeing their own reflections in the text, then reveal the readers' own faces behind the ridiculous characters. *Vanity* hails from a different poetic mode, one in between the pure satire of Pope and the vivid, penetrating, and more personal verses of Byron and Keats. At no point is the reader of *Vanity* encouraged to laugh. The direct condemnation of human folly and vice savors strongly of personal bitterness, while it places that bitterness onto the palate of the reader in a direct and unpretending manner that is quintessentially and uniquely Johnsonian. While Pope, and Johnson's other Augustan predecessors, document their human observations from a lofty, imperial, Augustan perch, detached from the subjects of the survey, Johnson writes his satires as if he is knee deep in the human affairs he describes. Such is not the nature of satire, and thus, Johnson's poems cannot rightly be called satire. It is in his imitations of Juvenal that the uniqueness of the Johnsonian mode becomes apparent. The other Augustans fit the ascribed mode of their literary era. The Romantics fit theirs. Johnson stands with one foot in each, with critical aspects of each, but not soundly enough to place him squarely in either.

Johnson's death is commonly held as the linear border between the Augustans and Romantics. It is unrealistic, however tidy, to draw such straight chronological lines between eras, whether literary, historical, or otherwise. In truth, Johnson did not hold the line of Augustan satire against the wave of Romanticism, as he is often credited with doing. He was rather a transitional poet, opening the doors for a more personal expression of the human experience. His "satire" remained true enough to Augustan form to gently acclimate readers to the onset of the Romantic mode before it hit in full force after Dr. Johnson's death. Bertrand Bronson writes of a "Pre-Romantic mode" but refuses to include Dr. Johnson in that mode with his contemporaries like Oliver Goldsmith [3]. Boyd writes of Dr.

Johnson's "sympathetic imagination," distinguishing it from his fellow Augustans, but declares that "it would be quite erroneous to assume that this tendency in any way constitutes a 'Pre-Romantic' element in Johnson's thought" [4].T. S. Eliot declares in 1930 that Dr. Johnson's poems are "purer satire than anything of Dryden or Pope, nearer in spirit to the Latin" [5]. He defends this, claiming that the satirist must be a "stern moralist" and declaring that "Johnson has a better claim to this seriousness than either Pope or Dryden" [5]. Eliot comes back in 1944 to claim Johnson as an inferior satirist to Pope and Dryden because of a weakness in satiric wit [6]. Eliot seems closer to the mark in 1944. Both *Vanity* and *London* are bereft of the dry and detached Augustan satiric wit that defines both the era and the genre, leaning Johnson even more toward the notion of 'Pre-Romantic' or at least 'Post-Augustan'. There is a distinct sense of tragedy in his 'satires', a trait separating his from all others in the genre.

Evidence of Johnson's intimate attachment to his poetic characters and the suffering of their circumstances can be seen in both *London* and *Vanity*. Rather than denounce the satirized characters as ludicrous, Johnson endears the reader to them through the tragedy of their failings. Literary critic, Northrop Frye writes that satire "breaks down when its content is too oppressively real to permit the maintaining of the fantastic or hypothetical tone" [6]. There is no fantastic or hypothetical tone in *Vanity*. It is real commentary on real people, set in imitation of Juvenal's satire for the purpose of displaying the universality of human folly and more importantly, the universality of the associated misery. There is an important distinction to be made between Juvenal's *X* and Johnson's *Vanity of Human Wishes*. Juvenal attacks human vanity. In Johnson's poem, it is not the humans that are vain but the wishes that are 'in vain'. So the 'vanity of human wishes' speaks more to the fruitlessness of desire than to the folly of self-interest. It is more of a testament to the toils of life than to the weaknesses of people, more akin to Keats' "Ode on Melancholy" than Pope's *Essay on Man*. This is not just a literary tool Johnson uses for the purposes of his satires. It is reflective of and dictated by his humanitarian nature with a

Romantic sense of despair and a Romantic intimacy with the author. In referring to Johnson's moral essays, W. J. Bate writes,

> Johnson was unable merely to observe, but had to participate and share; his own participation sets a bar to satire. The result, time and again in all his moral writings, is that we have anger, protest, even ridicule, always in the process of turning into something else. [4]

Johnson's proclivity for tragic narrative is reflective of a vision of Antiquity and the ruined reminders of fallen civilizations, far more aligned with that of the Romantics than with that of his fellow Augustans. His study of ancient languages and literature drew his attention keenly toward the fate of fallen greatness. Greece and Rome suffered a fall from splendor not entirely unlike that of Richard Savage or the tragic quartet of *Vanity,* albeit on a much larger scale. The Augustans' vision of empire, drawn from the study of Antiquity, focuses on the perpetual nature of Antiquity's legacy, the literature, the philosophy, the art, and the surviving architectural structures [7]. Even the crumbled ruins served more as a reminder of the living legacy of architectural advancements than a reminder of the ephemeral nature of human accomplishments, as portrayed in Percy Bysshe Shelley's "Ozymandias". The Romantics had a gloomier outlook on the lingering reminders of ancient civilizations. Referring to the Romantics, Goldstein writes, "Every high ideal represented by the Classical style contains a premonition of reversal" [7]. The ruins of Greece and Rome, which included the literature, did not promote a sense of patriotic nation-building in the minds of the Romantics, as it did with the Augustans. The expansion of the British Empire brought the ruins of Antiquity into intimate and daily proximity for British subjects. The effect of those artifacts on the psyche is one of the key distinguishing factors between the Augustans and the Romantics. Johnson's tragic narratives give strong clues as to which side of that divisive line he stood. The fall of empires impresses upon the Romantic mind the power and permanence of nature over human creations and the ephemeral nature of success and prosperity. This is why the poetry of the Romantics inclined toward a revered laudation of nature [7]. As a humanist, Johnson kept his focus on the human experience. Never removing the Romantic lenses, his writing told of the pathetic loser in the battle between man and nature. The theme of loss and decay permeated his writing.

Johnson's poetry more directly portrayed his inner thoughts, concerns, and frustrations than did any of his other published work, save maybe his familiar correspondence published long after his death. For the public that embraced and enshrined him, these verses were the strongest link between the deified hero and the mortal man. When his persona was raised as the banner of the industrial proletariat in the late Victorian Age, the image of Johnson and the mortal Johnson found their closest affiliation. The lofty observations of dry Augustan satire could never have such a gritty band of devotees. Pope's *Essay on Man* did not rally the hearts of the downtrodden, a demographic that found a personal connection to their hero through poetry lost in the border designations between literary ages. But it was this straddling of eras in Dr. Johnson's poetic mode that permitted his persona to be hoisted by multiple social factions, some more Augustan in sensibilities, and some more Romantic, in the course of the following historical ages.

Chapter 5
Romanticism's Relationship to Johnson

REGARDLESS OF WHETHER Samuel Johnson is to be considered in any way Romantic or pre-Romantic, much happened after his death that influenced English society and literature in ways he could not have influenced. Johnson died five years before the French Revolution, a cataclysmic event with profound effects on English literature. Social and political Enlightenment philosophy flourished in Johnson's lifetime. It would not have been difficult for a man of his connections and high literacy to read the writing on the wall. But the chaos of the French Revolution could not have been understood by those who did not live to experience it. The drastic changes in society and economy due to industrialization coincided with and contributed to the greatest age of socio-political upheaval in Western history. The generations after the Romantic Age were able to view these revolutionary events from a stoic distance, examining the architecture of the revolutionary Romantic Movement. Those living within the movement lacked that perspective. They could not see how Johnson fit into the greater picture. Johnson was of the past and the past could not be embraced or fully recognized amid the chaos of revolution. Revolutionary upheaval is a blunt instrument, swung with emotional violence. It is not a tool of precision. The past was the enemy of progress, regardless of the particulars of its members or of their philosophical affiliation. A current understanding of the Romantic atmosphere explains the zealous aversion some Romantic writers had to Johnson, despite the fact that they shared many of Johnson's core values. It is in this era that Johnson's image shifted toward the traditional, this polarized era that had to shove his image to one or the other extreme, as is an historically prevalent reaction in a revolutionary atmosphere.

The common perception of Johnson in the Romantic Period is not as easy to discern as in the Victorian Period. Romantic writers did not use Johnson as a compass to pinpoint the traits of their characters, as did the Victorians. The Johnsonian image is largely absent in Romantic fiction and poetry. Essays, letters, and journals of noted Romantics are the best sources for insight into the position and posture of the Johnsonian image in the generation immediately following Johnson's death, at least as it lived in literary circles. Although Johnson's figure was difficult to trace in the volumes of Romantic literature at the time of its publication, being so scarcely represented in popular literature and the literary focus so blinded to the immediate past by the swirling cloud of revolutionary chaos, his footprint in that era can be traced through an "archeological dig" of the surviving literature, now that the Romantic dust is long settled and with the hindsight of the social conditions of the time. To unearth the Johnson Romantic image requires an interdisciplinary viewpoint. The literary evidence alone tells little without the contribution of the social sciences.

The flourishing of classic liberalism in the latter half of the eighteenth century was the final result of generations of Enlightenment development. By the end of the 18th century, liberalism's dry, rational, detached, impersonal poetic mode ceased satisfying a reading public with an increasing desire for a reflection of the emotional element of the human experience. Liberalism's unaffected response to the problems of the Industrial Revolution was insufficient to the early Romantics. After all, liberalism had given birth to laissez faire capitalism, a socio-economic philosophy that gave great upward momentum to the middle class, while mandating by its design a massive and oppressed lower class. The high reason of Enlightenment liberalism kept its focus on the broader picture of society. It was blind to the squalor of society's lowest element and the immense suffering of the proletariat. The poetry of the Augustan Age reflected the reason and emotional detachment of Enlightenment ideals. The American Revolution, and the French Revolution shortly after, spread a revolutionary fever through England's early Romantic writers [1]. William Blake was a vocal supporter of the American Revolution [2]. William Wordsworth actively supported the French Revolution [3]. Percy Bysshe Shelley supported any movement that threatened to tear down establishment. The English literati were increasingly sympathetic to the causes of liberty. The political and commercial parts of English society still held to the promises of the Glorious Revolution, the "bloodless" revolution whose compromises narrowly averted bloody revolution more than a century earlier. The moderate Whigs responsible for the moderate Glorious Revolution responded to the problems of industrialization with slow and moderate reforms. This was too slow and too moderate for the Romantic writers, who were all too keenly in touch with industrialization's associated human suffering and clearly presented with the French example of a more rapid and dramatic path to reform. They defied the high Enlightenment ideals of the Augustans with reflections of human emotion, far more raw and personal than the Augustans. Human emotion and nature (industrialization's other arch-nemesis) were revered by the Romantic poets with religious fervor. Human imagination also became sacred, in direct opposition to the celebration of rationality displayed by Alexander Pope and John Dryden. John Keats wrote in a letter to Benjamin Bailey in 1817, "I am certain of nothing but the holiness of the heart's affections and the truth of imagination" [4]. Imagination and the heart's affections dealt more directly, and better suited to the popular tastes, with the problems of a rapidly changing society than did Pope's *Essay on Man*. Johnson's "Let observation with extensive view, survey mankind from China to Peru" [5] failed to connect the impatient, revolutionary Romantics to their desired degree of desperate urgency.

On many levels, ideals of revolution found their way into the heart of Romantic poetry. France's revolution had the English considering the possibility of a similar revolution in England. The French Revolution did not begin as a revolution of the proletariat.

It was born as a bourgeois revolution, not unlike the efforts of the English bourgeois Whigs in 1688. Lacking their own Dutch assistance, the French bourgeois effort ran out of fuel and required the support of the Parisian proletariat, a demographic without political connection and unable to affect the sort of internal change arranged and victoriously effectuated by the English Parliamentary Whigs in 1688 [1]. The revolutionary spirit that was spreading across the Western World at the end of the 18th century saturated beyond the political inclinations of English poets, into the heart of the period's poetic mode. From structure to content, English poetry was revolutionary. The Augustans tried to identify and express the universalities of the human experience. Even Dr. Johnson, like the Ancient Greeks and Romans he so ferociously studied, viewed human folly and tragedy as universal. The species was viewed as a whole, from a detached and academic distance. The poetry of the Romantics was more individualistic. The personal experiences of the individual poet became the focus. Poets like Wordsworth wanted their readers to understand and respect their feelings [1]. Romantic poetry is a reflection of self. William Blake famously wrote, "I must find my own system or be enslaved by another man's" [6].

The straight chronological line that is often drawn between the Augustan Period and the Romantic Period, generally marked by Johnson's death in 1784, is over-simplified and unrealistic. As ironic as it may sound, Dr. Johnson would have likely adored and supported Blake. The Johnson Canon identified earlier is highlighted by three precepts. 1. Poverty and obscurity offer shelter from the vices of vanity that haunt and hound the wealthy and renowned. 2. As a general rule in society, literary genius goes mostly unrecognized and underappreciated. 3. Vice and sloth can be handled and manipulated through the development of virtuous habits. Excepting the third, these precepts were lived by Blake. He died in obscurity. He has an unmarked grave, making the pilgrimages to his grave, so common with literary greats, impossible for enthusiasts of Blake [6]. His work never rose above obscurity during his lifetime. He was undereducated and from the lower classes. Like Keats, Blake was a Cockney. He was an impoverished scribbler whose situation and tale would have gripped Dr. Johnson's affections. Blake was a social revolutionary. Dr. Johnson often toasted, "Here's to the next insurrection of the negroes in the West Indies" [7]. Dr. Johnson's view of the poor, obscure talent, and the common sufferings of the human condition were shared by the Romantics. Dr. Johnson also championed the plight of the female writer. Although he was represented as a chauvinist by Boswell, a depiction of Dr. Johnson being refuted by current study, his relationships with women writers tells a drastically different tale.

In her 2001 book, *Johnson Re-Visioned: Looking Before and After*, Jaclyn Geller writes of the assistance and support Dr. Johnson gave to women writers of his day. Geller refers to Dr. Johnson as a "demanding mentor, collaborator, and editor, whose rigor was a form of respect and who encouraged women to stake their claim in eighteenth century literary society" [8]. His influence on feminist and revolutionary, Mary Wollstonecraft, is well documented. Wollstonecraft treasured her brief friendship with Dr. Johnson, just before his death, and her writing was greatly influenced by him. The Dr. Johnson that Wollstonecraft knew, kept in her memory, and allowed to influence her thinking, is very different from the Dr. Johnson that served the early Victorian novelists as a benchmark of conventionalism. Wollstonecraft met Dr. Johnson in 1784, not long before his final illness and death. In her memoirs, published in 1798 by her husband William Godwin, Godwin writes of her first encounter.

> It was during her residence at Newington Green, that she was introduced to the acquaintance of Dr. Johnson, who was at that time considered as in some sort the father of English literature. The doctor treated her with particular kindness and attention, had a long conversation with her, and desired her to repeat her visit often. This she firmly purposed to do; but the news of his last illness, and then of his death, intervened to prevent her making a second visit. [9]

This one visit was profoundly impactful to Wollstonecraft. In his 1996, Radical Affinities: Mary Wollstonecraft and Samuel Johnson, a chapter of the book *Tradition in Transition: Women Writers, Marginal Texts, and the Eighteenth-Century Canon*, James Basker writes that Wollstonecraft's response to meeting Dr. Johnson in person foreshadows the pattern of responses to his writings that she would later display, as she visits and revisits them through the rest of her life. In the abstract to the chapter, Basker writes of the three ways in which the Dr. Johnson/Wollstonecraft dynamic is most remarkable: "Wollstonecraft's deliberate affiliation with Johnson as critical authority; as commentator on the condition of women; and, in her own life, as kindred spirit and consoling presence during moments of personal crisis and depression" [10]. The notion of Dr. Johnson serving as consoling presence and kindred spirit for a Romantic pioneer and feminist flies in the face of many popular conceptions of Johnson, spanning from his own life into the twenty-first century. In Wollstonecraft's most famous and influential work, her 1792, *A Vindication of the Rights of Women*, she references Johnson in ways to affiliate herself with Godwin's "father of English literature". But it was not Dr. Johnson's literary philosophies that Wollstonecraft brings to her defense. It is the Johnsonian moral ideals. In Chapter 9 of *A Vindication of the Rights of Women*, on the rise of unnatural distinctions in society, Wollstonecraft mentions thinking as Johnson does on possible solutions. In Chapter 11, on parenting, she expresses an observation she has made of society's expectations of parents, injecting in conspicuous parenthesis, "(Dr. Johnson makes the same observation.)" [11]. In their brief acquaintance, Wollstonecraft took notice of and was inspired by the Romantic leanings of Johnson. Perhaps the face to face interaction gave Wollstonecraft an insight not conceived by those who evaluated Johnson solely on his published works or on Boswell's accounts of him. She saw that he was, in ways to which she could directly relate, Romantic.

In other ways, Johnson was quite Augustan and distant from the visions and sensibilities of the Romantics. He had the reputation of focusing his vision, and subsequently his writing, on generalities, of aiming his writing at the entire species, never zooming in enough to detect minute particulars of the human condition. Without a personal encounter like Wollstonecraft's, many Romantics had only Johnson's writings to evaluate, writings which, at least in structure and perspective, were easily aligned with Pope's and contrasted against their own. The Romantics told the human story in the minute details of individual circumstances, not exposing the universalities of the human condition to teach indirectly about the individual, rather to expose the details of the individual with the assumption of their universality. Although not entirely Romantic in this respect, Johnson is not entirely Augustan either. Dr. Johnson occupied a space between the fine focus of the Romantics and the lofty observations of Pope. Consider these lines from Pope's *Essay on Man*.

Observe how system into system runs,

What other planets circle other suns,

What varied being peoples every star,

May tell why Heaven has made us as we are.

But of this frame, the bearings, and the ties,

The strong connections, nice dependencies,

Gradations just, has thy pervading soul

Looked through? or can a part contain the whole? [12]

It is difficult to imagine a more distant perspective on the species. The perspective is narrowed by Johnson. These lines from Vanity of Human Wishes speak of humanity through a general example of a type of person.

The needy Traveller, serene and gay,

Walks the wild Heath, and sings his Toil away.

Does envy seize thee? Crush th' upbraiding joy,

Increase the riches and his peace destroy. [13]

Johnson expresses crushed joy and destroyed peace, far more personal and emotional observations that those of Pope. At the same time, they are not observations of a specific individual and whether or not he was reflecting personal experience, the lines are not expressions of self, but they do portray an easily imaginable moment, in contrast to Pope's cosmic perspective. Now consider lines from Wordsworth's Lucy.

Upon the moon I fixed my eye,

All over the wide lea;

With quickening pace my horse drew nigh

Those paths so dear to me. [14]

Not only are these lines in the first person. They express single moments in time. Wordsworth's vision is not of millennia of human development. It is of the minutest moments, and quite personal. Pope wanted to teach of the individual by showing the species. Wordsworth wanted to teach of the species by showing the individual. Johnson found a position between the two by moving up and down the scale of perspectives, from the very distant and detached to the up-close and intimate. The structure of the couplets is also indicative of the age in which they were written. Pope's lines are scientifically structured with mathematical precision. The structure is congruent with the lofty, impersonal perspective [1]. Of Wordsworth's four lines above, there are three different syllable counts. The structure and the content reflect the haphazard lack of order from Wordsworth's chaotic, revolutionary, and narrow focus.

Wordsworth's poetry was revolutionary in many ways. Poetry had been the solitary work of individuals. In 1798, Wordsworth published a collaborative volume, Lyrical Ballads, with Samuel Taylor Coleridge. The poems were Romantic in perspective. This trait would likely have been appreciated by Johnson. Even when Johnson wrote in third person narrative, he did so as if the narrator had an intimate, first person affiliation with the events. The emotional, first person perspectives in Lyrical Ballads would likely have appealed to his sensibilities. What he would not have appreciated was the pastoral nature of the work. Wordsworth wrote extensively on his beloved Lake District and its natural beauty. Wordsworth is thoroughly Romantic in Lyrical Ballads. These lines from "I Wandered Lonely as a Cloud" demonstrate the narrow Romantic perspective, first person intimacy, and a pastoral relationship with nature.

I wandered lonely as a cloud

That floats on high o'er vales and hills,

When all at once I saw a crowd,

A host of golden daffodils. [14]

Wordsworth gives the daffodils human characteristics, referring to them as a host and a crowd. As a humanist, Johnson would have criticized this brutally.

The Romantic inclinations toward the specifics of intimate moments and to the pastoral did not have need of Johnsonian references like those used in the Victorian Period and beyond. The Romantic eye was not set behind the present, or even ahead. It was on the moment. Johnson's public image in the Romantic Period is difficult to be discerned by a search for such references. He seems to have sunken beneath the waters of Romanticism, rising above the waters only as the revolutionary sentiments subsided. If there is an exception to this, it is in the writing of Romantic novelist, Jane Austen. Although fitting in the chronological shoes of a Romantic, Austen's sensibilities remained in the previous generation. She wrote of the miseries associated with conventional social practices, like primogeniture, but did not condemn them. They were simply the way of life, and are in the cases of most of her heroines, the very catalyst that propels them into heroism. Austen had a personal connection to

Dr. Johnson, one which attached Johnson permanently to her affections. Austen's maternal great-uncle, Dr. Theophilus Leigh, caught the eye of Dr. Johnson and Mrs. Thrale. In his 1869, *A Memoir of Jane Austen*, Austen's nephew, James Edward Austen-Leigh, writes copiously on Austen's affinity for Dr. Johnson. First he establishes the connection between Johnson and Dr. Leigh, writing, "Mrs. Thrale, in a letter to Dr. Johnson, writes thus: 'Are you acquainted with Dr. Leigh, the Master of Balliol College, and are you not delighted with his gaiety of manners and youthful vivacity, now that he is eighty-six years of age'" [15]. In Chapter 5, "Description of Jane Austen's Person, Character, and Tastes", Austen-Leigh describes Jane Austen's love of Johnson. He writes, "Amongst her favourite writers, Johnson in prose, Crabbe in verse, and Cowper in both, stood high" [15]. This is of particular note considering that it is the reading of prose that distinguishes many of Austen's heroines from the less admirable characters of her novels.

The documentation of Johnson's influence over Austen continues in 1913, with *Jane Austen: Her Life and Letters*. The book was co-authored by William Austen-Leigh, the son of Jane Austen's brother James, and William's son, Richard. They write that "Her 'dear Dr. Johnson' was a constant companion" [16]. It is important to note that Austen-Leigh puts "dear Dr. Johnson" in quotes, indicating that these are the words of Jane Austen being repeated to the reader. Jane Austen did not rely on her nephews to relate her affections for Dr. Johnson to posterity. She made it clear enough in her novels. In her 1814 novel, *Mansfield Park*, she references Johnson in a manner to assume that her readers' familiarity with Johnson must compare to hers. She writes,

> In a review of the two houses, as they appeared to her before the end of a week, Fanny was tempted to apply to them Dr. Johnson's celebrated judgment as to matrimony and celibacy, and say, that though Mansfield Park might have some pains, Portsmouth could have no pleasures. [17]

This reference to Johnson comes from one of two sources. In Boswell's *Life of Johnson*, Boswell quotes Johnson saying, "Even ill-assorted marriages were preferable to cheerless celibacy" [18]. The reference may come from Dr. Johnson's own pen. In Johnson's *Rasselas*, Chapter 26, the Princess says, "Marriage has many pains, but celibacy has no pleasures" [19]. Regardless of from which source, or combination of sources, Austen pulls this reference, she assumes that her readers are on board with her.

Austen references Johnson, in his role as the lexicographer, in her novel *Northanger Abbey*, not published until after her death. In Chapter 14, Eleanor Tilney warns Catherine Moreland of her brother's linguistic exactness. She tells Catherine, "The word 'nicest,' as you used it, did not suit him; and you had better change it as soon as you can, or we shall be overpowered with Johnson and Blair all the rest of the way" [17]. The "Blair" Austen refers to is Hugh Blair, a literary critic and contemporary of Dr. Johnson's. Austen portrays Henry Tilney as a kind-hearted, very proper but not stuffy, moral clergyman. With this reference, she paints her noble Mr. Tilney as distinctly Johnsonian.

Even Jane Austen, with her well documented affection for Johnson does not reference him in her novels to the level of the Victorian novelists. Austen largely leaves Johnson out of her work. The Romantic poets reference him very little in their work, but use him prodigiously in their personal correspondence. The writers of the Romantic Period were steeped in English literature. They studied Dr. Johnson. They referenced him and quoted him at length and in detail, in their personal correspondence and literary essays. In these places, the image of Johnson, between the time of Boswell's biography and the early Victorian references, can be reconstructed. It is in familiar letters that Johnson is used as a symbol of literary, social, and political affiliation, and in some cases, a point of strong contention.

The "Lake Poets", Robert Southey, William Wordsworth, and Samuel Taylor Coleridge, incited extreme bitterness from George Gordon Lord Byron, as is often and clearly expressed in Byron's brutal attacks of the pen. The bulk of Byron's brutality is directed toward Southey. He treats Wordsworth as Southey's simple-minded disciple. Coleridge seems spared much of Byron's derision and was eventually the recipient of his patronage and literary connections. Byron's respect for Coleridge increased with his disdain for Southey. His disapproval of Southey and Wordsworth is rooted in their polar sway from revolutionary Romanticism to staunch Tory-ism. But his criticism of them spread into other aspects of their lives and characters. Interestingly, but not surprisingly, the line in the sand between these poets seems to be drawn along the same line as their notions of Dr. Johnson.

Byron was proud of his noble heritage, a heritage that shared a connection to Dr. Johnson [20]. His aunt, Sophia Maria Byron, the sister of Byron's father, was unmarried. Her father, the Vice-Admiral Johns Byron, Fourth Baron Byron, was married to Sophia Trevanion Byron, who was in Dr. Johnson's and Mrs. Piozzi's circle [21]. This is the sort of distinction to which Byron would have clung. He did not receive the title from his father in direct decent. The title of Fifth Baron Byron belonged to his great-uncle. Although Byron's mother came from wealth, her husband squandered the family fortune. Prior to inheriting the title at age ten, he and his mother were living in poverty. Only after his inheritance could Byron afford an education at Harrow School and Trinity College, Cambridge. Byron held his education, the title, and any connection to the nation's elite, like his family's association with Dr. Johnson, quite near to his heart [20]. He was well read in literature from Antiquity to his own day. He references Boswell's *Life of Johnson* throughout his letters and journals. Byron held Johnson in high esteem, as in evident in the nature of his Johnson references.

Henry Lord Brougham (1778-1868) wrote a review of Byron for *The Edinburgh Review* in January of 1808. The article is entitled "Hours of Idleness." In the harshly unfavorable article, Brougham attests both to Byron's pride in his family name and to his affections for Dr. Johnson. Brougham writes,

His other plea of privilege, our author rather brings forward to wave it. He certainly, however, does allude frequently to his family and ancestors—sometimes in poetry, sometimes in notes; and while giving up his claim on the score of rank, he takes care to remember us of Dr. Johnson's saying, that when a nobleman appears as an author, his merit should be handsomely acknowledged. [22]

In Byron's letters, he remembers the recipients quite frequently to sayings of Dr. Johnson's, usually as reported by Boswell in *Life of Johnson*. Byron's response to the review did nothing to distance himself from Johnson. In a February 26, 1808 letter to the Reverend John Becher, he prepares his friend for Brougham's coming review, writing, "A most violent attack is preparing for me in the next number of the Edinburgh Review, this I have from the authority of a friend who has seen the proof and manuscript of the Critique" [21]. He brushed off the pending attack as he continues, "You know the system of the Edinburgh Gentlemen is universal attack, they praise none, and neither the public or the author expects praise from them" [21]. In a March 28 letter to Becher, after the release of the review, Byron defends himself with another quote from Dr. Johnson.

The Edinburgh Reviewers have not performed their task well; at least, the literati tell me this, and I think I could write a more sarcastic critique on myself than any yet published. For instance, instead of the remark – ill-natured enough, but not keen - about Macpherson, I (quoad reviewers) could have said "Alas, this imitation only proves the assertion of Dr. Johnson, that many men, women, and children, could have written such poetry as Ossian's." [21]

Byron is referencing a passage from Boswell's *Life*, in which Dr. Johnson replies, when asked if any man in the modern age could have written Ossian, referring to a translation of Ossian, by James Macpherson. Dr. Johnson replied saying, "Yes, Sir, many men, many women, and many children" [18]. Although this was a well-known saying of Dr. Johnson's, Byron quotes it directly and includes the context surrounding Boswell's quotation with the mention of Macpherson and Ossian [21]. This is the first of many indicators that Byron was thoroughly familiar with Boswell's biography.

References to Boswell's *Life* continue in a June 22, 1813 letter to Thomas Moore, a man Byron admired by reputation before meeting in November of 1811. Although Moore came to London to study law, his *Odes*, dedicated to the Prince of Wales, launched him in a career as a poet. Byron met Moore after avoiding a duel threatened by Moore because of some lines in Byron's 1809 *English Bards and Scotch Reviewers*, the same publication through which Byron insulted Southey, Coleridge, and Wordsworth [23]. In the letter to Moore, Byron is informing Moore that John Murray, Byron's publisher, wants to employ Moore as an editor of periodical work. Byron asks, "What say you? Will you be bound, like 'Kit Smart, to write for ninety-nine years in the Universal Visitor"[24]. Byron refers to an April 6, 1775 encounter detailed by Boswell, when Johnson tells of Christopher Smart. Boswell writes, "'Old Gardner the bookseller employed Rolt and Smart to write a monthly miscellany, called The Universal Visitor" [18]. Dr. Johnson concludes the tale, saying, "They were bound to write nothing else; they were to have, I think, a third of the profits of this sixpenny pamphlet; and the contract was for ninety-nine years" [18]. This reference to Boswell indicates both Byron's familiarity with Boswell and his expectation of Moore's familiarity with Boswell. In this case, as with most of Byron's quotes from Boswell, Byron places himself as the Johnsonian sage. He writes the references from Johnson's perspective, in each story likening himself to Johnson, while likening others to many other characters from Boswell's biography.

On February, 26, 1814, Byron wrote a letter to Samuel Rogers. Rogers was another poet admired by Byron. He was the son of a London banker who retired when his father died. He was already 48 years old when Byron met him in 1811. After his father's death, Rogers quit business for poetry. Byron was an enthusiast of Alexander Pope. He praised Rogers as being the embodiment of Popean elegance, carried into the nineteenth century. Rogers was one of the only poets to receive straight praise in Byron's bitterly critical literary satire, *English Bards and Scotch Reviewers* [23]. The post script to the letter Byron writes to Rogers reads,

> I will call for you at a quarter before seven, if that will suit you. I return your Sir Proteus, and shall merely add in return, as Johnson said of, and to, somebody or another 'Are we alive after all this censure? [25]

Sir Proteus, a Satirical Ballad (1814), by P. M. O'Donovan and Thomas Love Peacock, had a satirical inscription to Byron. The Johnson misquote is from an October 24, 1780 quotation from Boswell's *Life*. It reads,

> Once when somebody produced a newspaper in which there was a letter of stupid abuse of Sir Joshua Reynolds, of which Johnson himself came in for a share,—"Pray," said he, "let us have it read aloud from beginning to end;" which being done, he with a ludicrous earnestness, and not directing his look to any particular person, called out, "Are we alive after all this satire!" [18]

This is one of several passages from Boswell that Byron uses to liken himself to Dr. Johnson through the aspect of the Johnson Canon that states that literary genius goes mostly unrecognized, underappreciated, and is harshly criticized. Byron developed an adversarial relationship with English society, which, along with his early death, forbade him from the moderate shift that the Lake Poets went through as they aged. Johnson's early struggles to establish himself in the English literary world, followed by his rise to the heights of literary eminence, struck Byron in a personal and intimate manner. Byron deals with much of his literary criticisms and failings by looking in the mirror and seeing the younger, struggling Johnson.

Byron continues to associate himself with Johnson's struggles with the literary community in a September 25, 1815 letter to John Taylor. Taylor was the proprietor of *The Sun*, a Tory paper with whom he had quarreled prior to taking it over in 1813 [26]. Taylor wrote to Byron in July to apologize for some satiric verses toward Byron, written by Taylor's editor. Byron writes Taylor assuring him that he is beyond being affected by such criticism and takes no offense unless criticism of him involves his friends and those he respects. Byron writes, " In such a case – supposing it to occur – to reverse the saying of Dr. Johnson, 'What the law could not do for me, I would do for myself'" [25]. This is quite a telling use of Dr. Johnson by Byron. Although Byron attempts to convince Taylor that he is unaffected by the satire, the tone of his response is bitter, threatening, and disproportionate to the offense. In this emotional state, Byron, as usual, clings to Johnson. His initial, July 23, response to Taylor's apology was cordial and grateful for the compliments paid to him by Taylor. The September letter shows a growing bitterness. The original quote, as detailed by Boswell, is from the quarrel between Johnson and James Macpherson. After Johnson's critical assessment of Macpherson's *Ossian*, Macpherson wrote to Johnson. As Boswell explains it, "What words were used by Mr. Macpherson in his letter to the venerable Sage, I have never heard; but they are generally said to be of a nature very different from the language of a literary contest" [18]. Johnson's response to Macpherson shows that Macpherson's offense to Johnson was much more extreme, and possibly violent, than the mild satirical criticism of Byron by Taylor's editor. Johnson responded, "Mr. James Macpherson, I have received your foolish and imprudent letter. Any violence offered me, I shall do my best to repel; and what I cannot do for myself, the law shall do for me" [18]. Byron's reversal of this quotation truly reverses its spirit. Nevertheless, of all of Byron's vast reading, all of the characters in all of the stories in the whole of his extensive education, it is Dr. Johnson's defensive response to Macpherson, as detailed by Boswell, with which Byron chooses to associate himself in this clearly personal situation. When Byron's literary merits are questioned, he pulls from his pocket one of his many Johnsonian anecdotes. He holds Dr. Johnson as his membership card to literary authenticity.

On August 12, 1819, Byron responded to a request from his publisher, John Murray, for a plan of *Don Juan*, or as Byron called it, *Donny Jonny*. Byron writes, "You are too earnest and eager about a work never intended to be serious. Do you suppose that I could have any intention but to giggle and make giggle?" [27]. Byron's letter in response suggests that Murray had some apprehensions concerning the potential lewdness of *Don Juan*, a reasonable concern considering the alloy of Byron's nature and the well-known motif of the character of Don Juan. In standard form, Byron brings Johnson to his defense. Byron addresses Murray's concerns, adding, "and as to the indecency – do pray read in Boswell – what Johnson the sullen moralist – says of Prior and Paulo Purgante" [27]. Byron is remembering to his presumably well-read publisher a 1777 encounter recorded by Boswell in which Boswell recalls, "I mentioned Lord Hailes's censure of Prior, in his Preface to a collection of Sacred Poems, ... where he mentions, 'those impure tales which will be the eternal opprobrium of their ingenious authour'" [18]. Johnson answers, "'Sir, Lord Hailes has forgot. There is nothing in Prior that will excite to lewdness. If Lord Hailes thinks there is, he must be more combustible than other people" [18]. In challenge, Boswell brings up Prior's tale, *Paulo Purganti and his Wife*, to which Dr. Johnson responds, ". Sir, there is nothing there, but that his wife wanted to be kissed when poor Paulo was out of pocket. No, Sir, Prior is a lady's book. No lady is ashamed to have it standing in her library'" [18]. Byron wields Johnson as his shield against what he expects will be an onslaught of criticism against the licentiousness of *Don Juan*. By drawing his parallels to Prior, he resurrects Johnson to argue in his defense.

At times, Byron's Boswell quotations serve to liken Byron to Johnson. At other times, he uses the references to place himself within Johnson's elite circle, particularly in opposition to the more vulgar. He continually indicates a blend of elitism and self-deprivation. Haunted by his awareness of his faults, he clings to his elitism for balance. Another one of Byron's references to

Boswell, from the summer of 1819, betrays his true position on reform and helps to shine light on the enigmatic balance between his staunch traditionalism in one hand, and his Romantic ideals in the other. The letter is to John Cam Hobhouse, one of Byron's oldest friends. Byron and Hobhouse became friends in 1807, when they were just nineteen and twenty-one respectively. Hobhouse's father was a Whig Member of Parliament. Likewise John Cam was a liberal Whig until he and the party parted ways. He was elected to Parliament in 1820 as a radical or Reform candidate [21]. Hobhouse was challenged to a duel by seventy-nine year old, Major John Cartwright, for some perceived disrespect associated with the some reformers whom Cartwright connected with Hobhouse. Hobhouse was able to relieve the tension with an explanation and avoid the duel. On June 26, 1819, Byron writes to Hobhouse on the subject:

> To my great surprise, we hear that you have been challenged by Ancient Pistol Major Cartwright – this seems to me mere Midsummer madness – what had you to do with those Blackguard reformers who made you defy and leave the Whigs and make you lose your election, and then call you out as a reward for your trouble? [27]

Implying a complete disassociation with "those Blackguard reformers" seems out of character for a self-declared reformer like Byron. He quickly qualifies his comments, writing, "I am and have been for reform always – but not for the reformers" [27]. Although Byron gave a fiery 'reform' speech in the House of Lords, he would not be found hob-nobbing with reformers, as he explains in his reference to Dr. Johnson. "I saw enough of them at the Hampden Club – Burdett is the only one in whose company a Gentleman would be seen unless at a Public meeting – or in a Public house" [27]. He quotes Boswell, again likening himself to Dr. Johnson, in opposition to people less 'Johnsonian'. "'I shall have to bail my old friend out of the Road-house.' 'What a coalition!' as Davy said of Johnson and Beauclerk" [27]. In this extraction from Boswell, Byron refers to the unlikely friendship between Dr. Johnson and Topham Beauclerk. Beauclerk befriended Johnson's companion, Bennet Langton, Esq., in 1752, while both were studying at Oxford. Johnson had recently concluded his Rambler essays and was spending time with Langton at Oxford. It was in Langton's company that he met Beauclerk [18]. According to Boswell, Beauclerk was as ill-matched a companion for Langton as he was for Johnson. Boswell writes that Langton, "formed an acquaintance with his fellow student, Mr. Topham Beauclerk; who, though their opinions and modes of life were so different, that it seemed utterly improbable that they should at all agree, had so ardent a love of literature" [18]. The quote used by Byron is from Johnson's old friend and pupil, David Garrick, who thought Beauclerk's friendship an odd match for a stern moralist like Johnson. Boswell writes it as such, "the moral, pious Johnson, and the gay, dissipated Beauclerk, were companions. '"What a coalition! (said Garrick, when he heard of this;) I shall have my old friend to bail out of the Round-house.'" [18]. It is clear that Byron intends to liken Beauclerk to "those Blackguard reformers". It is difficult to say whether, in his mind, he places Hobhouse in the role of Dr. Johnson, with Byron being Garrick, or if Byron sees himself as the Dr. Johnson-figure. It is certain that the reference is intended to state that both Byron and Hobhouse are as socially detached from the reformers, regardless of their affiliation with them, as Johnson was with the scoundrel he befriended at Oxford. The reference also provides an ominous suggestion that Byron shares Garrick's fears of an ill wind with the association.

If Johnson served as Byron's shield to fend off attacks, in his August 12, 1819 letter to Murray, he is Byron's sword, to strike attacks of his own in a letter to the same recipient on September 11, 1820. Writing from Ravenna, Italy, Byron addresses the particulars of England's literary scene. Perhaps his time abroad elevated a keen awareness of his Englishness and intolerance for native contributors to the depravity of English literature. Byron writes to Murray, "What Gifford writes is very consolatory – 'English sterling, Genuine English', is a desideratum among you – and I am glad I have got so much left – though Heaven knows how I retain it – I hear none but from my valet" [28]. Clearly, these are the words of a lexicographer's disciple. Byron references William Gifford, a satirist and literary critic who wrote Baviad (1794) and Maeviad (1795), satirical works on contemporary writers. Byron revered the two works and used them as the models for *English Bards and Scotch Reviewers*, in which Byron brutally attacked the Lake Poets [28]. Referring to "genuine English", Byron continues, "I see none but in your new publications – and theirs is no language at all but jargon" [28]. He addresses the depreciation of language and its effect on England, which he refers to as "New Jerusalem", in a strikingly similar tone to Johnson's *Preface to the Dictionary*, when he writes, "Every year, New Jerusalem is terribly stilted and affected – with 'very very' – so soft and pamby" [28]. Byron, as Brougham put it, remembers Murray "of Dr. Johnson's saying, that when a nobleman appears as an author, his merit should be handsomely acknowledged" [22], taking a more aggressive posture, writing, "Oh, If I ever do come amongst you again I will give you such a Baviad and Maeviad, not as good as the old but even better merited" [28]. Here, Byron suggests that the need for harsh, satirical literary criticism is direr than when Gifford published his two works. He validates the comments of Brougham, writing, "There was never such a set as your ragamuffins – (I mean not yours only, but everybody's) what with the Cockneys and the Lakers" [28]. The two big Cockney poets of the time were William Blake and John Keats. The Lakers were Coleridge, Wordsworth, and Southey. Byron continues to Murray, "You are in the very uttermost decline and degradation of Literature" [28]. Next, Byron unsheathes his Johnsonian sword, writing, "I wish that Johnson were alive again to crush them" [28].

It is fitting that Byron should use Johnson as a weapon against the Lake Poets and fitting that he should draw a line in the sand where he and Johnson together stand opposed to the Lake Poets. The Lake Poets did not share Byron's admiration for Boswell's "venerable Sage". They, with the exception of Coleridge, assumed their own adversarial position against Johnson. There were many disagreements between Byron and the Lake Poets. Although no direct controversies on the subject of Johnson are present in their attacks on one another, Johnson stands conspicuously near the middle of the contest. Their respective positions on Johnson fueled the hostilities and began a tradition, in English literature, of using the image of Dr. Johnson as a beacon to display social, political, and literary standing points. The 1820s battle between Byron and the Lake Poets was handed in spirit directly to the next decade and the following literary era. Although the Lake Poets radically switched political affiliations, from republican revolutionaries, in support of the French Revolution to accepting, in Southey's case, a position appointed by the king, their early disgust for establishment, the moderate ideals of the Johnson Canon, and the literary mode of the Augustans were boldly proclaimed and published, opening them to a lifetime of attack from Byron and other literary traditionalists.

In contrast to Byron's obvious admiration for Boswell and Boswell's Johnson, Southey writes to Thomas Davis Lamb in January, 1793, "Canst thou in the society of brutes blockheads boobies beasts Boswells & all the rest of the Bs find wherewith to console thyself for the loss of all thy original friends" [29]? Boswell's is the only proper name here, in a list of broad and vague negative terms. Perhaps Southey had other writers in mind, represented by his other "Bs", but he allows no doubt as to his feelings for Boswell. In the same month, Southey writes to Grosvenor Charles Bedford, "Boswell might compile a few quartos from the loose memorandums but they would tire the world more than he has already done" [29]. It is not just Boswell whom Southey attacks. He bypasses Boswell for direct attacks upon Johnson. In February of 1794, he writes to Horace Walpole Bedford, in complaint of the damage done to English literature and tastes by Johnson's generation.

> A more vitiated taste prevails at present, since Johnson sonorized our prose & the imitators of Collins & Gray loaded our poetry with awkward imagery & cumbrous metaphor. Into this meretricious stile I know myself frequently to have fallen & am pleased to see myself daily reclaiming. [29]

These words came from the young, revolutionary Robert Southey, prior to his drastic rightward shift. Diarist, Henry Crabb Robinson documented Southey's response to the criticism of his turn-about. Robinson writes, "Many were ruined by the errors into which they were betrayed. Many also lived to smile at the follies of their youth. 'I am no more ashamed at having been a republican', said Southey, 'than I am of having been a child'" [30]. It is too bad the world cannot know what sort of evolution would have affected Byron's character, had he lived long enough to experience it. Southey's transformation, though not universal, was common, as noted by Robinson. Wordsworth experienced a similar transformation.

In a critical essay titled *Of the Principles of Poetry and the 'Lyrical Ballads'* (1798-1802), part of his publication of *Lyrical Ballads*, Wordsworth writes this criticism of Dr. Johnson.

> …as a fair example of the superlatively contemptible. Whence arises this difference? Not from the metre, not from the language, not from the order of the words; but the matter expressed in Dr. Johnson's stanza is contemptible. The proper method of treating trivial and simple verses, to which Dr. Johnson's stanza would be a fair parallelism, is not to say, this is a bad kind of poetry, or, this is not poetry; but, this wants sense. [31]

In this criticism, Wordsworth reminds the reader of his need for human emotion. Feelings made sense to Wordsworth. Dr. Johnson's and the Augustan's poetry, coming from, as Dr. Johnson put it, "Observation with extensive view", was distasteful to Wordsworth, even contemptible. Perhaps it was Johnson's humanism that Wordsworth disliked. After all, Johnson has a much more emotional mode of poetic expression than any of his contemporaries or predecessors. But it was all about humans with Johnson. Nature served merely as a habitat for human existence.

Coleridge's take on Dr. Johnson was quite different than that of his fellow Lake Poets. This is not surprising considering the similarities in Johnson's and Coleridge's education and background. In November, 1833, Coleridge writes the following criticism of Johnson.

> Dr. Johnson seems to have been really more powerful in discoursing viva voce in conversation than with his pen in hand. It seems as if the excitement of company called something like reality and consecutiveness into his reasonings, which in his writings I cannot see. His antitheses are almost always verbal only; and sentences in the Rambler may be pointed out to which you cannot attach any definite meaning whatever. In his political pamphlets there is more truth of expression than in his other works, for the same reason that his conversation is better than his writings in general. He was more excited and in earnest. [26]

Coleridge appears less discordant with Dr. Johnson's writing as he is concordant with his conversational mode, an aspect of the Johnsonian social phenomenon most widely known through Boswell's accounts of Johnson's conversations. Coleridge points out excitement as the key difference between Dr. Johnson's writing and his conversation. He shows that he requires, or at least respects, emotion, just as his poetic partner, Wordsworth. At the same time, Coleridge keeps an eye on structure, claiming that Dr. Johnson's excitement brings "consecutiveness" to his reasoning. The passage is not particularly harsh toward Johnson's writing, except perhaps the comment on the Rambler essays. The warmth of expression in his comments on Johnson's conversation suggests that Coleridge read and enjoyed Boswell's biography.

The differences between Southey's and Coleridge's notions on Johnson are not surprising. The differences between their tastes expanded beyond the bounds of literature. In Robinson's diary he writes, "Southey said that he and Coleridge were directly opposed in politics" [26]. Byron's criticism of the Lake Poets was comprehensive. But he later regretted his harsh words toward

Coleridge, noticing the differences between Coleridge and the others. In *English Bards and Scotch Reviewers*, Byron writes,

Yet let them not to vulgar Wordsworth stoop,

The meanest object of the lowly group,

Whose verse, of all but childish prattle void,

Seems blessed harmony to Lamb and Lloyd:

Let simple Wordsworth chime his childish verse,

And brother Coleridge lull the babe at nurse. [32]

Byron casually drops his hit on Coleridge as a minor side note to his vicious attack on Wordsworth. In his dedication to Don Juan, Byron brutalizes the Lake Poets again. His note on Coleridge is minor and not particularly bitter. Byron writes,

Bob Southey! You're a poet, poet laureate,

And representative of all the race.

Although 'tis true that you turned out a Tory at

Last, yours has lately been a common case.

And now my epic renegade, what are ye at

With all the lakers, in and out of place?

A nest of tuneful persons, to my eye

Like four and twenty blackbirds in a pye. [33]

Byron continues on Southey.

You, Bob, are rather insolent, you know,

At being disappointed in your wish

To supersede all warblers here below,

And be the only blackbird in the dish. [33]

He moves on to Wordsworth.

And Wordsworth, in a rather long "Excursion"

(I think the quarto holds five hundred pages),

Has given a sample from the vasty version

Of his new system to perplex the sages;

And he who understands it would be able

To add a story to the Tower of Babel [33]

His attacks on Southey and Wordsworth are harsh to a similar degree. He addresses Coleridge with a far slighter criticism.

And Coleridge, too, has lately taken wing,

But like a hawk encumber'd with his hood,

Explaining Metaphysics to the nation--

I wish he would explain his Explanation [33]

Besides sparing Coleridge the bulk of his criticism, Byron helps Coleridge, in his literary endeavors, with both money and connections. On the week of Easter, 1815, Coleridge writes to Byron, expressing plans for his upcoming literary projects and asking for Byron's help. He appeals to Byron's literary similarities, as Coleridge put it, "addressing himself to your Genius rather than your Rank" [34]. Byron helps Coleridge by sending him 100 pounds, suggesting an idea for a tragedy, and recommending him to John Murray [34]. In Byron's reply, he retracts his attacks from *English Bards and Scotch Reviewers*, writing, "It was written when I was very young and very angry, and has been a thorn in my side ever since" [25]. Byron distinguishes Coleridge from the other objects of the attack by writing, "The part applied to you is pert, and petulant, and shallow enough" [25]. He concludes the apology, writing, "I shall always regret the wantonness or generality of many of its attempted attacks [25]. In fact, in his years of regret, Byron tried to suppress the circulation of the satire [34].

In an October 17, 1815 letter, Coleridge accepts Byron's criticism, writing, "I am so little known to your Lordship that I scarcely dare venture to say what yet I know to be true-that your censure however extensive it should be, would be welcomed by me with unfeigned pleasure, as a mark of your kindness [34]. He attempts to distinguish himself from Wordsworth by adding that "I unexpectedly find my convictions widely different from that of Mr. Wordsworth as explained in the new Preface to his collection of his Poems [34]. On October 28, Byron writes to Thomas Moore, a review writer for the Edinburgh Review, making the following plea on Coleridge's behalf:

> Coleridge-who is a man of wonderful talent, and in distress, and about to publish two Volumes of Poesy and Biography, and who has been worse used by critics than ever we have-will you, if he comes out, promise me to review him favourably in the Edinburgh Review. [25]

In his letters to Coleridge and others, Byron displays affection for Coleridge. His 1815 apology and assistance shows the respect of a man who shares opinions and sensibilities. Dr. Johnson stands as one of the most distinguished shared opinions, linking them together as Johnsonites at the beginning of a long tradition in English culture and literature of defining one's self by one's position on Johnson.

Byron and the Lake Poets certainly disagreed and made their disagreements known. The line that is drawn at first, with Byron on one side and the Lake Poets on the other, is erased and redrawn along the precise line drawn by their respective positions on Dr. Johnson, with Byron and Coleridge on one side and Southey and Wordsworth on the other. Although they do not reference Johnson in their published works as prolifically as is seen in the following literary era, they begin a tradition of using

Johnson as the landmark by which to determine position on social, political, and literary matters. This is a tradition that continues through the Victorian Era, into the twentieth century.

Chapter 6

Dr. Johnson in the Victorian Age: Evolution of a Hero

THE VICTORIAN AGE began on June 20, 1837, when Victoria became queen, but there were a few major events in the decades preceding Victoria's ascension to the throne that sculpted British society and laid the path for the rise of the iconic Johnsonian persona. The first was Wellington's defeat of Napoleon at Waterloo in 1815. The second was the rapid advancement of the Industrial Revolution. The third was the Reform Bill of 1832 [1]. In 1840, Thomas Carlyle gave a popular and highly influential series of lectures titled *On Heroes, Hero-Worship and the Heroic in History.* The lectures, published the next year, spawned an ongoing debate on the nature of the national hero and the role of those who serve as the example of the national identity [2]. Dr. Johnson was one of Carlyle's national heroes, and the Johnsonian persona of the early Victorian Age took on the traits of Carlyle's ideal Englishman. As the age progressed and the various diverse demographics evolved, the role of the national hero evolved, taking the common perception of the Johnsonian persona with it.

Much like the defeat of Louis XIV in the Nine Years War with the 1697 Treaty of Ryswick, and again in the War of Spanish Succession with the Treaty of Utrecht in 1713 [3], the British people keenly felt the national pride that came with defeating the French and ascending to the undisputed position of Western Europe's dominant military and commercial nation. Young nobles were free to take the "Grand Tour" across Europe, with an acute awareness of their national dominance over the lands they traveled. All of this national pride set the British on the search for what is quintessentially British. A hero was needed to fit that mold and stand as a guide for a proud nation. Although many aspects of the Johnsonian character fit this demand, Johnson's *Dictionary* placed the nation's pride in its unique language into a single persona. The victory over France harkened the British back to the Grand Alliance that defeated Louis and the ideals and expectations of the Glorious Revolution. The merchant middle-class that drove the revolution and financed the defeat of Louis XIV became a British ideal. This ideal was also embodied in the Johnsonian persona.

In addition to raising Britain to the heights of world economic power, industrialization also created a massive, urban labor proletariat, a demographic that would eventually find a voice through the sympathies of England's dominant novelists and also find, by the end of the age, a hero in Dr. Johnson. All of this global dominance was put on display. In 1851, London hosted the first World's Fair in the magnificent Crystal Palace Exhibition, displaying the marvels of industrialization with a conspicuously patriotic British flavor [4]. In 1837, construction began on Charles Berry and Augustus Pugin's gothic design for the new Windsor Palace. It took more than 20 years to complete, finishing with the completion of the Victoria Tower in 1860 [4]. The very glimpse of these new and magnificent sights must have awed visitors and struck a patriotic chord in the hearts of the English. The face of London, therefore England, changed quickly under Queen Victoria. It was beginning to look like the world capital, in the fashion of Ancient Rome that it had become. But there was a dark side to industrialization that gained exposure through British literature.

The new industrial cities, and London herself, felt the perils of a sudden population boom before infrastructure could be brought to meet it. The beautiful Crystal Palace that held England's display of economic superiority and industrial leadership stood just a couple hundred yards from impoverished slums that could rival the very worst in Europe [4]. The Thames became so riddled with sewage and filthy street runoff that the stench was unbearable [5]. For every shining display of British splendor, there was a neighboring example of the associated squalor. By the end

126

of the Victorian Age, the impoverished side-effects of industrialization elevated Samuel Johnson to stand as their hero. Industrialization expanded their demographic, but the Reform Bill gave them a political voice and vindicated their desire for education.

The Reform Bill drastically increased the British voting body, propelling the nation toward democracy [6]. Suffrage and education discovered a powerful advocate under the administration of Liberal Party leader William Ewart Gladstone, elected to his first premiership in 1868 [7]. Gladstone's Chancellor of the Exchequer, Robert Lowe, was not a strong proponent of democracy but believed that the voting public should be brought up to the responsibility of the ballot. In a speech, he made the following argument about the necessity of educating a voting public.

> It appears to me that before we had entrusted the masses, the great bulk of whom are uneducated, with the whole power of this country, we should have taught them a little more how to use it. And not having done so, this rash and abrupt measure having been forced upon them, the only thing we can do is, as far as possible, to remedy the evil by the most universal measures of education that can be devised. I believe it will be absolutely necessary that you should prevail on our future masters to learn their letters. [8]

The Reform Bill increased debate and the socio-political rift between the three governmental ideologies that would come to define the 1840s. First there were the bourgeois Whigs, with their laissez faire capitalism, individualism, and promotion of progress. Second, there were the traditionalists, with their conventional social sensibilities and their sense of inherited duty and decorum. Third, there were those who rallied for reform, wanting full political democracy and social, economic equality [2]. Carlyle's popular *Heroes* demanded that each adopt a representative hero as the icon of their ideals. Especially for the conservatives, political ideals needed patriotic embodiment in a recognizable, embraceable figure. As reflected in the novels of the 1830s, 1840s, and very beginning of the 1850s, Dr. Johnson was adopted by that group. In often ironic contrast to his character, Johnson came to represent political conservatism, conventionalism, and traditional social etiquette, cemented by the early Victorian references to him, as detailed in the rest of this chapter. Johnson's staunch declarations of Tory-ism, as detailed in James Boswell's *The Life of Samuel Johnson, LL.D,* probably contributed to his adoption by the opposition to the sitting Whigs and bourgeois progression.

Conservatives suffered a few blows in the 1840s, further necessitating their need for a hero while initiating a push of the Johnsonian persona in the opposite direction. In 1846, Robert Peel fell from the top of the conservatives due to his support for the abolition of the Corn Laws [2]. The Corn Laws imposed heavy import duties on the import of grains, making it unpractical to buy cheaper foreign grains over locally grown [7]. However beneficial to the local farmers, such commercial regulations stood in staunch opposition to the bourgeois laissez faire capitalism. What was intended to be patriotic was deemed anti-British because it interfered with the flow of international commerce, denting the wallets of Whig businessmen. Peel took the fall. The 1848 Revolutions in Europe timed themselves with the British Chartism movement. Chartism was the first major labor movement in Europe, ending with the 1848 Chartist Petition. On April 10, a massive procession of thousands was organized to present Parliament with another labor petition. Such a show of labor solidarity was particularly frightening to conservatives in light of the major revolutions on the Continent [7]. 1848 also saw the monarchy of France's Louis Phillipe torn down by the hands of republicanism [2]. Conservatives needed an icon, unmistakably British, who could be embraced by the general public while being held to conservative ideals. Johnson was fashioned into that icon. In literature of the 1840s and early 1850s, he was pitted against the Whig equivalents. He was compared in sharp relief against all of the ideals and the follies feared and loathed by conventionalists, to the neglect of many of Johnson's personal beliefs. Those beliefs would surface later in the century as publications of intimate anecdotes from Johnson's life reached the bookstores, revealing the moderate, even liberal, views he had on the poor. Rather than associating conservative values with the heroic Johnsonian persona, the ultimate effect was to separate the enshrined British ideal icon from those values, beginning a migration of the Johnsonian persona toward more liberal values. The literary references to Johnson after the early 1850s reflect the migration.

All three of these major events leading up to and into the Victorian Age aided in the promotion of public education and literacy. As the demographic of literate Britons shifted down the socio-economic scale, the subject matter of British publications followed, as did the heroes represented in British literature. Wellington credited a higher educated officer corps for his victory at Waterloo and insisted that improvements in education would compensate for Britain's significantly lower population compared to the other world powers [8]. Industrial factory owners insisted that a higher educated workforce would improve efficiency and productivity and possibly stave off labor unrest. Lastly, the Reform Bill of 1832, and the century's subsequent acts to increase the voting population, inclined politicians to increase the literacy of the voting public [8]. As suffrage dipped more deeply into the depths of British society and politicians realized that the country would be run by the new labor proletariat, a new fervor for the education of that slice of society reached desperate attention. At the beginning of the Victorian Age, more than half of the British people could not read or write. This convergence of motivations lent a broad ranged political support to universal education, with profound results. By the end of the age, nearly all British citizens had at least basic literacy. The American Civil War (1861-1865) and the Franco-Prussian War (1870-1871) were strong evidence that a more educated fighting force held a distinct military advantage. These events created a greater push for education in the 1870s through the Education Act of 1870, which gave universal education through the age of thirteen [8]. Liberal minister, William Edward Forster, introduced the legislation, justifying it in Parliament with the following speech.

> Civilized communities are massing themselves together, each mass being measured by its force. And if we are to hold our position among the nations of the world, we must make up the smallness of our numbers by increasing the intellectual force of the individual. [8]

Education received a nationalistic, patriotic propaganda spin, garnering the endeavor universal appeal and attaching the literary and scholarly hero, Dr. Johnson, with a patriotic heroism. After all, with literacy as the new national objective, what better national hero could be raised than the writer of the English language's only dictionary? The attacks on linguistic decay and illiteracy Johnson bitterly presented in the preface to the *Dictionary* were echoed in this new cry for literacy and education.

A monumentally impactful feature of increased education on the nature of British literature was the advancements in women's education. London University began to admit women in 1848. In 1868, Oxford founded its first women's college. Cambridge followed suit the next year [8]. This was a tremendous advancement from the rural dame schools in the early part of the age, as accurately reflected in Charlotte Bronte's *Jane Eyre* (1847). Bronte's Lowood Institution was a vivid reflection of common conditions in these dame schools. Once again, an expanded educated demographic had its distinct effect on the literature of the age. An increase in female readers and in female writers added a feminine perspective and feminine qualities to the nation's body of literary works. The heroes of literature and the literate society had to embody the sensibilities of Britain's literate women in order to gain universal appeal. In the latter years of the Victorian Age, feminine sensibilities were allotted to the Johnsonian persona. This was lent credence by the release of the 1861 publication of *Autobiography, Letters and Literature Remains of Mrs. Piozzi*, by Hester Lynch Piozzi. Piozzi presented a more balanced account of Johnson's character and intimate moments than the more broadly read biography of James Boswell.

A drastic evolution in industrialization occurred in the 1850s, steering the nature of the British hero in a new direction. Labor unions were outlawed in 1799 with the Combination Acts, forbidding the gathering of laborers. They were designed to prevent the Jacobin activities that arose in revolutionary France [8]. Although the acts were repealed in 1824, laws against conspiracy remained in place. Laborers meeting for the purpose of union solidarity were often charged criminally under the conspiracy laws. As an example, Dorset farm workers, in 1834, tried to legally unionize. They were convicted of conspiracy and sentenced to seven years in the penal colony of Australia [8]. Large scale national unions attempted to form but were unable to coordinate until after the national railway was established after 1850. An evolution in the public perception of the Johnsonian persona began in the 1850s, as awareness of labor atrocities and the plight of the poor became common understanding through the networking provided by the national railway.

Carlyle explains that the hero charismatically and demonstratively embodies a system of values and beliefs held dear by his devotees [2]. It is not necessary that the system adhere strictly to the true traits of the mortal who has been enshrined. Carlyle poignantly writes, "They were the leaders of men, these great ones; the modellers, patterns, and in a wide sense, creators, of whatsoever the general mass of men contrived to do or to attain" [9]. The key phrase, "whatsoever the general mass ... contrived" explains the pliable constitutions of public heroes. Dr. Johnson's constitution proved pliable, as it evolved dramatically with the dramatic changes of the Victorian Age. As the literate public expanded to incorporate a much more varied swath of British society, so did the Johnsonian persona, as reflected in popular literature. As the 1850s brought changes in education, labor, and public awareness of the toils of the proletariat, the decade also steered the Johnsonian persona away from its conservative public and literary perception of the 1830s and

1840s. In some ways, the hero steers the people. It is clear in the case of the Victorian Johnsonian persona that the people also steer the hero. Popular literature and lectures like Carlyle's established Johnson as the representative of the intrinsic British national ideals. As the definition of "intrinsically British" changed, rather than find a new hero for the new set of values, the British public simply altered the hero they already had to fit the new national identity.

In some of Carlyle's many descriptions and heroic comparisons of Dr. Johnson in *Heroes*, he aligns Johnson with conventionalism. This was a dominant feature of the Johnsonian persona in the first two decades of the Victorian Age, as reflected in the references to Dr. Johnson in the novels of that time. Carlyle writes, "Johnson believed altogether in the old; he found the old opinions credible for him, and in a right heroic manner lived under them" [9]. Although representing only a part of the character of the mortal Samuel Johnson, and contrary to much of the Johnson Canon, this image represented a generation of Victorians uneager to relinquish old customs in the wave of dramatic social changes caused by industrialization, modernization, and the passage of time. The Johnsonian image became the anchor to which that generation tied itself to ride out the storm of change. Dr. Johnson came to represent the "old opinions" and all who held them.

The first Victorian novelist to employ the conservative Johnsonian image was Benjamin Disraeli (1804-1881). Although Disraeli was not the first politician to leap into the world of imaginative literature, he was one of the most successful, publishing 11 novels from 1826 to 1881. Numerically speaking, he surpasses some of the popular great novelists of Victorian fiction, like Thackeray and Eliot [10]. He was a political conservative whose views on politics were reflected in his literary works. His election to Parliament in 1837 ensured a political circle of friends rather than a literary circle like those of Dickens and Thackeray, Tennyson and Browning [11]. Accordingly, his associations, conversations, and literary achievements centered on the political sphere. There are distinct references to Dr. Johnson in three of Disraeli's novels of the 1830s and 1840s. As the British political pendulum swung back from its extreme of the Romantic Era, a conservative like Disraeli found his arguments had traction in references to the Augustan icon. Disraeli used Dr. Johnson to express his political and social conservatism while unofficially employing him as a campaign supporter the way current candidates use a similarly politically aligned celebrity as a campaign spokesman. His novels employed the popular image of Dr. Johnson to its fullest in seducing the affections of the generation of Victorian conventionalists.

As an English conservative of his era, Disraeli favored empire building, by military means if necessary [12]. The Augustan association of Britain with Rome remained firmly in his political point of view. This is evident in the many Roman references throughout his fiction. He also continuously harkens his readers back to the cherished ideals of the previous century. In his 1837 novel *Henrietta Temple*, he shows this in his description of the Viscountess Dowager Bellair, calling her "the last remaining link between the two centuries." Disraeli draws a picture, with the Viscountess, of the best member of the best generation, writing,

> All that had been famous for beauty, rank, fashion, wit, genius, had been gathered round her throne; and at this very hour a fresh and admiring generation, distinguished for these qualities, cheerfully acknowledged her supremacy, and paid to her their homage. [13]

He associates her with three primary English figures, each of a different genre of public acclaim, writing, "distinguished both for her beauty and her wit, she had reigned for a quarter of a century the favourite subject of Sir Joshua; had flirted with Lord Carlisle, and chatted with Dr. Johnson" [13].

Johnson is placed in elite company in this attempt to associate the character with the greatest public figures in the fields of art, politics, and social elitism. As a "favourite subject of Sir Joshua," Disraeli refers to the painter, Sir Joshua Reynolds. Reynolds was the eighteenth century's leading portraitist, first president of the Royal Academy, established in 1768, and as it happens, a good friend of Dr. Johnson's [14]. Lord Carlisle was George William Frederick Howard, seventh Earl of Carlisle. Carlisle was a powerful politician and champion of the repeal of Jewish disabilities [15]. Disraeli, being Jewish, could probably think of no more noble political company to include in this trinity of social icons. If her beauty made her a favorite of Reynolds's, it was her wit Disraeli wished to boast by writing that she "chatted with Dr. Johnson." Johnson was known far more for his conversational mode and witty banter than anything he published, save perhaps his *Dictionary*. His company was desperately sought by those who wished to be associated with the socially elite [16]. To have 'chatted', implying a comfortable encounter as equals, with Dr. Johnson places her conversational wit on an equal footing with her attributes that connected her with Reynolds and Carlisle.

An earlier Johnson reference comes in Disraeli's 1831 novel, *The Young Duke*. In Chapter 7, Disraeli argues to the follies of youth, listing among them their loose grasp on what had become the lost art of conversation. He writes, "[D]o not think, as many young gentlemen are apt to believe, that talking will serve your purpose. That is the quicksand of your young beginners." Disraeli brings his readers back to Johnson's circle of intimate acquaintance and their coveted conversation. He continues, "All can talk in a public assembly; that is to say, all can give us exhortations which do not move, and arguments which do not convince; but to converse in a private assembly is a different affair." He prepares his readers for his Johnson reference with more imagery of the lost Socratic gathering of minds by writing, "The high style of conversation where eloquence and philosophy emulate each other, where principles are profoundly expounded and felicitously illustrated, all this has ceased." Then he ties it into Dr. Johnson by noting that "It ceased in this country with Johnson and Burke, and it requires a Johnson and a Burke for its maintenance" [17].

Disraeli's 1844 novel *Comingsby* is brimming with references to ancient Roman glory. Of course, such Augustan sentiments would be incomplete without a mention of Johnson. The character, Princess Lucrecia, is undoubtedly meant to remind the readers of the story of the suicide of the Roman Lucrecia and the founding of the Roman Republic. In the Roman legend, Lucrecia was the wife of Collatinus, a nobleman and friend of the Roman prince, Tarquin. Collatinus and Tarquin were involved in a bet as to which of them had the most pure and chaste wife. Collatinus won the bet. Tarquin could not abide such a pure woman being out of his reach. He propositioned her and was refused. Her noble character was too much for him to resist. He defiled her purity by raping her. Lucrecia was afraid that future Roman women would use her story as an excuse for licentious behavior so she stabbed herself in the heart. Collatinus' friend Brutus took Lucrecia's body, still dripping with blood, to the center of the city and rallied the Roman people against the king. Thus, the Roman Republic was born [18]. Disraeli's Lucrecia was a similarly revered noble.

The character Sidonia becomes enthralled with Lucrecia after earlier having had no prurient interest in her. Disraeli credits the change to Lucecia having become Marchioness of Monmouth. He attests to his readers that, "an affair of gallantry with a great lady is more delightful than with ladies of a lower degree." To nail this notion down, he feels it best to quote Dr. Johnson, writing that, "certain it is that Dr. Johnson announced to Boswell, 'Sir, in the case of a Countess the imagination is more excited.'" The parallels to the Roman legend are clear and Johnson again is attached to the English associated identity with Roman greatness.

Charles Dickens (1812-1870) had a novel writing career that spanned from 1837 to 1870. In that time, Dickens experienced many changes in his personal life and his socio-political positions. Like Disraeli, Dickens referenced Johnson in his novels for specific reasons, and reflective of the writer's beliefs. His characters, and even his narrators, struggle with language and understanding each other [19]. This is why a lexicographer, one who puts native speakers on the same linguistic page, is a powerful symbol in Dickens' books. The expressive isolation that causes much of the turmoil in Dickens' novels would find mitigation in the universal embrace of Johnsonian ideals of language. Some of his references to Johnson hint at such a solution. There is an ugly awkwardness to Dickens' London and to his characters. Some Dickensian references to Dr. Johnson allude to the beauty, or at least the brilliance, that can be found in awkward, ugly people and places.

Dickens' first reference to Johnson comes in his 1838-39 serial, *The Life and Adventures of Nicholas Nickleby.* In the story, Nicholas' uncle secures him a situation with a boys' boarding school in Yorkshire. Chapter 4 bears the heading, "Nicholas and his Uncle (to secure the Fortune without loss of time) wait upon Mr Wackford Squeers, the Yorkshire Schoolmaster". Dickens describes the one-eyed villain, Mr. Squeers, in a manner to immediately repulse. He writes, "The blank side of his face was much wrinkled and puckered up, which gave him a very sinister appearance, especially when he smiled, at which times his expression bordered closely on the villainous." Nicholas is immediately apprehensive. He tries to overcome his apprehension by reminding himself, "' He is an odd-looking man,' thought Nicholas. 'What of that? Porson was an odd-looking man, and so was Doctor Johnson; all these bookworms are.'"[20] The Porson to whom Nicholas refers is Professor Richard Porson, a Greek scholar and Cambridge University professor from 1792-1808. Porson is known as the eminent Greek scholar of his age [21]. By Dickens' reference, he must have had some physical peculiarities. Johnson was known to be physically awkward, as well as having some quirking mannerisms that would have been considered uncouth, if not for his social eminence. To place Johnson in with a Cambridge professor as someone who is of premium quality despite the first impressions of outward appearances, speaks to Dickens' understanding of his readers' image of Johnson. When Nicholas took comfort in comparing the repulsive schoolmaster to Porson and Dr. Johnson, he wanted the reader to feel the relieved apprehension that he intended for Nicholas. He employed the image he thought best would serve that end. Dr. Johnson and Porson must have been endearingly awkward to English society for Dickens' reference to serve its purpose.

In Dickens' 1849-1850 *David Copperfield,* Dr. Strong, a man of some advanced years, is married to the much younger Annie. In a Chapter 45 argument between Dr. Strong and Annie Strong's mother, Mrs. Markleham, Mrs. Markleham comments on the age difference between her daughter and Dr. Strong, expressing pleasure in the fact that Dr. Strong does not expect his wife to be at the same intellectual level. She appreciates that he does not expect "as many elderly people do expect, old heads on young shoulders" [22]. She implies to Dr. Strong that her daughter must be informed by her husband, referencing Johnson and giving his *Dictionary* credit for people knowing the meaning of simple, commonplace words. She says, "Without Doctor Johnson, or somebody of that sort, we might have been at this present moment calling an Italian-iron, a bedstead." Obviously, language is used accurately by people who have never lifted a dictionary. Giving the lexicographer credit for the correct use of language in common society is an exaggeration of his contribution. It is not likely that Dickens had such an unrealistically lofty opinion of *Johnson's Dictionary.* Through this reference, he recognizes the existence of such opinions in his readers, particularly on the part of people of Mrs. Markleham's age, with one foot in each century. *Johnson's Dictionary* stood as the standard dictionary of the English language for more than a hundred years. Having completed and published such a tremendous literary feat as documenting the English language, it is not difficult to see how Johnson's literary achievements alloyed with his socially iconic stardom to create a notion like Mrs. Markleham's. Without Dr. Johnson, some felt, people would be mumbling confusion, with no idea how to use the language. This reference implies the larger-than-life, almost divinely heroic nature of the Johnsonian image in the 1840s, crediting Johnson for the existence of linguistic order in England the way Americans might credit Washington's fabled incident with the cherry tree for American honor.

William Makepeace Thackeray (1811-1863) greatly admired Disraeli, long wishing to make his acquaintance [11]. Arethusa Milner-Gibson, the wife of one of Disraeli's old schoolmates, was the leader of a society whose salon was frequented by Thackeray and other literary giants of the time. She expressed in a letter to Mrs. Disraeli how much Thackeray admired her husband. Thackeray wrote the review of Disraeli's political novel *Coningsby* for the *Morning Chronicle*. Milner-Gibson wrote in her letter that Thackeray "throws himself at my feet (in a note) to know if he may make your acquaintance-he is an odd man!-he spoke of Coningsby in raptures" [11]. It is not surprising that Thackeray's image of Dr. Johnson would be influenced by Disraeli's expression of him. In his review of *Coningsby,* Thackeray wrote of the book's "wonderful truth" and "vivid correctness" [11]. Thackeray takes Disraeli's political use of the Johnsonian image to a more personal level, betraying an intimate reverence for Dr. Johnson and his works. In short, Disraeli's intended use of the Johnsonian image had its desired propaganda effect on Thackeray. No Victorian novelist enshrined the Johnsonian image to such a degree, deifying, gilding, and polishing the image before presenting it to his readers, like Thackeray.

In 1844, Thackeray presents the Victorian literati with what could be the most bizarre references to Dr. Johnson in his story, *The Luck of Barry Lyndon,* written in the first person. This narrative technique precludes him from the commentary asides he used to delineate the characters of his other novels, characters like Becky Sharp, whose follies were given regular criticism in the words of an omniscient narrator. Thackeray had to present the satirical nature of the story directly through the words and actions of the narrating main character, Barry Lyndon. The character, having little negative report of himself, had to present his story in a way that the satirical message of the story would not be lost to the readers [23]. Immediately upon the novels opening, Lyndon presents his family story. He begins by claiming that he may have found himself wearing the crown of a free and independent Ireland if not for some particular misfortunes. Lyndon is presented as a con artist, swindler, and scoundrel from Chapter 1, by his attempts to con the reader into believing his lofty lineage, just as he later assumes the identity of a wounded Prussian army officer in another of his long line of dishonest schemes.

In the middle of presenting his early history, he interrupts himself to recount a tale in defense of his failed education. After admitting to the readers that he failed at the Classics, he narrates, "So six weeks' was all the schooling I ever got. And I say this to let parents know the value of it; for though I have met more learned book-worms in the world". The thought is never finished. He goes on to claim an intimate encounter and ensuing friendship with Dr. Johnson. The quotation continues, "[E]specially a great hulking, clumsy, blear-eyed old doctor, whom they called Johnson". To be certain the reader understands the reference to be of Dr. Samuel Johnson the lexicographer, he adds, "and who lived in a court off Fleet Street, in London, yet I pretty soon silenced him in an argument (at 'Button's Coffeehouse')". Lyndon then lists a series of academic fields at which he claims to excel. If there was any taller tale than besting Dr. Johnson in a battle of wits, it was finding intimacy within his circle. To establish this, Lyndon adds, "[H]e was accompanied by a Mr. Boswell of Scotland, and I was presented to the club by a Mr. Goldsmith". Anyone with such a claim would indeed command the respect of his audience, considering that the coveted company of Johnson's inner circle had grown in legend since the last London coffeehouse had echoed their conversations. Unlike with Miss Sharp, the absurdity of Lyndon had to come from his own words. Thackeray could not have established it better than he did with Lyndon's tale of his dealings with Dr. Johnson. He continues, "'Sir,' said I, in reply to the schoolmaster's great thundering quotation in Greek, 'you fancy you know a great deal more than me, because you quote your Aristotle and your Pluto". Next, Lyndon challenges Dr. Johnson, asking him, "[C]an you tell me which horse will win at Epsom Downs next week?—Can you run six miles without breathing?—Can you shoot the ace of spades ten times without missing? If so, talk about Aristotle and Pluto to me.'" Lyndon's tale reaches its ridiculous climax after he belittles Boswell, as any good Irishmen would do. Lyndon claims, "'Hold your tongue, Mr. Boswell,' said the old schoolmaster. 'I had no right to brag of my Greek to the gentleman, and he has answered me very well.'" Lyndon presents Dr. Johnson with the following riddle, "'Doctor,' says I, looking waggishly at him, 'do you know ever a rhyme for ArisTOTLE'" [24]. Goldsmith solves the riddle and orders a "bottle" of port. Lyndon and English society's most elite social circle share six bottles of port before the evening is over.

The entire tale of the coffeehouse encounter occurs in Chapter 1. In Chapter 17, Lyndon recounts more intimate encounters with Johnson, this time painting him and his circle in an uglier light. He tries to associate himself with the greatest literary circle of their time by claiming, "I had always a taste for men of letters, and perhaps, if the truth must be told, have no objection to playing the fine gentleman and patron among the wits." In a tale not well aligned with his account of Dr. Johnson in Chapter 1, he says, "I was introduced to a score of these gentlemen, and their great chief, Mr. Johnson. I always thought their great chief a great bear." He sets the insult up by setting the scene in his own house. "He drank tea twice or thrice at my house, misbehaving himself most grossly". Entirely unlike his description of Johnson's behavior in the coffeehouse, Lyndon speaks of Dr. Johnson "[T]reating my opinions with no more respect than those of a schoolboy, and telling me to mind my horses and tailors, and not trouble myself about letters." Lyndon adds one more poke at Boswell, saying, "His Scotch bear-leader, Mr. Boswell, was a butt of the first quality" [24]. Thackeray had to establish Lyndon's degree of wretchedness through the character's own words and does so masterfully through his accounts of Johnson and associates. His attack on English society's beacon of scholarship, wit, common sense, and reliable conventionalism served Thackeray's need to establish his character and serves current readers as insight into the Victorian public's ideas of Johnson and his circle. Lyndon's reports of his encounters with Johnson established his character for Victorian readers in three ways. First, only a lying con artist would dare to claim intimacy with such an elite circle. Second, only a character of gross vanity, either real or portrayed, would attempt to place Dr. Johnson and his circle beneath him in any way. Third, Lyndon's own account of the insults Johnson threw at him would have dictated the sentiments of a Victorian reader. Throughout Victorian literature, in both the novel and the essay, people are measured by the reported opinions of Johnson. Probably the most revealing aspect of the novel's view into the iconic nature of Johnson's Victorian persona is the fact that, aside from the brief mention of a couple historical figures, Johnson and his circle are the only non-fictional characters presented in the novel. They are certainly the only ones presented at that length and intended to serve as a primary means of establishing the main character.

Thackeray continues his use of Johnson's public image to establish his characters in his most popular novel, his 1848 *Vanity Fair*. Just a few lines into the novel, he references Johnson in establishing the virtues and eminence of a character that will stand in contrast to the follies of the primary character throughout the story. The characters are Becky Sharp and Miss Sedley's school mistress, Miss Pinkerton. Thackeray, in omniscient narrative, describes Pinkerton as "that majestic lady; the Semiramis of Hammersmith, the friend of Doctor Johnson, the correspondent of Mrs. Chapone herself" [25]. Just as Disraeli placed Johnson with Joshua Reynolds and Lord Carlisle, Thackeray places him with Semiramis and Hester Chapone. As with Disraeli's use, the intended use of Dr. Johnson can be put into perspective through an understanding of the other two references. Semiramis was an Assyrian queen of Greek legendary invention and the title character of the 1823 Rossini opera already popular by the time *Vanity Fair* was published. According to Babylonian legend, Semiramis was half goddess, half human. She lends her name to many monuments of the Babylonian Age, including the Wonder of the Ancient World, the Hanging Gardens of Babylon, also called the Hanging Gardens of Semiramis [26]. Hammersmith is a section in the western part of London. Hester Chapone was an advocate of women's rights in the Augustan age. To understand Thackeray's intentions in connecting Miss Pinkerton to Chapone, one needs look no farther than the first line of Chapone's memoirs. "The design in presenting examples of women whose endowments or whose conduct has reflected lustre on the sex, has been to excite a noble emulation in the cause of truth, virtue, and philosophy" [27]. Sandwiched between an Assyrian queen and Hester Chapone is Dr. Johnson. To be noted as a friend of Dr. Johnson's established an immediate notion of the woman's character for the Victorian reader. Also of note is the fact that Johnson is the only man in the reference. Johnson might seem out of place with a Babylonian demigoddess and a popular women's rights advocate, two potently feminine figures. Such was the universal appeal of the Johnsonian image in Thackeray's mind.

A little farther into Chapter 1, as Sedley and Sharp were leaving the school, "Miss Pinkerton proceeded to write her own name, and Miss Sedley's, in the fly-leaf of a *Johnson's Dictionary*—the interesting work which she invariably presented to her scholars, on their departure from the Mall" [25]. Thackeray intended Pinkerton's relationship to Johnson to be so close that Johnson was meant to have supplied the copies of his *Dictionary* to Miss Pinkerton himself for that very purpose, evident in the next line, "On the cover was inserted a copy of 'Lines addressed to a young lady on quitting Miss Pinkerton's school, at the Mall; by the late revered Doctor Samuel Johnson'". Next, Thackeray establishes that all of Pinkerton's esteem, made clear in such abundance, was due entirely to her association with Johnson. He writes, "In fact, the Lexicographer's name was always on the lips of this majestic woman, and a visit he had paid to her was the cause of her reputation and her fortune" [25]. Pinkerton was not particularly fond of Becky Sharp and did not intend to send her with a copy of the *Dictionary*. Pinkerton would never willfully present such an undeserving academic with such a symbol of academic excellence. Nevertheless, she gives Sharp a *Dictionary* by the urging of Sharp's friend, Miss Sedley. Becky Sharp proves Pinkerton correct at the end of the chapter. The chapter ends with a sound establishment of Sharp's insolence. She throws her copy of *Johnson's Dictionary* out of the carriage window as they ride away from the school. The *Dictionary* held sacredness not unlike a treasured national symbol, such as a flag, a fact Thackeray drives in the chapter's final lines. "This almost caused Jemima to faint with terror. 'Well, I never'—said she—'what an audacious'—Emotion prevented her from completing either sentence" [25].

Many parallels have been drawn between Thackeray's *Vanity Fair* and Bunyan's *Pilgrim's Progress,* primarily because Vanity Fair is a location that Bunyan's character Christian encounters in his journey. Of all of the faulty people Christian encounters, none have Becky Sharp's ambition. Thackeray's novel draws closer parallels to Johnson's *Vanity of Human Wishes* [28]. Walter Jackson Bate (1918-1999), Pulitzer Prize winning Johnson biographer, incidentally describes Becky Sharp exactly in his synopsis of Dr. Johnson's poem:

> Its general subject is the enormous clutter of fitful desires and rival ambitions, of fears, projections, envy and self-expectation that human feelings create in their confused impulse to assert themselves and find satisfaction. To this is added the unwelcome discovery, which we naturally try to resist, that even to attain our wishes brings languor or indifference afterward, while at the same time we are inspiring envy and hostility in others, and moving into the decay that seems so rapid and remorseless to a conscious being. [28]

Bate was not thinking of Becky Sharpe when he wrote the passage, and obviously Thackeray did not model Sharpe after Bate's description of Johnson's *Vanity*. Nevertheless, the passage could serve as a vivid description of Sharpe, providing further evidence of the saturation of "Johnsonian-ness" in Thackeray's narrative.

In Chapter 48, Thackeray relays his respect for Johnson in words difficult to misinterpret. In a chapter titled "In Which the Reader is Introduced to the Very Best of Company", Thackeray writes, "Others have seen Napoleon. Some few still exist who have beheld Frederick the Great, Doctor Johnson, Marie Antoinette, &c." Here, Thackeray lifts Johnson beyond the spheres of Sir Joshua Reynolds or Hester Chapone. His eminence is compared with key figures of Western history. A comparison of Bate's summary of Johnson's *Vanity* with Thackeray's apparent intended message in his novel, combined with the manner in which Johnson's name is dropped during the novel and used in the establishment of characters, serve to proclaim some combination of Thackeray's own notions of Johnson and his understanding of that of his readers. In any case, study of Thackeray's *Vanity Fair* remains incomplete without an understanding of how Johnson's iconic persona guides and saturates the narrative.

From Disraeli's efforts to hearken his reader back to their memories of Augustan virtues to Dickens' reliance on an established public perception in the building of his characters, to Thackeray's lofty comparisons of admired social and historical figures and his emulation of Johnsonian themes, a strongly present public sentiment of Dr. Johnson's image is both reflected and perpetuated in the great novels of the 1830s and 40s. As those two decades came to a close, the Johnsonian image seemed to expand in both scope and potency, propelling it into the 1850s with a force to sweep the Victorian English reading public into a Johnsonian frenzy. The novels of the 30s and 40s established Johnson as the polar magnet toward which all literary compasses pointed and held him as the comparison point from which many major literary characters were established.

References to Johnson evolve tremendously in the 1850s in both volume and nature. In some novels, his name appears nearly as often as those of the stories' protagonists. It is the nature of a social icon for the public perception to drift from the truths of the actual life of the icon to a position best suited to fit the needs of those who worship the idolized version. At the beginning of his fame, after the publication of his 1755 *Dictionary*, Johnson's public image revolved around the man himself, his works, and the magnetism of his elite inner circle of scholars, artists, and others. In particular, his brilliant conversation was legendary and coveted in his own lifetime [29]. Having been so commonly the topic of personal and public discourse, personal letters detailing encounters with Johnson or contemporary opinions of him are great resource into the nature of his public image. Also, many letters to and from Johnson have also survived. Conversely, in the Victorian Era, the story of Johnson's public persona is far less a story about Johnson himself than one about the early Victorian public's need to enshrine him, using the fabled and often exaggerated aspects of the Johnsonian identity as a banner for the ideals of an aged generation clinging to the old, idealistic hopes of the Glorious Revolution of 1688 and Augustan imperial pride. By the 1850s, this was particularly true. As industrialism further polarized English society, Johnson's identity in the public came less and less to represent a man than to represent a generation in fear of losing their own identity and their cherished, definitive ideals.

Even during his life, Dr. Johnson's character greatly outweighed his published works in its impression on the public. Any attempt to grasp his common image as an entity in itself must begin with an intentional turn away from literary criticism of his published works. Macaulay's assertion that "The memory of other authors is kept alive by their works. But the memory of Johnson keeps many of his works alive" [30] looks more closely at the person as an historical figure and less at writings. But it holds as true for the literary and sociological legacy of Johnson. The academic study of Johnson does not often break through the sphere of literary study into the social sciences, although it should. His impact on the British culture and people was immense, taking particular hold in the 1850s. With Macaulay's quotation guiding research away from the confines of strict literary study, the broader sense of Johnson's impact is more comprehensively observable. The rise of a powerful and vocal middle class in England fostered the conditions for the cult of Dr. Johnson, which focused on his humble beginnings and gradual climb from destitution to prosperity and public influence [31]. This is quite a turnaround from the elitist image employed by Disraeli. As the arm of industrialism reached out from its initially urban hubs in the 1850s, Johnson was the talisman worn by the slice of society hoping to ward off the frightening changes. He began to belong less to elite academics and more to the common people with their common daily concerns.

The 1850s increased the number of literary references to Johnson, per narrative, indicating a more thorough saturation of his persona in the public mind. This happened as the ideals associated with Dr. Johnson became a more consistent part of daily common thought and conversation. Thackeray's 1848-50 serial, *The History of Pendennis,* is as notable for the number of Johnson references, sprinkled evenly throughout the novel, as for the variety of ways Thackeray employs the Johnsonian image. Johnson is mentioned in ten different chapters, in a variety of manners, and for a variety of purposes. In Chapter 3, the main character, Arthur Pendennis, called 'Pen', now a young man, encounters an old schoolmate named Henry Foker. Foker is quite improved since Pen had seen him a year earlier. To establish this degree of improvement, Thackeray puts Foker in an impressive costume. Before describing this costume in detail, he prepares the reader, writing that Foker appeared "in one of those costumes to which the public consent, that I take to be quite as influential in this respect as *'Johnson's Dictionary,'* has awarded the title of 'Swell.'"[32] When Becky Sharp threw the *Dictionary* out of the carriage window at the beginning of *Vanity Fair,* Thackeray represented the *Dictionary* as an item sacred to the character of Miss Pinkerton and to Thackeray himself. In this reference to the *Dictionary*, he alludes to its degree of influence on a larger, public scale. To compare the influence of Dr. Johnson's *Dictionary* to that of the "public consent" would have been quite enough of a testament to the book's sacred position in society. Thackeray compares the people's affections to the *Dictionary*, as if the *Dictionary* is the standard and the thoughts of the public are measured by it.

In Chapter 5, Thackeray establishes the "common knowledge" nature of some of the finer details of Johnson's career. Pen finds himself romantically entangled with the actress Emily Fotheringay. Thackeray establishes that Emily is poorly read in drama and only familiar with the parts she has played on stage. He drives the point home with an anecdote from Emily's past. "A wag once told her that Dante was born at Algiers: and asked her,—which Dr. Johnson wrote first, 'Irene,' or 'Every Man in his Humour.'" *Irene* is a tragedy written by Johnson in his youth, of which he was not proud [16]. *Every Man in his Humour* is a play written by Renaissance playwright, Ben Jonson [33]. This joke that the "wag" played on Emily was meant to demonstrate to Thackeray's readers the extent of Emily's ignorance in the field of dramatic literature. His point would be lost if the reader is not fully aware of both Dr. Johnson's and Benjamin Jonson's works and aware of the public expectation of a common knowledge of the distinction. To accentuate the pathetic nature of the ignorance, Thackeray had to choose works and writers with which any reader should be familiar.

The Chapter 6 reference might seem less significant at first glance. Pen introduces Emily to Shakespeare. Thackeray adds that Pen's father said that Shakespeare's plays had "more poetry than in all 'Johnson's Poets' put together." This may not seem like a profoundly important or telling reference to Johnson. When considering the illustrious names covered in Dr. Johnson's *Lives of the Most Eminent English Poets*, names like Milton, Dryden, Pope, Addison, and Swift, the question arises as to why Thackeray did not just list some of the poets. Why call them "Johnson's poets"? Two insights into Thackeray's notion of the public perception of Dr. Johnson come through this reference. First, Thackeray makes the assumption that his readers were familiar with Dr. Johnson's biographies on the poets and knew which poets were covered. Without knowledge of the biographies, the compliment to Shakespeare holds no power. Second, by referring to the poets as "Johnson's", the literary reference is not to anything actually written by Milton, Dryden, or Pope. These poets and their works were well known to a literate Victorian audience. The reference is to a publication of Johnson's, therefore comparing Shakespeare less to the poets covered by Johnson's biographies than to Johnson's generous portrayal of them in his biographies.

Not only did Thackeray portray Johnson as the herdsman of the great, he still clung to the gilded Dr. Johnson, who sat as a polished bust in the hallowed halls of academia. The Chapter 18 reference is in the style of Disraeli's description of Viscountess Dowager Bellair. An association with Johnson is used to establish a character's eminence. When Pen leaves home to study at St. Boniface College, Thackeray describes the portraits of the establishment's most prestigious graduates lining a hallway of the College. He describes six portraits, in each case listing the subject's particular point of notoriety. He describes one portrait as "Doctor Blogg, the late master, and friend of Doctor Johnson". This theme of denoting a character's status by an intimacy with Dr. Johnson is among the most common uses of Johnson references in early Victorian literature. It seems to have been the best way to establish a character's elite social status or level of scholarly achievement.

By Chapter 30, the reader begins to again see evidence of Johnson's transformation from an unreachable ideal, placed upon some high shelf to be honored but not touched, to a fellow scholar to whom the common youth may feel a personal connection, still maintaining his connection to an idealized past. This gradual trend explodes into a full evolution in the Johnsonian image in the next few decades. Pen moves to London, where he meets journalist George Warington, with whose help Pen intends to support himself as a writer. George and Pen take residence in a cheap but lively part of town. Thackeray describes the area as antiquated, with a nostalgic respect for traditions. He writes, "A well-ordained workhouse or prison is much better provided with the appliances of health, comfort, and cleanliness, than a respectable Foundation School a venerable College, or a learned Inn." He defends the charm the area holds for writers, continuing, "[B]ut the man of letters can't but love the place which has been inhabited by so many of his brethren." He continues to describe Pen's area of residence as beings as lively "as old Samuel Johnson rolling through the fog with the Scotch gentleman at his heels on their way to Dr. Goldsmith's chambers in Brick Court." This serves as a reminder of the sacred position such men of letters held in Augustan society. The image of Johnson and his circle bustling around the literary havens had to be alive and fresh in the minds of Thackeray's readers. The image of Johnson, the Scottish Boswell, and Goldsmith must have still represented the epitome of scholarly and literary achievement or the image would not have served Thackeray's intentions. The charmingly dilapidated neighborhood is excused by its connection to Augustan achievement, an achievement whose essence is personified in Dr. Johnson. In this reference, Johnson is not placed in the parlor of some elite swell, but in the bustling literary neighborhoods of the city. This foreshadows the Johnsonian trends of the next few decades.

Thackeray again tries to place the image of the living Dr. Johnson, in the mind's eye of his readers, among the well-known local scenes. In Chapter 50, Pen finds himself strolling into Temple Garden, in Central London. Thackeray describes the area and the people there. He writes of the lawyers coming and going with no mind for the historical significance of the Garden. He writes, "Only antiquarians and literary amateurs care to look at the gardens with much interest." He continues, detailing what these interested parties might have in their imaginations as they gaze down the streets. One example reads as follows:

> Treading heavily on the gravel, and rolling majestically along in a snuff-coloured suit, and a wig that sadly wants the barber's powder and irons, one sees the Great Doctor step up to him (his Scotch lackey following at the lexicographer's heels, a little the worse for port wine that they have been taking at the Mitre). [32]

This image is not intended for the sole understanding and enjoyment of such "antiquarians and literary amateurs" among Thackeray's readers. It is an image for the common reader to associate with "antiquarians and literary amateurs", but one understandable by the common Victorian reader. The meticulously sculpted and gilded image of the 1830s and 1840s has transformed into the ragged and unkempt picture Thackeray presents in the Chapter 50 reference. Understanding Thackeray's devoted admiration for Dr. Johnson dissolves any notion that the reference is intended to belittle Johnson in any way. It is clear that Thackeray wishes to offer a claim of affiliation with Johnson to a slice of society unable to approach Disraeli's Johnson, just as education and suffrage were working their way into that same slice of society.

After a couple more quaint images of Johnson's circle, Thackeray writes, "Sir Roger and Mr. Spectator are as real to us now as the two doctors and the boozy and faithful Scotchman" [32]. In addition to Dr. Johnson's circle, the reference is to Addison's daily publication, *The Spectator,* and its primary character Sir Roger de Coverley. In March of 1711, Addison published the first number of *The Spectator,* in which the Spectator was an imaginary person, living in London, who was an observer of manners and behavior [34]. He released the results of his observations in the form of sketches. The sketches were primarily of one group of friends, primary among which are Sir Roger de Coverly and Will Honeycomb. *The Spectator* also included critical articles. The series was brought to a close in 1712 with the death of Sir Roger, the marriage of Honeycomb, the breakup of the group, and eventually the death of the Spectator [34]. It is not difficult to recognize the parallels to Johnson and his circle. First, Addison was an Augustan. He approached his work from the same angle of the objective observation of human tendencies that was distinctive of the literature of his era. Sir Roger's group was not dissimilar to Dr. Johnson's elite circle of literary friends and colleagues. It is difficult to guess whether this reference meant that the Spectator and Sir Roger have become less fictional or Johnson and Boswell have become more fictional. Since the *Spectator* had been around since the early 1700s, it is unlikely that the social perception of it would have changed. It is more likely that Thackeray meant that the perception of Johnson had come to resemble that of Addison's fictional creations. He would have been keenly aware of the transitions in Johnson's image as they occurred. He represents those transitions in his references in *The History of Pendennis.* Much can be speculated about Thackeray's Johnson by the mention that Addison's fiction and the factual Johnson are "as real to us."

The *Pendennis* references to Johnson round off with a simple Chapter 66 reference to the *Dictionary* (interestingly mentioned with the Bible as a "must buy" book for the characters) and a Chapter 73 reference comparing the qualities of literary men such as Johnson to the much softer standards of Pen's generation of literary figures. It was sort of a "back in my day" speech given by Mr. Bows, an old man and professional fiddler, in which Thackeray writes:

> Doctor Johnson has been down the street many a time with ragged shoes, and a bundle of penny-a-lining for the Gent's Magazine. You literary gents are better off now—eh? You ride in your cabs, and wear yellow kid gloves now [32].

If compiling a list of running themes throughout this novel, the Johnsonian persona must appear near the top. It is as consistently present and as deeply relevant as the novel's main characters. Most importantly, *Pendennis* christens a voyage that Johnson's image takes from a polished bust to a real, struggling writer "with ragged shoes, and a bundle of penny-a-lining."

The running Victorian theme of Augustan nostalgia versus social change and industrialization was personally and poignantly experienced by Elizabeth Gaskell (1810-1865). Her novels not only adhered to the social concerns and literary tastes of the era, but they also reflected her own observations of polarization caused by industrial technology, expansion, and economy. She grew up in the small town of Knutsford, in Northwest England. After marrying a minister in 1832, she moved to the industrial city of Manchester, which exposed her to the vivid differences between her backward town and the rapidly changing and growing industrialization of Manchester [35]. Her struggle to reconcile these vastly disparate societies is reflected in her writing. In *North and South* (1855), her protagonist moves from the rural South to an industrial city. In *Cranford* (1853), the reverse occurs, as the narrator settles in to the small town of Cranford, the residents of which are reluctant to change, religiously clinging to the social conventions of the previous generations. It is set in the 1830s, when Dickens' *Pickwick Papers* is a new and popular comic serial [34]. The social polarization caused by industrialism is less boldly presented than in Gaskell's later novels. In *Cranford*, the polarization is represented by the literary tastes of the characters.

Cranford begins a series of Gaskell novels and novellas that deeply entangle Johnson's Victorian persona in their plots. These went beyond the drop of Johnson's name to create an image in the readers' minds or establishing the social prominence of a character by a social association with the Great Doctor. Gaskell uses Johnson as the champion of a set of ideals that are vehemently, and sometimes violently, defended by her characters. *Cranford* pits Johnsonian literature, society, decorum, and conventionalism against the time's current writers, like Dickens, and the evolutions in etiquette, all before the backdrop of a town trying to remain frozen in Dr. Johnson's England amid the expanding railroad and the encroachment of industrialization. It is in these novels that Johnson's persona drifts furthest from the mortal man who wrote the first English dictionary. Dr. Johnson becomes the very countenance of a way of life that seeps down to the core of Gaskell's characters. The characters affixed to Johnson are thoroughly Johnsonian, paying a religious homage to a Johnsonian image even more gilded, polished, enshrined, and removed from mortal folly than Disraeli's and Thackeray's Dr. Johnson. It is the contrast against what it perceived as anti-Johnsonian that pushes the Johnsonian pendulum so far from moderate reality. This push will eventually cause a swing in the opposite direction in the following decades, as the Johnsonian image becomes gritty, common, and tangible to the common folk. Gaskell's petty character disputes reflected the same issues that occurred on a much larger scale around them. She wasted no time intertwining Johnson into the plot.

Chapter 1 of *Cranford*, titled "Our Society" establishes the key characters and their rules of unchanging etiquette. Among the characters introduced is Captain Brown. Gaskell spends many paragraphs establishing the fact that Brown, a newcomer to Cranford, does not fit in well with the ladies who dominate the

Cranford social scene. Decorum is the rule in Cranford and the term 'vulgar' is given to anything outside of their expectations. The scene is set as Brown violates some of Cranford's conversational taboos. On the larger parallel, Brown is connected with the railroad, that symbol of progress, the arch-enemy of a town clinging to the 18th century. Most of the women of Cranford are able to accept Brown into their society despite his social vulgarity. His simple, sincere manner endears him to the ladies, all but Miss Jenkyns. In Chapter 1, Brown, in the same innocently intended manner as all of his offenses are delivered, speaks highly of Dickens' *Pickwick Papers.* He introduces the topic with a childlike enthusiasm, like a boy showing off his latest birthday present. His intention is to delight his audience of Cranford ladies with something new that he is certain they have not yet encountered but will thoroughly appreciate. If it is new, however, it is vulgar to the Cranford ladies, especially to Miss Jenkyns. She is the daughter of a deceased rector, who "on the strength of a number of manuscript sermons, and a pretty good library of divinity, considered herself literary, and looked upon any conversation about books as a challenge to her"[36]. She admits to Brown that she has read Dickens. With a great deal of excitement at entering into a discussion on such a topic, Brown asks Miss Jenkyns what she thinks of Dickens. But Brown is doomed, because he and Miss Jenkyns do not come to the topic with the same excitement and intentions. As Gaskell writes it, Miss Jenkyns saw the introduction of a controversial literary topic "as a challenge to her." This was no open symposium. Brown giddily asks Miss Jenkyns, "And what do you think of them?", "Aren't they famously good?" to which she responds with what could only have been a carefully rehearsed lecture, "I must say, I don't think they are by any means equal to Dr Johnson." Left alone, this would have been an invitation for rational debate. However, she follows up with, "Still, perhaps, the author is young. Let him persevere, and who knows what he may become if he will take the great Doctor for his model?"

Brown's enthusiasm for Dickens and the prospect of bearing his Dickensian gifts to the fairer sex was not dampened. He points out to Miss Jenkyns that Dr. Johnson and Dickens are quite different, suggesting that they should not be compared in this way. Miss Jenkyns intends this to be a showdown between Dr. Johnson and Dickens, fought by their appointed champions, despite Brown's reluctance to take it in that direction. Brown displays his boyish infatuation with 'the new', begging for an opportunity to win over the crowd. "'Just allow me to read you a scene out of this month's number,' pleads he. 'I had it only this morning, and I don't think the company can have read it yet.'" Brown reads from *The Pickwick Papers* while Miss Jenkyns "sat in patient gravity". Gaskell continues, "When it was ended, she turned to me, and said with mild dignity – 'Fetch me Rasselas, my dear, out of the book-room.'" When Brown read his passage, he had no intention of tossing Dickens into the ring against Johnson. Nevertheless, that is what he has done. Before beginning, Miss Jenkyns qualifies her reading by saying, "the present company can judge between your favourite, Mr Boz, and Dr. Johnson." Mr. Boz is the narrator in Dickens' *Sketches by Boz*. In his early publications, Dickens experimented with narrative techniques. Mr. Boz was one of those experiments [37]. The *Pickwick Papers* was Dickens' first novel following the success of *Sketches by Boz*. That is why Dickens is referred to here as Boz. Interestingly, *Pickwick Papers* was quite similar to Addison's *Spectator*. Both were meant to portray ordinary London life through the eyes of a fictitious narrator. Dickens wrote a letter to John Macrone, the publisher of *Sketches by Boz*, in which he wrote, "Let me beg your particular regard for this specimen of London life 'Sam Weller'" [37].

After Miss Jenkyns' recital from *Rasselas*, she gives one more stab at Brown's tastes, saying, "I consider it vulgar, and below the dignity of literature, to publish in numbers." This remark is presumably a response to Brown's indecorum during the length of their acquaintance to which apparently she had previously bitten her tongue. Miss Jenkyns' indignation finally pulls Brown from his puerile fervor to a state of apparent perturbation. She finally has her duel. Brown refers to Dr. Johnson's writing as "pompous" after Miss Jenkyns admits to having modeled her own epistolary style after him. Miss Jenkyns takes it as a personal insult. The argument and the chapter end as, "She drew herself up with dignity, and only replied to Captain Brown's last remark by saying, with marked emphasis on every syllable, 'I prefer Dr Johnson to Mr Boz.'" This entire encounter becomes more interesting to the reader with the added knowledge that Dickens edited *Cranford* when it was published in the weekly magazine, *Household Words,* for which Dickens served as editor in the 1850s [39]. Ironically, Browns 'vulgar' mannerisms are not dissimilar to Dr. Johnson's social peculiarities as expressed by Boswell.

The dispute over literary tastes lingers in Chapter 2, which covers a large swath of time. Brown tries to make amends for any affront by hand-crafting a wooden fire shovel as a gift for Miss Jenkyns, who he had heard complain of the irritating sound of her iron shovel. This does not appease the lady. After he leaves, she demands it be thrown in with the lumber, claiming,"...no present from a man who preferred Mr Boz to Dr Johnson could be less jarring than an iron fire-shovel." Even when Brown drums his fingers, Miss Jenkyns views it as "very disparaging to Dr Johnson." While preparing an apple with cloves as fragrance for the room of Brown's infirmed daughter, she utters a Johnsonian line with the insertion of each clove. "Indeed, she never could think of the Browns without talking Johnson." The relationship was complex. Miss Jenkyns performed many kindnesses for Brown and his daughters, while clinging to the insult of the literary argument. As the chapter continues, Brown is killed by the railroad. He was, of course, reading *Pickwick* when he saw a child on the track with the train approaching. He pushes the child off of the track and is killed by the train. This is the novel's first hard attack on industrialization. Chapter 2 ends with a much older, feeble, and ailing Miss Jenkyns being read Dr. Johnson's *Rambler* by Flora, Captain Brown's grand-daughter. In her last babbling speech before her death, she promotes *Rambler* as being a wonderful book and productive for Flora, putting the final punctuation on the old literary dispute, calling *Rambler,* "better than that strange old book, with the queer name, poor Captain

Brown was killed for reading." The line in the sand has been drawn by Gaskell. Although the two sides have come closer to each other, neither crosses the line. Brown's granddaughter reading *Rambler* to Miss Jenkyns suggests a passing of the Johnsonian baton to the younger generations. But Gaskell includes one last shadow of the old dispute, with no apparent loss of fervor, as if Miss Jenkyns was baptized a Johnsonian at her birth and must live and die as an ardent devotee to her religion.

The death of Dr. Johnson's champion, Miss Jenkyns, does not put an end to the Johnsonian presence in the novel. After the initial confrontation, the works of Johnson are almost evangelized, furthering the religious nature of Johnsonian-ism. Chapter 3 is spent in the description of life in the wake of Miss Jenkyns' death, particularly for her sister, Miss Matilda, and of an old love affair between Miss Matilda and Mr. Thomas Holbrook. Chapter 4 details a visit Miss Matilda made to Mr. Holbrook. Miss Matilda and Mr. Holbrook also discuss Johnson, but far more amiably than did Miss Jenkyns and Captain Brown. The next Johnson reference serves to conjure an image for the reader, with the assumption of a preconceived picture of a Johnsonian library in the minds of the readers. Miss Matilda is brought to one of Mr. Holbrook's rooms, which is filled with dusty old books. She comments, "I think it must be like one of the great Dr Johnson's rooms." The Victorian reader must have had some preconceived image of a Johnsonian room interior for this quote to have usefulness. In the discussion of one of the books, Miss Matilda says she is reminded of a Dr. Johnson poem her sister used to read. The spirit of Miss Jenkyns lives in her sister. Mr. Holbrook admits unfamiliarity with Johnson's poems, but sets himself to the task of learning them.

In Chapter 5, the Johnsonian side moves closer to the line in the sand as Miss Matilda discovers that her parents were perhaps less Johnsonian than her sister would have liked to admit. While Miss Matilda was perusing her parents' old letters, a literary reference to Johnson stands out among the many cultural references in them. The letters are said to be written in short, fresh sentences, "very different from the grand Latinised,

Johnsonian style of the printed sermon." Although the social Johnsonian image, dominated by his ideals and mannerisms, seems to have dominated Victorian literature, the occasional reference to the Doctor's writing style appears, again with an assumption of the readers' understanding of what this means. To stand the letters in contrast to the "Johnsonian style" was enough description in Gaskell's opinion as not to necessitate elaboration. In Chapter 15, the next to last chapter, Miss Matilda donates her father's library. She keeps only two books for herself, the same two, sacred, 'must buy' books from Thackeray's *Pendennis*, the Bible, and *Johnson's Dictionary*. *Cranford*, while maintaining consistency with the Johnsonian image of the 1830s and 1840s, prepares the Victorian readers for an evolution in Johnson's persona. It is arguable that Gaskell has caused the evolution by pushing the pendulum so far in one direct as to necessitate its counter-swing. The Johnsonian literary saturation established by Gaskell in *Cranford* is carried forward by Thackeray, a writer needing no sharp conversion.

In Thackeray's 1855, *The Newcomes*, released serially over a 23 month period, he revisits the theme of youthful vanity and materialistic greed versus Augustan respect and conventionalism [40]. Gaskell's line in the sand remains. The board is cleared of its *Cranford* pieces and reset for a new match with new characters. The Newcome family members battle with that Victorian English, upper middle-class struggle between virtue and wealth. They are continually faced with decisions between goodness and the material goods that signify respectability in their society [40]. Again, Johnson holds the banner of his generation and his ideals. Thackeray's opinion of Johnson evolved at this point, from the admiration he displayed in *Vanity Fair*, to a more knowledgeable and far more personal affection. In Chapter 4, Colonel Thomas Newcome and old friend, Mr. Warrington, address the Colonel's son Clive on these middle-class issues. Upon recalling tales of Warrington's social eminence, Clive admits expecting greater wealth to accompany the fame. He confesses, "I thought you must have chambers in the Albany, and lots of horses to ride, and a valet and a groom, and a cab at the very least." Warrington is said to respect no work of modern genius, but the Colonel rebukes his son, saying, "I hope it is not your practice to measure and estimate gentlemen by such paltry standards as those. A man of letters follows the noblest calling which any man can pursue." Although Thackeray's opinion on this matter can by no means be considered unbiased, it is Johnson he throws forth in defense of this claim. He has the Colonel defend impoverished scholars by adding, "Who would not be poor if he could be sure of possessing genius, and winning fame and immortality, sir? Think of Dr. Johnson, what a genius he had, and where did he live?" The Colonel continues to describe the paltry but pleasant apartment of Dr. Johnson. A few paragraphs later, the narrator promotes Johnson while connecting him to the greatness of Roman Antiquity. Referring to Colonel Newcome, he writes, "I found he believed Dr. Johnson to be the greatest of men: the Doctor's words were constantly in his mouth; and he never travelled without Boswell's *Life*. Besides these, he read Caesar and Tacitus." Within a few lines, the narrator connects Johnson to his Augustan predecessors by adding Addison's *Spectator* to the list. Tacitus, Caesar, and Addison are connected to Johnson here, but they are only used in support of Johnson, the flag bearer of their ideals. It is James Boswell's *Life of Johnson* that the Colonel carries with him. This furthers the transition of Victorian references to Johnson meant more to display his humanity than his divinity.

The conversation continues with Clive's attempts to have his father expand on his literary preferences. He asks the Colonel for his opinion of Henry Fielding (1707-1754). The Colonel maintains his loyalty to Johnsonian ideals and opinions with an argument about Fielding almost identical to the one recounted in Boswell's *Life of Johnson* between Boswell and Johnson. In the latter, Johnson degrades Fielding fiercely, calling him a 'blockhead'. His main point of contention is that Fielding's characters lack any true representation of the human heart. Boswell writes of Johnson's words. "Sir, there is more knowledge of the heart in one letter of Richardson's, than in all Tom Jones" [41]. Johnson is referring to Fielding's novel *A History*

158

of Tom Jones, a Foundling (1749). Thackeray writes Colonel Newcome in an identical tone as when Boswell recalls Dr. Johnson. The Colonel says, "I read them when I was a boy, when I kept other bad company, and did other low and disgraceful things, of which I'm ashamed now". The Colonel displays his knowledge of Boswell, saying, "But I forgot that I need not speak. The great and good Dr. Johnson has settled that question. You remember what he said to Mr. Boswell about Fielding?" In Thackeray's previous references to Johnson, he holds his idol in a third person comparison to opposing ideals and traits. Here, he echoes Johnson's voice in a narrative taken almost directly from the biography that would have been Thackeray's primary source of knowledge about Johnson, Boswell's *Life of Johnson*. A clear evolution in Johnson's persona, at least as it lived in the mind of Thackeray, can be seen in comparing the Dr. Johnson referenced in the 1848 *Vanity Fair* to the same author's novel seven years later. Whether it is believed that the novelist creates or reflects the thoughts of the readers, this change in Thackeray's affection and embrace of Johnson would surely have been found in the minds of his Victorian readers.

Thackeray drops Johnson's name here and there over the next several chapters, always in reference to Colonel Newcome's personal attachment to him. In Chapter 19, he uses the Colonel's words to reference Johnson in a third person comparison, much as Disraeli did. The Colonel is speaking in support of artists, saying, "'an artist is any man's equal,' he said. 'I have no prejudice of that sort; and think that Sir Joshua Reynolds and Doctor Johnson were fit company for any person, of whatever rank'". In this reference, Thackeray exalts Johnson to a level in society where no member may outrank him. The notion that anyone would be too good for the Doctor's company is absurd to Thackeray. But unlike Disraeli's social claims on Johnson's behalf, Thackeray uses Johnson's image in the promotion of poor artists, a demographic increasingly akin to the Johnson image. Chapter 21 gives the reader another literary where Johnson, Alexander Pope and other attendees of Oxford University are held in comparison to their Cambridge University literary rivals, particularly Lord Tennyson. Again, the Colonel's words bear a Johnsonian tone reminiscent of that recorded by Boswell. The debate begins when a character named Honeyman, who the narrator calls, "well enough read in profane literature, especially of the lighter sort," says to the Colonel, "Dr. Johnson, talked admirably, but did not write English". Thackeray disparaged his seedier characters in the most potent way he could consider, by setting them against Dr. Johnson. The following decades' successful attempt to associate Johnson, not with the loftiest members of society, as was the trend in the early Victorian Age, but to the lowliest, most common figures in society, constitutes a shift as revolutionary as the political upheaval occurring in Europe at the time. Colonel Newcome's Dr. Johnson does not fall, per se, in the following decades. He changes socio-political affiliation. His quality does not change, only those who carry his banner.

Chapter 7

The Later Victorian Era: a New Johnsonian Demographic

THE NUMBER AND IMPORTANCE of scenes in Victorian literature that depict these sorts of debates about the merits of literary icons must signify to some degree a similar phenomenon in the Victorian public discourse, especially considering the popular literary style was the reflection of daily English life. Johnson sits at the heart of these debates, in the Thackeray and Gaskell novels, and is usually the focus of the most heated emotions. It is no stretch of the imagination to impose these fictional representations of English society onto the factual persons the Victorian novelists attempt to reflect. Johnson must have been a frequently and fiercely debated topic in the 1850s, based on the polarization his image is used by writers to establish and on the demonstrative swing from the Johnson references of the decades prior and those of the 1850s. A more universal embrace of Johnsonian-ism in the remainder of the Victorian Age begins as the image of Johnson evolves, or at least expands to encompass more universally British traits. The line in the sand is erased by this evolution and expansion, and the Johnsonian icon becomes tangible to a struggling lower class that finds kinship in the tales of Johnson's humble beginnings and confrontational bouts with established authority. The real Samuel Johnson begins to show through the gilding. He is associated less with elite decorum and more with the one thing for which Britons are universally proud — the English language.

The evolution of Dr. Johnson can even be seen in Thackeray's later works. Johnson's literary bequests begin to dominate the references. In Chapter 14 of his 1855 novel, *The Rose and the*

Ring, Giglio is going off to the university. Thackeray establishes that Giglio has only brought the bare essentials in a bag, which contains "a student's cap and gown, a writing-book full of paper, an inkstand, pens, and a Johnson's Dictionary, which was very useful to him, as his spelling had been sadly neglected."[1] It is not easy for current scholars to fully grasp what a powerful symbol *Johnson's Dictionary* was for Victorian readers. The only aspects of the Johnsonian image as deified as the *Dictionary* were Johnson's social circle and conversational mode. These, plus references to his humble beginnings, dominate Johnsonian literary references in the later Victorian period. Giglio's humble simplicity, reflecting Johnson's own experiences at Oxford, were as much 'Johnsonian' as the *Dictionary* itself.

The changes in the Johnsonian persona owe some debt to dramatic improvements in British literacy rates. A convergence of different social and political motivations brought national literacy rates to the political forefront. Not surprisingly, drastic increases in literacy coincided with the establishment of a national system of elementary schooling [2]. Literacy rates measured by the signatures on marriage registries nearly doubled in the Victorian Era. In 1840, half of the registered brides and one third of the registered grooms made crude marks on marriage registries. In 1900, 97 percent of all marriage registries were signed with a signature [2]. The "Ragged School Union" may take credit for much of this lower-class literacy. Formed in 1844, Lord Shaftesbury as chairman, the confederation of lower-class schools began with only sixteen schools but grew to 176 by 1861 [3]. This demographic of newly literate had but one dictionary, Dr. Johnson's. Johnson's letter to Lord Chesterfield, refuting Chesterfield's claim of patronizing the *Dictionary*, served as a *David and Goliath* story for the many small people who finally had the literacy to embrace a literary hero.

Johnson's letter to Chesterfield is referenced in Elizabeth Gaskell's 1857 *Life of Charlotte Bronte*. Again, the reference comes with no explanation, on the assumption of a universal public understanding. In the description of Bronte's life in the immediate aftermath of the publication of *Jane Eyre*, Gaskell writes, "Any author of a successful novel is liable to an inroad of letters from unknown readers, containing commendation."[4] Already, the reader picks up a slight aroma of Lord Chesterfield. She continues, "sometimes of so fulsome and indiscriminating a character as to remind the recipient of Dr. Johnson's famous speech to one who offered presumptuous and injudicious praise."[4] Earlier in the biography, Gaskell relays the tale of Bronte's harsh criticism of Johnson, when Bronte made the claim that "Johnson hadn't a spark of cleverality in him." But despite the mixed feelings and stances on Dr. Johnson, the letter to Lord Chesterfield was a rallying cry to Victorian writers and many seemed to bear some degree of affection and gratitude for it and for its author.

Dickens continues the Johnsonian trend away from the enshrined and into the tattered pockets of the working class. While Thackeray's affection for Johnson is clear, Dickens' is fogged by ambiguous references. He often puts his Johnsonian references in the mouths of his seedier characters. Nevertheless, the references are there and they point the Johnsonian image in a downward angle on the social scale. While Disraeli's social and political views are clear and documented, in great part due to his involvement in government and his famous letters to the queen, and his views and use of the Johnsonian image are clear, leaving no ambiguity in interpreting his thoughts on Johnson or the intentions behind the Johnsonian references in his novels, Dickens' references require a study of the changes in Dickens' life and his disdain for the British socio-political system. Dickens' relationship with the Victorian Johnsonian persona is far more complex and enigmatic than Disraeli's because Dickens' political and social opinions were complex and enigmatic. His disgust at the inefficiencies of the British parliamentary government and the shameful by-products of a limitless capitalism led him toward affection for the French. He noticed the stark contrast between the seemingly clogged arteries of republican government and the efficient movements of Napoleonic France. By 1854, he was becoming an avid Francophile. He took a villa in Boulogne that summer, where he left two of his children in school when he returned to London [5]. The following February, he spent two weeks in Paris with Wilkie Collins and returned again in the fall when he stayed for seven months. He showed his admiration for the Parisians in an article for *Household Words*, contrasting them with the deficiencies of the London Court of Common Council. Although he had a personal dislike of Napoleon III, his inclinations toward the French increased as his interest in politics increased and his faith in parliamentary government waned [5]. Just as the Johnsonian image was used by Disraeli for the purposes of patriotic rhetoric, Dickens, having such opposing views, used it to opposing ends.

Dickens supported social, political, and administrative reform in England. For over twenty years, he was editor and controlling owner of a series of periodicals, all stressing the importance of honesty in publication [6]. The greatest of his periodical publications enjoyed a larger circulation than the *London Times* did at the time. Dickens' periodicals were *Bentley's Miscellany*, 1837- 1839, *Master Humphrey's Clock*, 1840-1841, *Household Words*, 1850-1859, and *All the Year Round*, 1859-1870 [6]. War is never a time for reform, and when Britain declared war on Russia in the Crimean War in the spring of 1854, Dickens accurately predicted that it would be used as an excuse to delay reform [7]. His confidence in the government fell further when reports of the army's failures in the war made it to Dickens' ear. Dickens was far more concerned with how military failures would affect daily life in London. He took keen notice of the plight of the impoverished and had no faith that the necessary reforms for them would be enacted in Parliament. He wrote in 1854, "As to Parliament, it does so little and talks so much" [7]. Eighteen months later, in a letter to his friend, John Foster, he wrote, "I really am serious in thinking … that representational government is becoming a failure with us … and that the whole thing has broken down since that great seventeenth century time" [7]. He was referring to the beginning of British parliamentary dominance in government with the Glorious Revolution of 1688. Less than a year before his death in June of 1870, Dickens made a speech to that effect, saying, "My faith in the people governing is infinitesimal. My faith in the people governed is, on a whole, illimitable" [7]. Dickens aligned himself with Carlyle in the drive for reform. His relationship with the Johnsonian persona was as varying as the Johnsonian persona itself. One moment, Johnson is a model of conventionalism. The next, he is a champion of the working-class, crushing the established order with a single letter to an Earl. Johnson was a staunch Tory [8]. Perhaps Dickens' French leanings and loss of faith in parliamentary government helped him to relate to the Tory aspect of the Johnsonian persona. In any case, Johnson's smug affront to the aristocracy in his letter to Lord Chesterfield must have been admired by a writer in support of social change. In 1855, Dickens gave his support to a society formed to advocate administrative reform. In a June meeting of that society, he denounced the Prime Minister, Henry John Temple, 3rd Viscount Palmerston, for heartlessness in the face of national disaster [7]. In a letter written after the meeting, Dickens wrote, "The first is to carry the war dead into the Tent of such a creature as this Lord Palmerston and ring it into his soul … that Dandy insolence is gone forever" [7]. One month later, he began writing his greatest social satire, *Little Dorrit*, a monthly serial from December, 1855 to June, 1857 [7]. In it, Johnson belongs to the lowest of characters. Dickens robs from the Johnsonian shrines of Colonel Newcome, Miss Pinkerton, and Miss Jenkyns and gives to the poor of his own creation.

Little Dorrit contains two references to Dr. Johnson, which seem to be used as compliments to despicable characters. This is the sort of ambiguity that makes it hard to firmly press a finger on Dickens' interpretation of, and contribution to, the Johnsonian persona. The first reference is used in the description of Tite Barnacle, head of the Barnacle family who run the Circumlocution Office. Parallel to Dickens' newest notions of Parliament and of governmental bureaucracy, the Circumlocution Office is inefficient, filled with redundant procedures, where nothing ever gets done. The precise intention of the reference is difficult to discern. Dickens writes, "Mr Tite Barnacle, who, like Dr Johnson's celebrated acquaintance, had only one idea in his head and that was a wrong one, had appeared by this time."[9] The character of Tite Barnacle represented everything Dickens had come to loathe about the British bureaucracy. Although Johnson's "celebrated acquaintance" probably referred to Boswell, as a bash on his character and position among the aristocracy, it places Johnson in the possession of a different breed of person than those who held him dear just a few years earlier and begins a widening of the Johnsonian image, and a transformation from a divisive symbol to a pan-British icon which, like education, now belongs to the entire scope of social strata.

The other reference relates to the character Christopher Casby, also known as the Patriarch. Casby is a landlord who, by self-admission, "squeezes" his tenants for money. In a conversation with Mr. Pancks, Casby's clerk and debt collector, the Patriarch is reminding Pancks of his duty to squeeze money out of the indebted. Casby tells Pancks that he must be sharper with people. Pancks replies, "Don't I squeeze 'em? …What else am I made for?" Dickens writes Casby's response: "You are made for nothing else, Mr Pancks. You are made to do your duty, but you don't do your duty. You are paid to squeeze, and you must squeeze to pay." Next, Dickens uses a Johnsonian reference to paint the character. The reference has many layers and its meaning is more difficult to interpret than the less ambiguous references of Disraeli or Thackeray. He writes, "The Patriarch so much surprised himself by this brilliant turn, after Dr Johnson, which he had not in the least expected or intended, that he laughed aloud."[9] The reference is to brilliance, but in the hands of infamous villainy. Again, it is the same Dr. Johnson of the 1830s through the early 1850s, but on much fouler lips. The only certainty of this reference is that it is dropped casually, without elaboration, indicating that Dickens uses it with the assumption that his intentions are met with his audience's understanding and the dramatic change in the type of character flinging Johnson's name and quotes as their conversational wildcard. As with the multitude of other Victorian Johnsonian references, the references in *Little Dorrit* prove the commonness of the Johnsonian persona in the public discourse. Dickens' relationship with that persona is ambiguous, however. Both of the references in *Little Dorrit* were used in the establishment of ridiculous and unsavory characters. The reference with Casby is more layered. It is the wit of his reply to Pancks that is particularly Johnsonian. Dickens called it a "brilliant turn, after Dr. Johnson". And Casby was surprised by his Johnsonian brilliance. In these respects, the reference reflects positively on Dr. Johnson. The fact that the only two references to Dr, Johnson in this novel are connected to distasteful characters that Dickens was using to represent his most hated aspects of British society adds thinly veiled sarcasm to what appears on the surface to be a compliment.

Other known inclinations of Johnson's endeared Dickens to him. Dickens, Carlyle, and Johnson shared similar notions on slavery. Such a passionately driven topic tended to cement like minds in an embrace of admiration. Dickens harbored and expressed an unyielding distain for tyranny of all kinds. It is not surprising that he included American slavery in his contempt after his first visit to the U.S. in 1842 [10]. From that first visit until the end of his second trip in 1868, he spoke openly on the issues that arose from the institution of slavery.[10] In addition to sharing with Dr. Johnson a distaste for elitism, Dickens shared the Doctor's opinions on slavery. Dr. Johnson's thoughts on slavery were not well publicized, but he maintained a frequent toast of "Here's to the next insurrection of the negroes in the West Indies" [11]. It seems that Dickens felt a kinship with the real Dr. Johnson while feeling an irritating opposition to the Johnsonian persona of unyielding conventionalism and Augustan imperial tyranny. The views of writers like Disraeli, who supported empire building through military tyranny, if necessary, were projected upon the Johnsonian persona in their literary references to him, to be run up the imperial flagpole for all to see. This could help clarify the enigmatic purpose of the *Little Dorrit* references. Dickens seems to be complimenting the real Dr. Johnson while ruthlessly assaulting what he would consider the disillusioned public's twisted image of the Johnsonian persona in the Victorian Age. He had to smash the elitist Johnsonian shrines constructed by the likes of Disraeli in order to hand the common public a hero that should belong to the whole of British society. He did that with his quirky and ambiguous references, setting the Johnsonian persona on a path toward universal British possession and a comprehensive British endearment. Johnson was one of the elite commodities that Dickens wanted to see evenly distributed. His position as popular author gave him the tools of distribution. Gaskell's pendulum had finally swung to the other side.

Little Dorrit began an evolution of the Johnsonian persona that seems complete by the 1860s, as the literary references to him took on a different tone. Before 1860, they were used to align characters to one side or the other of the great socio-political divide that was expanding in the increasingly industrial English cities. After 1860, a transition in the English public's image of Johnson drew literary references in another direction. There were more references to his mannerisms, dress, and conversational mode, with less regard for political affiliation. He appears more often as a vivid description of characters, based on a social figure all readers would be certain to understand. Johnson ceased to be the proverbial socio-political 'line in the sand' by which characters are identified by their creators, as Gaskell used him in *Cranford*. Similarly, he seems to be no longer tied to a political agenda, as Disraeli used him, or so intimately validated as an academic ideal, as Thackeray used him. He became more comprehensively embraced as the common ground of universal Brit-ism shared by all the British, regardless of social or economic standing, regardless of profession or locale.

As long as Johnson's image was used by authors to separate and distinguish one brand of Brit from another, his appeal remained partisan. The Johnsonian persona was moving toward one that could be revered by both Captain Brown and Miss Jenkyns. The transition away from that partisan use of his public memory opened the doors for a broader appeal. The Johnsonian quotes present in Victorian literature from this point on were aimed at a wider audience. Johnson's wit no longer belonged to the Augustan-minded, those throw-backs to the age of unbridled imperial expansion, or the socially conservative. It did not belong only to the working man or the literary elite. Whether an author was putting a Johnsonian quote on a character's lips or a Johnson publication in a character's hands, the purposes in doing so lacked the motivation of social segregation and elitism as seen in the earlier Victorian novels.

There is evidence that the displays of Johnsonian wit by literary characters in the 1860s and beyond are reflections of (or reflected by) contemporary events. Dr. Johnson became a national institution and was quoted and misquoted by those in just about every level of society. In his 1913 book *Dr. Johnson and His Circle*, John Bailey relays a poignant anecdote to this effect.

> A few years ago, a lover of Johnson walking along a London street passed by the side of a cabmen's shelter. Two cabmen were getting their dinner ready, and the Johnsonian was amused and pleased to hear one say to the other: "After all, as Doctor Johnson says, a man may travel all over the world without seeing anything better than his dinner." The saying was new to him and probably apocryphal, though the sentiment is one which can well be imagined as coming from the great man's mouth[12].

This tale occurred decades after the 1860s, but indicates the direction upon which the Johnsonian persona was bound. The first evidence of a turn in that direction comes in the form of the 1860s literary references to Dr. Johnson. Bailey continues, "But whether apocryphal or authentic, the remark well illustrates both the extent and the particular nature of Johnson's fame"[12]. Bailey makes it clear that a quote would not have to come directly from Johnson to be "Johnsonian". Johnson came to represent all wit and common sense as well as the beauty that comes in an awkward, unsightly package. Bailey expresses that Johnson held something "broadly and fundamentally human about him which appeals to all and especially to the plain man"[12]. Also of particular interest is the wording of the cabman when he declares "Doctor Johnson says" instead of "Doctor Johnson said". This shows an inhabitation of Johnson's spirit, living and current, in the minds of the cabmen. Bailey continues by challenging his reader to consider any other literary figure to whom a cabman would ascribe a shrewd and witty saying, and testifies that neither Pope nor Milton could receive the honor. Quotes like the cabman's and the quotes used in Victorian literature after 1860 are as often from Johnson's daily discourse as from his published works. Although the *Dictionary* was still an iconic symbol to the English people, inseparable from the enshrined persona of Dr. Johnson, the Doctor evolved from a literary figure to a social figure, with more emphasis placed on the Socratic wit he portioned out to his devotees in the coffeehouses than on his body of published works. Just as Socrates left no writings, and current understanding of him comes primarily through the writings of his student Plato, Johnson's writings were becoming a smaller source of his fame and appeal. His celebrity was more about the writings on Johnson by his devotees. As Bailey's anecdote demonstrates, it also became about stories that never made it to print.

There was a humanization of Johnson's image as it appeared in published writings. Elizabeth Gaskell displays this in her 1860 short story collection, *Curious If True: Strange Tales.* In the titular short story, "Curious If True", when Richard Whittingham gets lost in the French countryside, he stumbles upon a chateau, asks for assistance, and is surprised when the porter welcomes him, saying that he was "long expected". In the chateau, Whittingham encounters a lively party of varied company, peculiar by their rustic accents and other traits that defy gentility. Among them is a tiny but well-proportioned man, underdressed for the occasion. Whittingham describes the man with a reference to Dr. Johnson.

> He had the awkward habit—which I do not think he could have copied from Dr. Johnson, because most probably he had never heard of him—of trying always to retrace his steps on the exact boards on which he had trodden to arrive at any particular part of the room. [14]

The reference is to what has come to be known as Obsessive Compulsive Disorder (OCD), of which Dr. Johnson is thought to have had a severe case [14]. Boswell's *Life of Johnson* reports evidence to this effect:

> Upon every post as he passed along, I could observe he deliberately laid his hand; but missing one of them, when he had got at some distance, he seemed suddenly to recollect himself, and immediately returning back, carefully performed the accustomed ceremony, and resuming his former course, not omitting one till he gained the crossing. [15]

Boswell writes that this sort of behavior "was his constant practice"[15]. For Gaskell to make the reference, these peculiarities must have been a commonly understood part of the Johnsonian persona. The deified Dr. Johnson of Disraeli's and Thackeray's novels would never have presented with such a human weakness. Thomas Carlyle compared Dr. Johnson with the god Odin in his 1841 book *On Heroes, Hero-Worship, and the Heroic in History,* of which Dr. Johnson is a constant and integral part[16]. OCD is not a trait commonly associated with the gods of myth. It is however a trait of ordinary, flawed people and Dr. Johnson was making the transition from mythical god to common man. This would account for his more universal appeal in this era, especially among the simpler folk. Whittingham's description of his tiny acquaintance included tattered boots and a sir name without the preceding *de,* the French mark of gentility. Whittingham's first thought was that the man may have been paying tribute or imitating Johnson with his quirky mannerism. Such was the common person's affection for the Doctor, as seen much later in Bailey's cabmen.

As Johnson's awkward mannerisms became a more common point of Johnsonian references in Victorian literature, so did his Socratic, coffeehouse wisdom he doled out to his disciples, as recorded by Boswell and others. The image of the sage presiding over witty banter, in the most commonplace locations of Fleet Street, echoed in the novels of the 1860s and beyond. Thomas

Peacock's novel *Gryll Grange* (1861) makes several such references. In Chapter 1, the Rev. Dr. Opimian is conversing with Mr. and Miss Gryll about the follies of the British establishment. After a few stabs at Parliament, Opimian informs Miss Gryll of a lecture Lord Curryfin will be giving to a group of fisherman on the particulars of their own trade. There is some discussion about the absurdity of the very notion of such a lecture, followed by attacks on the concept of lecturing lords. This attack on the upper establishment, reflective of Dr. Johnson's letter to Lord Chesterfield, had to include a Johnsonian reference. Mr. Gryll says, "Doctor Johnson was astonished at the mania for lectures, even in his day, when there were no lecturing lords"[17]. Mr. Gryll follows with a very witty and distinctly Johnsonian poke at the affectation of expertise shown by lecturing lords.

> He thought little was to be learned from lectures, unless where, as in chemistry, the subject required illustration by experiment. Now, if your lord is going to exhibit experiments in the art of cooking fish, with specimens in sufficient number for all his audience to taste, I have no doubt his lecture will be well attended, and a repetition earnestly desired.[17]

A reader can almost place Mr. Gryll's quotation directly in the mouth of Dr. Johnson. The transition from the conservative symbol of empire and establishment, as Dr. Johnson's image was used before 1860, to the sage of the common people and the humbler of the pretentious elite is evident in this reference. The topic is closed with Opimian's in-turn response, also referencing Dr. Johnson and presented in a distinctly Johnsonian fashion.

> But I agree with Doctor Johnson, that little is to be learned from lectures. For the most part those who do not already understand the subject will not understand the lecture, and those who do will learn nothing from it.[17]

These uses of Johnson are more reminiscent of Byron's Boswell quotes from his personal letters than of the literary exploitation of Johnson's name in the decades immediately following.

The casual dropping of Socratic Johnsonian quotations continues in Chapter 5. Opimian is visiting the home of Algernon Falconer. After dinner, the two men adjourn to the drawing-room. Opimian notices some musical instrument about the room and asks if Falconer plays. Falconer becomes the third character in the novel to reference Dr. Johnson with a bit of his signature coffeehouse wit. He says, "I have profited by the observation of Doctor Johnson: Sir, once on a time I took to fiddling; but I found that to fiddle well I must fiddle all my life, and I thought I could do something better"[17]. Peacock promotes the lower classes again when Falconer informs Opimian that the instruments are there for the use of the servants, who he boasts are well educated and accomplished musicians. The entire novel reflects the evolved Johnsonian image. Proud and confident lower classes pass witty banter, often at the expense of the elite, in a wise and witty format that had come to be considered bequeathed directly to them by Johnson.

The notion of Johnson's words as a bequest directly to the common people continued in the literary references of the 1870s. Samuel Butler (1835-1902) represents the 1870s Victorian relationship to the Johnsonian persona through references to Johnson in a few of his 1870s novels. In 1913, R. A. Streatfeild wrote an introduction to Butler's 1873 novel *The Fair Haven*, referring to the novel as Butler's most characteristic work and wrote, "Few of his works, indeed, show more strikingly his brilliant powers as a controversialist and his implacable determination to get at the truth of whatever engaged his attention" [18]. It is the controversial facet of Butler's character that endears the Johnsonian persona to him. To engage absurdity with truth is the cornerstone of Johnsonian-ism. It is unlikely Butler would have employed the Johnsonian persona had he written in the earlier part of the Victorian Era, when Johnson's image was more akin to Odin than to Socrates. The narrator of *The Fair Haven* presents the memoirs of his elder brother. In Chapter 3, he displays his brother's thoughts on the moral advancements of society from Augustan Rome to his own time with examples of the differences in common opinion. He quotes a passage from his brother's writing. "'Every man,' said Dr. Johnson, 'has a right to his own opinion, and everyone else has a right to knock him down for it'"[18]. This quotation is evidence of an enormous evolution in the Johnsonian persona. The earlier Victorian Dr. Johnson was the banner of Augustan ideals with their connections to Antiquity. In this passage, the narrator insists, through his brother's memoirs, that a natural evolution in society has brought his contemporaries to a moral platform above that of the best of the Augustan Romans. He uses Johnson's wit to make his point. It not only shows the evolution in Johnson's persona; it delivers an interesting irony in the comparative evaluation of the two Johnsonian images.

Gaskell portrayed Johnson's evolved persona through his quirky mannerisms. Peacock and Butler used his coffeehouse wisdom with what would now be considered 'blue-collar logic'. Thomas Hardy (1840-1948) referenced Dr. Johnson's dress in the establishment of humbleness in a character. In his 1874 novel, *Far From the Madding Crowd,* Hardy references Johnson in page one. He describes the simplicity of his protagonist, Farmer Oak. The establishment of Oak's rustic simplicity is paramount to the story. Oak is a working man, identified by that trait above all. Hardy writes, "Oak's appearance in his old clothes was most peculiarly his own"[19]. He explains that his neighbors' mental image of him is always in that sort of rustic, rural dress. Among the simple, practical clothes for a simple, commonsense working man, Hardy describes Oak as wearing "a coat like Dr. Johnson's"[19]. This small and subtle reference demonstrates two points of interest in the research of the Johnsonian persona in the 1870s. First, Johnson has come to represent the simple, common man, with his name attached to commonsense practical efficiency. Second, Hardy has an expectation that his readers will form an instant image of Oak's appearance from this slight reference. "A coat like Dr. Johnson's" was apparently enough information, without elaboration on the topic, to grant a vivid image. This one simple reference makes a profound statement toward the universality of the physical Johnsonian image. Other references to Johnson have revolved around what can be read or heard about the man. This reference depends upon a pictorial image. By this point, images like the 1848 painting by Edward Matthew Ward, of Dr. Johnson at Lord Chesterfield's house, had met the public eye. "A Scene at the Mitre" by Eyre Crowe (1857) depicts Johnson, Oliver Goldsmith, and James Boswell at the Mitre Tavern[20]. The circulation of images of Johnson gave the writers of Johnsonian references an additional tool. The visual image of Johnson could accompany the notions of his character traits. Hardy alloys Johnson's rustic, working-class pictorial image with his public association with commonsense simplicity to set the essential traits of character in the first page of his novel.

The 1860s and 1870s witnessed an extreme evolution in the common perception and representation of Johnson. In some senses, the Dr. Johnson of that time stood in contradiction to the essential traits of his image just a decade earlier. Rather than being used to identify the divisions in society, by setting characters on one side or the other of perceived Johnsonian ideals, the Dr. Johnson of the 1860s and 70s was used to unite a public behind the common ideals of industriousness, working-class pride, and universally applicable commonsense. The evolution from the gilded, polished, enshrined idol portrayed by Thackeray and Disraeli to, as Johnson referred to himself, the simple, "uncourtly scholar," with tattered clothing and a wise but simple vision of society, continued in the 1870 and 80s, through the end of the Victorian Age and into the 20th century. The Johnsonian image began to align itself with the Johnson Canon, as Johnson's image was discovered through the readings of the newly literate demographics, rather than being dictated by the educationally elite of the previous generations. The early Victorian Dr. Johnson represented the literary elite. His circle of friends sat upon their Fleet Street thrones like the gods of Olympus. Thomas Carlyle promoted the image, deifying Dr. Johnson in his 1841 *On Heroes, Hero-Worship, and the Heroic in History*. Carlyle's representation of Dr. Johnson reflected and promoted the popular image more than it created it, as is seen in the similar references to Johnson at the time of Carlyle's publication and just before. It gave support to a growing notion of an elite, untouchable hero, to be worshiped more than imitated, that lasted for about two decades. Even Gaskell's Dr. Johnson was an ideal character, out of the reach of mere mortals. By contrast, however, the Dr. Johnson of Collins, Butler, Peacock, Hardy, Gissing, Meredith, even the unconventional George Elliot represented the more obtainable set of ideals of a common-sense working class. Simple clothes, sharp-tongued distain for elitist aristocracy, compassionate association with the poor, and simply stated, unpretentious bits of everyday wit became the common Johnsonian references in the later Victorian Age, bringing Johnson down from Olympus and back into the coffeehouses and taverns he frequented during his life.

It is common for the image of public figures to drift from the realities of their lives toward the enshrined images that spring to the thoughts of posterity at the mention of their names. It is the plaster bust, rather than the flesh and bone, that remains in the public mind. Dr. Johnson made the same ascension only to return to the gritty reality of real people. His image experienced a re-humanization in the late Victorian Age, initiated by the publication of tales from his life and perpetuated by frequent references in late Victorian literature. 1861 saw the publication of *Autobiography, Letters and Literature Remains of Mrs. Piozzi*, by Hester Lynch Piozzi, Dr. Johnson's friend Hester Thrale. Included was "Anecdotes of the late Samuel Johnson LL.D." Piozzi's work familiarized the public with the more human and sympathetic, humanitarian Dr. Johnson, telling tales of his compassion for the poor. She writes, "Severity towards the poor was, in Dr. Johnson's opinion (as is visible in his *Life of Addison* particularly), an undoubted and constant attendant or consequence upon whiggism"[21]. Dr. Johnson wanted not only to keep the poor alive, he also wanted them to experience some of the pleasures of life. Piozzi continues, "He was not contented with giving them relief; he wished to add also indulgence. He loved the poor as I never yet saw any one else do, with an earnest desire to make them happy"[21]. If current readers wonder why Johnson and his ideals have a timeless relevance, they need only read the following passage from *Anecdotes* and notice the current familiarity.

> "What signifies," says someone, "giving halfpence to common beggars they only lay it out in gin or tobacco."

> "And why should they be denied such sweeteners of their existence?" (says Johnson) "It is surely very savage to refuse them every possible avenue to pleasure, reckoned too coarse for our own acceptance. Life is a pill which none of us can bear to swallow without gilding; yet for the poor we delight in stripping it still barer, and are not ashamed to show even visible displeasure, if ever the bitter taste is taken from their mouths."[21]

She writes of Dr. Johnson's keeping "whole nests" of poor people in his house and, "treating them with the same, or perhaps more ceremonious civility, than he would have done by as many people of fashion"[21]. Piozzi makes no mention of these "nests" of people having any personal relationship with Dr. Johnson. She states, "[T]he lame, the blind, the sick, and the sorrowful found a sure retreat from all the evils whence his little income could secure them"[21]. These are not tales of an enshrined bust of a distant, unapproachable hero. Rather, these are evidence of the good Doctor's compassion and empathy. Dr. Johnson, who had been touted by the conservative conventionalists in both the social and political realms of the 1830s into the 1850s, was raised as the banner of the common folk in the 1860s. This would remain his identity through the century and fiction of the period would reflect it.

By the 1880s, Johnson's connection to the poor dominated the literary references to him. Both Wilkie Collins and Arthur Conan Doyle have allusions in this mode. In December of 1883, Collins (1824-1889) published *She Loves and Lies* in the New York periodical, *Spirit of the Times,* and in 1885 in Doyle's *Tales from Many Sources Vol. 4* [22], which was later published as *Mr. Lismore and the Widow.* Collins tells of a businessman, Mr. Lismore, in the prime of his life whose business is failing and prospects are bleak. He is discovered by a rich widow, Mrs. Callender, who he had saved from a fire six years earlier. She offers to save him from financial ruin if he will marry her. Her husband's will demands that she marry in order to maintain her fortune. When he visits her house, he expects to see the typical extravagances of a wealthy home. Collins uses Dr. Johnson's persona to disparage the wealthy in his description of Mr. Lismore's expectations.

> What Dr. Johnson called "the insolence of wealth" appears far more frequently in the houses of the rich than in the manners of the rich. The reason is plain enough. Personal ostentation is, in the very nature of it, ridiculous; but the ostentation which exhibits magnificent pictures, priceless china, and splendid furniture, can purchase good taste to guide it, and can assert itself without affording the smallest opening for a word of depreciation or a look of contempt. If I am worth a million of money, and if I am dying to show it, I don't ask you to look at me, I ask you to look at my house. [23]

He is delighted to discover that she lives in quite modest elegance. This adds to the respect he had already begun to develop for her. They marry and move to Munich where he meets a beautiful young lady. He is enamored but appalled at the way the young lady speaks of his wife. When he rejects the young lady in defense of his wife, she reveals that she is in fact his wife all along. The rich "wife" is a young actress who disguised herself as the old Mrs. Callender, in order to ensure Lismore's character. The entire story warns of the perils of capitalism and the temptations of monetary greed. The point made with the Johnsonian reference could have easily been made without mention of Johnson. In fact, the inclusion of a factual person in this fiction is almost awkward. Johnson is the only real person mentioned in the story. The Johnsonian "insolence of wealth" put a bitter flavor concerning the rich on the palate of Collins' readers. When the poor man's Johnsonian banner was raised, the desired, positive feelings were raised in the hearts of the reader.

Perhaps the best evidence of Johnson's evolution from the banner of Augustan conventionalism to the icon of the common folk is his embrace by George Eliot (1819-1880), Mary Anne Evans. In Eliot's most famous novel, *Middlemarch* (1874), heroine Dorothea is obsessed with improving the conditions of the poor in her community. Her life takes her in some unexpected directions, but she continues to return to that calling. Although Dorothea comes from a wealthy family and ends up an independently wealthy widow, her tastes remain modest throughout the story and her only consistent ambitions are for the betterment of the poor. In this novel, Eliot establishes her sympathy for the plight of the poor and also her opinion on the humanitarian obligations of the wealthy. Eliot's other novels all feature humble, working-class protagonists. They all stress the virtues of hard work and moderate living. Her essays focus equally on moderation and the human obligation of aid to the poor. They also speak frequently of Dr. Johnson.

In the 1883 essay, *German Wit: Henry Heine*, Eliot lauds Dr. Johnson's commonsense reasoning. Although he is more commonly lauded for his wit, Johnson here is commended for the same sort of moderate reasoning that Eliot features in the heroes and heroines of her novels. She writes this of Johnson:

> Some of Johnson's most admirable witticisms consist in the suggestion of an analogy which immediately exposes the absurdity of an action or proposition; and it is only their ingenuity, condensation, and instantaneousness which lift them from reasoning into Wit—they are reasoning raised to a higher power. [24]

In this quotation, Eliot ascribes to Johnson the same steady reasoning and exposure of the ridiculous that she uses to endear Dorothea to her readers. She displays a similar set of qualities in her heroes as she describes in Johnson. Although it might be a stretch to claim that Dorothea was modeled after Dr. Johnson, it is clear that Eliot sees them in a similar light of admiration and affection.

George Gissing (1857-1903) continued Johnson's association with the poor, describing Johnson's own struggles with poverty in his 1889 novel, *The Netherworld.* Gissing also reminds his readers of the early fledgling career of Johnson, further peeling him from Thackeray's gilded throne. Gissing writes, "A hundred and fifty years ago, one Edward Cave, publisher of the Gentleman's Magazine, and there many a time has sat a journeyman author of his, by name Samuel Johnson" [25]. *The Gentleman's Magazine,* founded in London by Cave in 1731, was where the young Johnson found his first employment as a writer [26]. Gissing humbles the imminent Doctor further: "There it was that the said Samuel once had his dinner handed to him behind a screen, because of his unpresentable costume, when Cave was entertaining an aristocratic guest" [25]. In this passage, Johnson has fully made the transformation from deified idol to the humbly impoverished. Gissing's use of Dr. Johnson's new, gritty Victorian identity was not intended to disparage the public image of Johnson. It, like its many similar contemporary references, uses Johnson's image to raise respect for the poor and struggling, by showing that even some great people were once impoverished.

Gissing continues this line of Johnsonian references into the next decade. In his 1891 novel, *New Grub Street,* the two primary characters are writers. The title refers to London's Grub Street, where impoverished writers for small publications worked and lived in the Augustan Age. Johnson defined Grub Street as a place "much inhabited by writers of small histories, dictionaries, and temporary poems; whence any mean production is called Grub-street"[27]. In the novel, Gissing again references Johnson's poor attire in the description of Mr. Quarmby: "He made a fair living, but, like Dr Johnson, had no passion for clean linen" [28]. The reference continues and is augmented by a Johnsonian accolade. He writes of Johnson's industriousness noting "Dr Johnson's saying, that a man may write at any time if he will set himself doggedly to it" [28]. Here Gissing deflates the over-inflated craft of writing with the notion that in fact any industrious person may do it well. He adds to that thought in a later chapter, again using the "every man's" Dr. Johnson to prove the point. He refers to literature in the words of his character, Yule. "His dictionary, I believe, defines the word as 'learning, skill in letters'—nothing else" [28]. Through this, Gissing allocates the once elite craft of writing into the hands of the common people, and he uses Dr. Johnson to do it.

Gissing portrays the Johnsonian persona as one with both a connection to and compassion for the poor and carries it into the 20th century and to the close of the Victorian Age. In his 1903 *The Private Papers of Henry Ryecroft,* Gissing defends the poor directly through words he ascribes to Dr. Johnson.

> "Sir," said Johnson, "all the arguments which are brought to represent poverty as no evil, show it to be evidently a great evil. You never find people labouring to convince you that you may live very happily upon a plentiful fortune." [29]

Again in the same chapter Gissing cites Johnson. "'Poverty,' said Johnson again, 'is so great an evil, and pregnant with so much temptation, so much misery, that I cannot but earnestly enjoin you to avoid it'" [29]. In the next chapter, Gissing writes of Johnson, the humanitarian. In the private writings of Gisssing's Henry Ryecroft, Henry confesses a lack of bravery in denouncing absurdity and misanthropy. Gissing closes out the literary era with a poignant appraisal of the nature of the Johnsonian persona at the time, in Henry's words.

> Brave Samuel Johnson! One such truth-teller is worth all the moralists and preachers who ever laboured to humanise mankind. Had he withdrawn into solitude, it would have been a national loss. Every one of his blunt, fearless words had more value than a whole evangel on the lips of a timidly good man. It is thus that the commonalty, however well

clad, should be treated. So seldom does the fool or the ruffian in broadcloth hear his just designation; so seldom is the man found who has a right to address him by it. By the bandying of insults we profit nothing; there can be no useful rebuke which is exposed to a tu quoque. But, as the world is, an honest and wise man should have a rough tongue. Let him speak and spare not! [29]

Using citations and actual Johnson quotes like these, Victorian writers crafted Dr. Johnson's persona to work in the defense of the poor and obscure, and to battle the misanthropic hypocrisy of the elite, completing the transfer of the possession of Johnson's persona from a select few to the masses. He had finally become public property and was no longer owned by Disraeli's Viscountess Dowager Bellair and Sidonia. Dr. Johnson did not rest in the pocket of those claiming greatness, like Thackeray's Barry Lyndon. He no longer served as a gift of potential greatness to be handed out by Miss Pinkerton to the Becky Sharpes of the world. He did not signify eminence for the Arthur Pendennises or serve to distinguish the Captain Browns from the Miss Jenkynses. He belonged to Bailey's cabmen, the poor writers of Grub Street, and the man "behind a screen, because of his unpresentable costume." He belonged to the simple Farmer Oaks and to those who stood against "the insolence of wealth". He belonged to the sort of people he kept "in nests" in his own home during his lifetime.

Chapter 8

From Image to Artifact

REFERENCES TO JOHNSON in literature and criticism show little change in nature until the second half of the 20th century. Essays and biographies written after that point have the benefit of more recent understandings in the fields of the social sciences. Many of Johnson's quirks that were unexplainably peculiar to Macaulay have sound diagnoses when these latter biographies were written. Not only are Johnson's quirks explainable, the commonness of his ailments is better known, striking the peculiarity from them. These developments in understanding Johnson's behavior have served opposing functions. They have acquitted Johnson of much of his earlier criticism, while simultaneously removing the mystique that kept his larger-than-life persona alive in the public discourse.

Macaulay, writing from an historian's perspective, rather than that of a poet, novelist, or literary critic, had the intention of reconstructing the history of his subject's life. Carlyle, and his predecessors, including Boswell and Johnson, wrote from the perspective of a literary man, seeking to expose a truth and make a point deeper than the reconstruct of facts. Facts were secondary to the truth they sought to relay. The transition in the standards of biography from Carlyle's perspective to Macaulay's continued to the present day. Present day biographies present evidence in the manner of historical reconstruction and no longer read like fiction or lead the reader to a moral conclusion, like Johnson's *Savage*. They no longer construct heroes, like Boswell's *Life*. These changes, plus the inclination to hold famous figures of the past to current social sensibilities, have led Johnson's once iconic persona down the road to near oblivion.

At the beginning of the 20th century, Johnson's image was still rooted in the common folks' ability to relate to him. Already, Johnson's quirky behavior lost its peculiarity and served as common ground between a literary giant and the impoverished masses, struggling for an identity. John Bailey's 1913 biography, *Dr. Johnson and His Circle*, betrays the transition, distinguishing itself from Macaulay with much more moderate views of both Johnson's greatness and his weaknesses. Bailey writes, "We can all imagine that under other conditions, and with an added store of brains and character, we might each have been Doctor Johnson" [1]. This declaration cements the common perception at the time of Johnson's station as a representative of the English masses. Johnson's persona seems to have led the way in the humanization of biographical subjects. Bailey continues, writing, "Before we could fancy ourselves Shelley or Keats the self that we know would have to be not developed but destroyed. But in Johnson we see our own magnified and glorified selves" [1]. Perhaps Bailey was right, and the decline of Johnson's iconic persona is a result of a public's lost desire to recognize a magnified or glorified image of itself. In a world where so many seek their moment of fame, where individualism and self-sovereignty are such important parts of the public identity, admitting a glorified version of self, in the image of a hero, is to admit an inferior and reduced self in comparison. Perhaps the literary figure simply ceased filling that role, yielding to heroes of the modern age, heroes no longer representing an exalted version of the common, individual citizen. Many of today's literary heroes come from other planets or have mutated, super-human powers. We cannot become them by altering ourselves. Following the precepts of the Johnson Canon will not grant laser vision or the ability to fly. Today's society is not as quick to liken themselves to their heroes, as Byron did with Johnson. There is evidence to this in the current desire to elevate heroes only to violently rip them from their heights. The hero is no longer sacred because it no longer is an aggrandized reflection of the common individual. At any rate, Johnson's persona still loomed large in 1913. Bailey writes that the, "name of Samuel Johnson is, of course, not the greatest in English prose, but even today, when he has been dead more than a century and a quarter, it is still the most familiar" [1]. It would be fair to say that Johnson's name was not only the most famous name in English prose. At that time, and the several preceding decades, it led all genres of heroes. Bailey eludes to this, writing, "He is still for us the great scholar and the strongly marked individuality, but he has gradually attained a kind of apotheosis, a kind of semi-legendary position, almost rivaling that of the great John Bull himself, as the embodiment of the essential features of the English character" [1].

Bailey links Johnson with Boswell, still claiming for Boswell's biography fatherhood of the Johnsonian image. By 1913, many essays and biographies were written of Johnson, both as literary criticism and personal exposés. Bailey recognizes that and does not try to construct a hero in Johnson, like Boswell did. The evolution in the nature of biography was not lost to him. Boswell's biography was personal and poignantly reverent. *Life of Johnson* was a shrine, built by Boswell, for Boswell and his readers to meet in paying homage to Johnson. Johnson's *Lives of the English Poets*, although all biographies within are more censuring than Boswell's, had an equally intentional purpose, a purpose that would have been clouded or lost altogether by the boundless research criteria and hazy or absent agendas of current biographies, beyond that of raw documentation. Bailey writes of Boswell, "[W]e know him as well as we know Johnson, as we know no other two men, perhaps, in the history of the world" [1]. Perhaps it is the incessant injection of opinion, in Boswell's *Life*, that not only links Boswell and Johnson, but distinguishes the Augustan mode of biography from that of Macaulay and beyond. This distinction begs the question: Is biography literature or a social science? Biography today certainly bares the traits of historical reconstruction. Bailey was not yet under the scrutiny of current biographical expectations, freeing him to laden his book with opinion and employ those opinions toward a solid and easily discernible authorial agenda.

Bailey's praise of Boswell and his marked attempts to credit Boswell for Johnson's fame display his mode of biography, one more like Carlyle than Macaulay. Bailey writes, "He and Johnson are now linked together for all eternity; and everybody who takes an interest in Johnson is interested in Boswell too" [1]. This notion is not without precedent. Would anyone know Savage without Johnson? Certainly Johnson's eminence was far beyond that of Savage's, during their respective lifetimes. But living icons are easily forgotten after death, unless they are immortalized by the living, and the tool of their immortalization is regularly renewed. This is where Augustan biography stands apart in its function from biographies of today. The biographer's opinionated agenda affects more than it informs, and facts become less important than truths. Bailey betrays his allegiance to this mode, writing, "Without Boswell, we should have respected Johnson, honoured him as a man and a writer, liked him as 'a true-born Englishman,' but we could not have known him enough to love him" [1]. To foster love for a biographer's subject is not in the standard criteria of current biographies. By current standards, such a biography would be met with stern criticism, claiming bias. The Augustan response would be, "What is wrong with bias?" Boswell places, in quotes, words of Johnson's that could not possibly have been recorded to the letter. By today's biographical standards, that would be considered weak scholarship at best. Boswell does nothing to veil his agenda of fostering reverence, and yes, even love, for Johnson in the hearts of his readers.

Bailey gives a good reason for the acceptance of Boswell in the 19th century more than the 20th. Boswell can be read in short segments and picked right back up without a loss of the author's intended flow. Bailey writes,

> But is there any time which is not the time for Boswell? He does not ask for a mood which may not be forthcoming: he does not demand an attention which it is inconvenient to give. We can take him up and lay him down as and when we will. [1]

Perhaps this is the reason for his fame during the age of poetry, periodical essays, and the serialized novel and his loss of fame in the age of the full length movie and the epic length novel. Maybe

Johnson's diminished fame is due to Boswell's and they truly are, as Bailey put it, "linked together for all eternity". One thing can be said for certain. None of the many 20th century biographies and essays on Johnson promote Johnson's iconic persona, seek to spawn affection for Johnson, or even acknowledge Johnson's time atop the public discourse like Boswell's quasi-faithful, moderately fictional biography. Boswell served his purpose, and if it is still considered the greatest of biographies, then the aroma of hypocrisy would permeate from all current biographies, for Boswell's *Life* would not see publication if released for the first time today. Bailey makes that precise point about Boswell:

> The fact is that justice will never be fully done to his memory till Macaulay and some others have been called up from their graves to do penance for their arrogant unfairness. Carlyle did something, but not enough; and he stands almost alone. Yet after all, considering what we owe Boswell, if there be any blindness in our view of him, it surely ought to be blindness to his faults. We have heard enough and to spare of his vanity, his self-importance, his entire lack of dignity, his weakness for wine and worse things than wine. But we have heard very little, far too little, of the kindness and genuineness of the man's whole nature, the warmth of his friendships and the enthusiastic loyalty of his hero-worship, of the reverence for religion and the earnest desire after being a better man, which, though often defeated by temptation, were profound and absolutely sincere. [1]

Boswell may have been less than scientific, but all Johnson biographies lean on him to some degree. Boswell's worth can be put into perspective by considering how much less would be known of Johnson's life and how much less significant the Johnsonian phenomenon would have been without Boswell's contribution.

It is interesting to ponder what Johnson would think of Boswell's biography and all of the many biographies since.

Johnson had strong opinions on the proper style and purpose of biography. Johnson writes in *Rambler 60*, "… the business of the biographer is often to pass slightly over those performances and incidents which produce vulgar greatness, to lead the thoughts into domestick privacies and display the minute details of daily life" [2]. Boswell adhered to his hero's regulations. His image of Johnson was painted by thousands of minor brushstrokes, each a word or phrase from Johnson's mouth, delivered during the minute moments of his life, to produce in concert a mural that lasted in public popularity for more than a century. Recent articles of criticism have focused on Johnson's major personality issues and bigotries that, while offensive today, were on par with the sensibilities of his age. Much is made of Johnson's views on women and the woman's place in society. Certainly, a quirky, physically awkward, crusty old Johnson, spouting those opinions in a modern coffeehouse or restaurant would rightfully meet the derision of the bulk of current society. But Johnson did not live in the 21st century. His own times must be considered. What is today considered the antiquated sensibilities of Johnson, must bear the bulk of the responsibility for the fall of Johnson's iconic stature. Similar criticism is made toward American Founding Fathers, who spoke and wrote of freedom while owning slaves. Those men are still revered but many look at their image with the disapprobation they would have for someone who owned slaves today. Johnson unintentionally argues in his own defense in this case against him. He writes in *Dryden* that, "To judge rightly of an author, we must transport ourselves to his time" [2]. He implores his readers to "examine what were the wants of his contemporaries, and what were his means of supplying them" [2]. Paul Alkon suggests through the words of Johnson that time distorts communication between generations. He writes, "Time's greatest disservice to literature, Johnson suggests, is in obscuring the meaning of words as they go out of fashion [3]. Johnson's anti-feminism was not anti-feminism at the time and, like many of his other opinions, must be translated, not into a different language, but into a modern social paradigm. If one were to replace, for a moment, Johnson's social notions with his fashions, the same criticisms would not hold. Johnson wore clothes that would look ridiculous in current settings. Nobody claims that he had no fashion sense because his clothes were not in line with current fashions. However, other aspects of his character suffer the same scrutiny.

Johnson is attacked, in many articles and biographies of the second half of the 20th century, as if he walked our current streets with 18th century opinions. In such a case, the criticism would be justifiable. What Boswell, Piozzi, and Carlyle offer, which is not offered in the latest biographies, is insight into Johnson's heart. That insight, far more than any facts from his history or even Johnson's own words, allows modern scholars to translate Johnson into modern sensibilities. A rising issue of Johnson's time was the plight of the poor. Boswell, Piozzi, and Carlyle all write copiously on Johnson's tenderness and humanitarianism regarding the poor. The plight of women was not on the mind of the Augustan public. Mary Wollstonecraft's *A Vindication of the Rights of Woman: with Strictures on Political and Moral Subjects* was written in 1792, eight years after Johnson's death, and was considered radical for its time, yet Johnson still influenced her, more as a woman writer than simply as a writer.

O'Flaherty wrote in 1967, in an article about Johnson's satires, "For the satirist is in theory a stern moralist, castigating the vices of his time or place, and Johnson has a better claim to this seriousness than either Pope or Dryden" [4]. The key words of O'Flaherty's quotation are "the vices of his time and place". With the intimate understanding of Johnson's inner-character, provided in detail by Boswell, Piozzi, and Carlyle, and indirectly through Bailey and even O'Flaherty, it is safe to imagine that had many of today's social issues been larger and more visible issues of Johnson's time, he would have embraced them with as much personal fervor as he embraced the problem of poverty and the other issues of his day. A supposition of what Johnson's views on current issues would be if he lived today, based on his social leanings in 18th century matters, provides greater insight into his character than a word for word interpretation of his writing under the lamp of current sensibilities. The Victorians did just that. They did not so much alter Johnson's image to fit their agendas.

They translated Johnson documented sensibilities to contemporary situations, albeit not always accurately. But supposition is not within the accepted criteria of current biography. Current biographers are reconstructing historical fact, without Boswell's enamored bias. Historical fact can present an ugly picture of Johnson, committing the error of, as Alkon put it, "obscuring the meaning of words as they go out of fashion".

In the second half of the 20th century, many literary scholars came to view Dr. Johnson's death in 1784 as the end of the Augustan Age [5]. The literature about the 18th century began to refer to "Johnson's London" or "Johnson's England" to denote the time when Johnson stood as the patriarch of the London literary scene. Johnson quotes and Johnson letters became the era's representatives in anthologies of literary genres. A few later scholars dedicated years of research, focusing their careers on a Johnsonian persona that had lost clarity and recognition in the public mind. They tried to pull Johnson's image out of enigmatic obscurity with remarkably comprehensive biographies. While these efforts serve as priceless resources in the study of Johnson and his time, they have failed in reviving the breathless corpse of the Johnsonian persona that reigned supreme and deified for well over a century. Now they exist like ruins of the temples of gods long forgotten, to be visited by the curious, no longer serving as the centers of worship as in their pinnacle.

One of these Johnson scholars is Bertrand Bronson (1903-1986). Bronson focused much attention on the use of Johnson to divide the Augustan and Romantic ages. The inability to draw a straight chronological line between the Augustan Age and the Romantic Age has been a common subject in literary journals. In an essay from the *Journal of English Literary History*, Bronson suggests that no line should be drawn to divide the ages. Rather a short buffer age should be inserted between the two. His 1953 essay, *The Pre-Romantic or Post-Augustan Mode*, focuses primarily on Johnson, singling him as the spokesman for this newly labeled age of literature. The contention is that Johnson's writing style is inconsistent with those of the other Augustans. To consider Johnson 'Post-Augustan', by viewing his place in the

Augustan Age simply from a literary angle, denies the influence of the other important angles that place him squarely as an Augustan. Johnson must be viewed as much more than the body of his literary accomplishments. Bronson hints toward this point with the acknowledgement that the bulk of Johnson's poetic work was written before 1850. He presents this as evidence that Johnson's poetry could not be used to mark the end of an age that perpetuated beyond the bulk of his work. It serves far better as evidence that Johnson's character and the public response to his character are the greater parts of Johnsonian influence. If his poetry is the mark, the age would have ended with the publication of his great poetry and not with his death. Marking the end of an age with his death shows that Johnson's image is more social than literary. To aid in placing a finger firmly on Johnson and his place in literary history, scholars like Bronson perpetuated and advanced the biographical trend of employing the social sciences in their endeavors, a trend initiated by Macaulay.

One unique perspective, encompassing historical, biographical, psychological, and literary study, comes in the 1977 Lawrence Goldstein book, *Ruins and Empire: The Evolution of a Theme in Augustan and Romantic Literature*. Writers from both ages held an intimate connection to the civilizations of Antiquity. Goldstein demonstrates how the shift from Augustan literature to Romantic accompanied a shift in writers' views of the ruined evidence of those civilizations. This perspective sheds revealing light on the driving prides and fears of writers from the two ages. According to Goldstein, the Romantics saw the ruins of Antiquity as evidence of the natural and inevitable decay and eventual destruction of society, as is evident in his statement that "Every high ideal represented by the classical style contains a premonition of reversal" [6]. Whereas the Augustan image of Antiquity discerned no reversal of high ideals. Vergil's writings live. Augustus' ambitions live. All of the ideals, philosophies, writings, and social, political, and artistic advancements of Antiquity live on in the English Augustan who proudly takes the baton passed by Rome. New societies are built upon the ruins of old, not in place of them. This was the Augustan image of Antiquity's ruins [6]. As a humanist, Johnson based his moral code on the lessons of the past. His faith in progress was based on his study of Antiquity and what he considered its continuing progression through time. Without detailing reasons for the difference, Goldstein contrasted the Romantic vision of the lessons of demolished Antiquity. The notion of promoting the national glory seemed distasteful to a proletariat who was left out of contemporary pleasures and whose pessimistic views of the fragility of state forbade them from anticipating future glory. A desperate 'now or never' attitude led to the literary transition from Augustan state building and the Johnsonian reverence for steady additions to conventionalism to the free and immediate pleasures of nature, as is seen in the many poems to nature by Wordsworth and his fellow Romantics [6].

This biographical expansion of form can be easily contrasted to works of the first half of the 20th century. In their 1935 book, *Literature and Life: Volume 4, English Literature*, authors Miles, Pooley, and Greenlaw draw the ever important lines between literature and its historical parallels. Each chapter begins with an introduction of the key historical factors affecting public demand and literary forms. The focus is significantly more literary than historical. The historical events referenced are strictly of a political nature to the neglect of social history and the lower classes. Important lines are drawn between the English national sentiment, resulting from the tumultuous 17th century, and the associated literary trends. The chapter on Johnson begins with this question: "How did Dr. Samuel Johnson strive to maintain the reign of form?" [7]. In this chapter, the authors indicate tendencies toward Romanticism following the deaths of Pope and Swift and credit Johnson with holding off the collapse of the cerebral, sophisticated Augustan form. They simultaneously support and conflict with Bronson's notion of a Johnson dominated, post-Augustan mode. They are synchronized with Bronson's argument that the Johnsonian mode was unlike that of Johnson's contemporaries. Bronson used this notion to drive home his point that Johnson's death cannot be used to signify the end of the Augustan Age because the age ended when the Johnsonian mode ceased to be the literary standard. They conflict with Bronson by citing the dominance of Johnson's literary circle. The fact that the majority of literary works during Johnson's later years were not particularly Augustan is overshadowed by the fact that during Johnson's life, those works remained hidden by the shadow of Johnson's iconic persona and the powerful influence of his circle on the English public's identity. All works cited in the sections covering Johnson's later years were either written by a member of Johnson's circle or referencing Johnson in some way. They argue that Johnson succeeded in staving off the approach of the Romantic Age of literature, perpetuating the Augustan mode as the dominant form of literary expression, despite its numerical minority [7]. If one pulls the eye away from the microscope focused on individual words and letters written by Johnson, and views the Johnsonian social phenomenon as a whole, and Johnson's writing as simply one contributor to the phenomenon, Johnson's role as the literary usher comes clear. Johnson did not stand as an armed sentry at the border of an age. He did not carry a sword. He carried a flashlight, ushering literature forward in time. It was his character, not his writing that held the flashlight. His character held influence long after 1755, when the bulk of his writing was already published. With the Johnsonian character weighing more heavily than the Johnsonian literary mode, biography becomes as important to the research of the Johnson phenomenon as poetry. Miles' vision of Johnson, congruent with the early 20th century, maintained a literary focus, with blinders to the broad perspectives of later studies of Johnson and almost entirely excluding the light cast by the social sciences.

The second half of the 20th century saw the publication of work dedicated to cultural aspects of Johnson's age. Johnson is used in these works to epitomize his age and genre. In 1953, *The Oxford Book of English Talk*, edited by James Sutherland, was published. The book gives examples of formal and familiar discourse, throughout English history, in presenting the evolution of English language usage. It is a wonderful example of the immerging trend of hybrid disciplines of study. The book is certainly literary while undoubtedly historical. Letters from such prominent names as Jonathan Swift to those of obscure lady's maids expose the range of English usage through an expansive swath of time and social strata. As the book enters Johnson's age, the Johnsonian aroma permeates. A servant of David Garrick's is quoted in 1758 and in 1776, Johnson's dinner with Mr. Wilkes, as reported by Boswell, serves as the example of English discourse of the literary elite.

In 1966, a similar book was released, entitled *The Familiar Letter in the Eighteenth Century*. As the title suggests, the book covers only familiar letters of one century. It is no surprise that Johnson's portrait serves as the cover art. With 20th century researchers surfacing more and more letters of Johnson's, the editors had numerous examples to include. The introduction, titled, *The Correspondence of the Augustans*, betrays the literary and linguistic genre intended to be presented by the book. Covering literary, political, and social figures, from Pope and Swift to Lady Montagu and Lord Chesterfield, it is Johnson's letters that dominate in both pages and prominence. The Johnson chapter is titled, "Dr. Johnson: the Public Guise of Private Matters." The title alone gives great insight into the nature of the Johnsonian phenomenon. The editors suggest that "The reader curious to see Dr. Johnson without any intervening elements has three sources to examine" [8]. Those sources are Johnson's notes on Shakespeare, the *Diaries, Prayers and Annals*, edited by McAdam in 1958, and the *Letters of Samuel Johnson*, edited in three volumes by R. W. Chapman in 1952. This suggestion also points toward the expansion of biographical study beyond what is presented by Carlyle and Macaulay. Johnson's letters are not only presented as quintessentially Augustan; they are contrasted to those of fellow Augustans only in superiority and quintessence, contrary to Bronson's arguments.

As the 20th century progressed and evidence of the peripheral aspects of Johnson's life continued to surface, literature on Johnson and his life and times became far more comprehensive than what was presented by Macaulay, Carlyle, even Boswell. Walter Jackson Bate's 1975, Pulitzer Prize-winning biography serves as a definitive example of the evolutionary resting point of what should now be considered the science of biography. Bate broadens the scope of study to include the extreme peripherals of Johnson's life. The thoughts and comments on Johnson's life, character, history, writings, and even many quirky anecdotes have been recorded from sources from the well-known Boswell biography to personal letters and obscure writing only recently discovered at the time of publication. As much emphasis is placed on Johnson's peripheral contacts as on his inner circle. These contacts, while individually minute and seemingly insignificant, combine to reveal more about the building blocks of Johnson's character, leading to a better understanding of the reasons for his impact on popular society than previous Johnson studies, which focused primarily on his literary influence. Through this grand scope, Bate reveals a more comprehensive vision of Johnson, from his staged appearances to the very incidental. Although Carlyle would probably have disliked such a comprehensively humanizing portrayal of Johnson, the work does not contribute to Johnson's fall from enshrinement. If read with the fall of Johnson's image in mind, it provides an understanding of the fall by illuminating the differences between scholarly thought while Johnson's image reigned and the academic expectations of today. It rather explains, in very practical, understandable, human terms, the inner workings of Johnson's very personal side. A perusal of the biography allows the reader to draw the lines between Johnson's ideals, his quirks, the events in his life, his familiar contacts, his literary achievements and his elevation to the height of social prominence. Although the biography does not extend past Johnson's death, the final chapter covers the preparations Johnson and others made in anticipation of his death. It leads the reader into the development of what Bate calls "The Johnson Legend". He describes ambitious people "lurking outside the house looking for private information about Johnson's life" [9]. This image of lurking people and of the commonness of collecting pieces of Johnson's life for later use, hints at the development of the Johnson social phenomenon without diving deeply into it.

An historical, literary, psychological, and sociological study of Johnson's image, presented in congruence with current biographical trends, beginning with the historical events that fertilized the social soil that grew the Johnsonian persona and covering the peripheral connections and minor Johnson references through the early 20th century will serve as a continuation of the biographies of Bate and his contemporaries. The story of Samuel Johnson ends with Johnson's death, but the story of the Johnson phenomenon is so much more expansive. The culmination of previous biographies, from Piozzi to Bate, and the uses to Johnson as the mark of his age and genre, as employed in *The Oxford Book of English Talk* and *The Familiar Letter in the Eighteenth Century* and the countless references to Johnson in novels and essays from his death to today, all present a mosaic of Johnson's story, a story with a beginning, middle, and as far as a grand social acclaim is concerned, an end. This is the story of Johnson and the purpose of this study.

Although Samuel Johnson's public persona was steered in great part by common public discourse and references to Johnson in fictional literature, creating a quasi-fictional character of Johnson in Johnsonian lore, the biographies of Johnson provided a cord of connection between the ever expanding and evolving Johnson image and the factual man, with all of his faults and quirks. While the Johnson references in English fiction focused on the mythological Johnson, as he stood in the public eye and as he represented his brand of literary figure, many sources sought to capture the factual Johnson. This attempt most often focused on Johnson's faults, producing the humanizing effect of exposing the faults of a legendary social icon. Some of these sources came in the form of pure biography. Others provided biographical contributions in other forms, such as prefaces to new editions of Johnson's work, or as members of the host of Johnson related articles in literary journals. All added pieces of the mosaic that became the Johnsonian image. Ultimately, the gilded image of Johnson fell from its lofty shrine into the gutters of social obscurity. The humanizing agenda of latter publications on Johnson succeeded in exposing the factual Johnson, scouring off the layers of gilding poured on by the committee of hero makers, from Boswell to Carlyle and all of the fictional references that used Johnson's image as a beacon of quintessential British traits and scholarly excellence, like those used by Disraeli and Thackeray. The point of this study is not to side with either the hero-builders or the more recent trends in biography, but rather to understand the image of Johnson as it sits in the mind of each.

Rather than fending off the onset of Romanticism with pure Augustan-ism, just as the "Old Guard" of any genre clings more tightly to its traditions in the face of its collapse, Johnson's literary achievements and the reports of his character in his earliest biographies, convene to establish a 'Pre-Romantic' Johnson, more escorting the entrance of the new era than hiding behind the old Augustan ramparts, dug in for a battle to the death. Johnson was the bridge that allowed English literature to walk peacefully from Pope to Shelley. It was the standards of a new kind of biography, one that read less like the moral essays of Johnson's *Lives of the English Poets* or Boswell's hero-building *Life of Samuel Johnson*, and more like the chronicles of historical reconstruction. Piozzi's intimate exposure to the public of Johnson's Romantic, sometimes revolutionary, personal inclinations and behaviors allowed readers of Johnson's published works to view them in a Romantic light. With this lens, the staunch, conservative, Augustan sentry melts away to expose a quirky quasi-Romantic who bucks convention more than defends it. The later biographies on Johnson employ Piozzi, Boswell, and Johnson's own annals in exposing the factual Johnson. This exposed figure may be analyzed for the point of denoting his precise place in literary history. This has been the focus of recent Johnson studies, placing Johnson on literary and historical scales alongside other key figures. The failure in this approach comes in the denial of the mythological image of Johnson that dominated English literature and the public discourse for over a century. It is easy to understand the scholarly merits of actualizing the Johnsonian image and debunking the mythology. A better understanding of the factual man is important to understanding Johnson. But the study of Johnson must include the whole of the Johnson phenomenon, and what is considered noble fact-finding, destroying the mythology of Johnson, is in fact destroying facts about the English people and their relationship to their hero.

So many of the biographies on Johnson focus, as current psychology tends toward, on establishing Johnson through a thorough establishment of his early life. Bate spends over 140 pages just to get Johnson out of Oxford. This is evidence of the invasion of the social sciences into literature. Of course there is merit to establishing Johnson's youth in understanding his character. But when the whole of the Johnson phenomenon is in focus, Johnson's youth is an infinitesimal speck of the whole study. Johnson references in Victorian literature focus almost entirely on the Johnsonian image from after the *Dictionary* through the height of his elite circle, toward the end of his life. To the Victorians, this was the only Johnson that concerned them and served their literary needs. There are few references to the struggling youth so vividly and extensively described in Bate's biography. For the purposes of their Johnson enshrinement, Johnson was born with plume in hand, huddled over countless volumes of literature, in his Gough Square home. There is no Johnson without Boswell hanging out of his back pocket. The journey of the Victorian Johnson social phenomenon can be plotted precisely through the references to Johnson in Victorian fiction.

The gradual evolution and the sudden mutations in the Johnsonian image are reflected accurately in the many uses of the image in Victorian fiction. In the 20th century, Johnson's name fell out of fiction. His name was perpetuated in other genres of literature. The biography and literary journal essay took the Johnsonian baton from the likes of Hardy and Dickens. Once Johnson's name was no longer used in establishing the attributes of fictional characters or used to align the characters with certain social agendas and it was taken from the author and given to the literary critic, the search for the factual Johnson began. Freud's work in the 20th century popularized psychology, running the Johnsonian image through a Freudian filter. What concerned

Freud was of no concern to Elizabeth Gaskell and those who used the Johnsonian image as a literary tool. Gaskell's literary tools were of no concern to those who wished to dissect Johnson as a living, breathing man. The utter debunking of the mythological Victorian Johnson by the Freudian filter and the psychological leanings of the new generation of biography were the primary contributors to the death of the iconic Johnson image. But a comprehensive study of Johnson's image is actually a study of the English people and the embrace and employment of Johnson's image, both for literary purposes and for social identification. It is a study more in sociology than psychology, more in societal trends than in literary criticism. With the Johnson moral canon on one end and the rise of Johnsonian mythology flowing from his elite circle on the other, the true story of Johnson may begin in Lichfield on September 18, 1709, but it does not end in London on December 18, 1784, as it does in the biographies on Johnson. It continues as Johnson's image faced the rising sensibilities of Romanticism. It stood when those sensibilities receded and British Imperialism found its pinnacle. It stood through the social changes of industrialization and public education. It was the rope in a tug-of-war between ever dividing factions of English society. Johnson's image was raised as the definitive banner of diverse and often opposing social movements, from the extremely conservative to the revolutionary. Johnson's story continues into the 20th century, when it drastically changed its nature. It aged and withered with the humanizing effects of extensive biography. Eventually, it died as it became so real, so true to life that it no longer served as an extraordinary tale, with profound social and political implications. Now Johnson exists in literary academia as a eulogy to a writer, mostly disconnected by biographical trends from the profoundly iconic and socially colossal image that loomed so long over the English social and literary scenes. Johnson is the boy born in illness in Lichfield. He is the literary lion holding court in the coffeehouses and taverns of Fleet Street. He is Disraeli's picture of literary elitism and Carlyle's Oden. He is Thackeray's deified sage. He is Gaskell's soldier of conventionalism, Dickens' common man's connection to the language, and Hardy's simple farmer. He is the factual man portrayed in 20th century biographies, and he is the corpse of an icon, an icon born in the coffeehouses of London, who antiqued, worn and withered in the vividly humanizing pages of psychological biography.

References

Chapter 1

[1] Bucholz, R. (2009*)*. London a short history of the greatest city in the Western World. Chantilly, Virginia. The Teaching Company.

[2] Herlihy, D. (1997). The Black Death and the Transformation of the West. Cambridge. Harvard University Press.

[3] Cantor, N. (2001). In the Wake of the Plague: The Black Death and the World It Made. New York, New York. The Free Press.

[4] Pamuk, S. (2007). The Black Death and the origins of the 'Great Divergence' across Europe, 1300-1600. *European Review of Economic History, 11*(3), 289-317.

[5] Vallance, E. (2008). The Glorious Revolution: 1688: Britain's fight for liberty. Berkeley, California. Pegasus Books.

[6] Baugh, A. ed. (1948). A Literary History of England. New York, NY. Appleton-Century-Crofts.

[7] Cohn, S. (June, 2002). The Black Death: End of a Paradigm. *American Historical Review*. Volume 107, Issue 3, p. 703–738.

[8] Benedictow, J. (2005). The Black Death: The Greatest Catastrophe Ever. *History Today, 55*(3), 42-49.

[9] Lord, I. (1970). The Diary of Samuel Pepys. Eau Claire, Wisconsin. E.M. Hale & Company.

[10] Pincus, S. (2009). 1688: The First Modern Revolution. New Haven Connecticut. Yale University Press.

[11] Jenkins, S. (2011). A Short History of England: The Glorious Story of a Rowdy Nation. New York, New York. PublicAffairs.

[12] Bucholz, R. (2006). Foundations of Western Civilization II; A History of the Modern Western World. Chantilly, Virginia. The Teaching Company.

[13] Humphreys, A. (1954). The Augustan World: Society, Thought, Letters in Eighteenth Century England. New York, NY. Harper Torchbooks.

[14] Olsen, K. (1999). Daily Life in 18th Century England. London, UK. Greenwood Press.

[15] Bronson, B. ed. (1952). Samuel Johnson: Rasselas, Poems and Selected Prose. New York, New York. Holt, Rinehart and Winston, Inc.

Chapter 2

[1] Bronson, B. (1951). The Double Tradition of Dr. Johnson. *Journal of English Literary History.* Vol. 18, No. 2, pp. 90-106.

[2] Macaulay, T. (1896). Macaulay's Life of Samuel Johnson along with his essay on Johnson. New York, NY. Longmans, Green, and Co. Retrieved from https://archive.org/stream/macaulayslifesa01beuhgoog#page/n12/mode/2up

[3] Kniskern, W. (1985). Satire and the "Tragic Quartet" in The Vanity of Human Wishes. Studies in English Literature, 1500-1900. Vol. 25, No. 3, pp. 633-649.

[4] Bronson, B. (1952). Samuel Johnson: Rasselas, Poems and Selected Prose. New York, New York. Holt, Rinehart and Winston, Inc.

[5] Johnson, C. (1984). Samuel Johnson's Moral Psychology and Locke's "Of Power". Studies in English Literature, 1500-1900. Vol. 24, No. 3, pp. 563-582.

[6] Greene, D. (1984). Samuel Johnson Major Works including Rasselas. Oxford, U.K. Oxford University Press.

[7] Hardy, T. (1987). Tess of the D'Urbervilles. London, UK. Laurel Press.

[8] Thackeray, W. (2001). Vanity Fair: A Novel Without a Hero. Hertfordshire, U.K. Wordsworth Editions Limited.

[9] Lacey, R. (2006). Great Tales from English History. New York, New York. Little, Brown & Company.

[10] Gaskell, E. (2005). Life of Charlotte Bronte. Retrieved from http://www.gutenberg.org /files/1827/1827-h/1827-h.htm.

[11] Hitchings, H. (2005). Defining the World: The Extraordinary Story of Dr Johnson's Dictionary. New York, New York. Farrar, Straus, and Giroux.

[12] Bate, W. (1975). *Samuel Johnson*. New York, NY. Harcourt Brace Jovanovich.

[13] Boswell, J. (1904). Life of Johnson. Oxford, U.K. Oxford University Press.

[14] Uzgalis, William, "John Locke", The Stanford Encyclopedia of Philosophy. Edward N. Zalta (ed.), URL = <http://plato.stanford.edu/archives/fall2012/entries/locke/>.

[15] Alkon, P. (1966). Robert South, William Low, and Samuel Johnson. Studies in English Literature, 1500-1900. Vol. 6, No. 3, pp. 499-528.

[16] Johnson, S. (1996). The Works of Samuel Johnson in Sixteen Volumes: Volume IV. Retrieved from http://www.gutenberg.org/cache/epub/577/pg577.html.

[17] Johnson, S. (2004). The Works of Samuel Johnson, LL.D. in Nine Volumes: Volume the Fourth. Retrieved from http://www.gutenberg.org/ cache/epub/12050/pg12050.html.

[18] Kolb, G. (1951). The Structure of Rasselas. *PMLA,* Vol. 66, No. 5, pp. 698-717.

[19] Hartdegen, S. (1970). The New American Bible. Nashville, TN. Thomas Nelson Publishers.

[20] Preston, T. (1969). The Biblical Context of Johnson's "Rasselas". *PMLA,* Vol. 84, No. 2, pp. 274-281.

[21] Richard, J. (2003). "I Am Equally Weary of Confinement": Women Writers and "Rasselas" from "Dinarbas to Jane Eyre". *Tulsa Studies in Women's Literature.* Vol. 22, No. 2, pp. 335-356.

[22] Kelly, R. (1968). Johnson Among the Sheep. *Studies in English Literature, 1500-1900.* Vol. 8, No. 3, pp. 475-485.

[23] Lynch, J. (2002). Samuel Johnson's Dictionary. London, UK. Levenger Press.

[24] Kallich, M. (1954). The Association of Ideas in Samuel Johnson's Criticism. *Mosern Language Notes.* Vol. 69, No. 3, pp. 170-176.

[25] Griffin, D. (1997). Regulated Loyalty: Jacobitism and Johnson's "Lives of the Poets". *Journal of English Literary History.* Vol. 64, No. 4, pp.1007-1027.

[26] Rogers, P. (1980). Johnson's Lives of the Poets and the Biographic Dictionaries. *The Review of English Studies.* Vol. 31, No. 122, pp. 149-171.

[27] Pope, A. (2007). An Essay on Man: Moral Essays and Satires. Retrieved from http://www.gutenberg.org/files/2428/2428-h/2428-h.htm.

[28] Knoblauch, C. H. (1979). Coherence Betrayed: Samuel Johnson and the "Prose of the World". *Boundary 2*, Vol. 7, No. 2, pp. 235-260.

[29] Ruml, T. (1985). The Younger Johnson's Texts of Pope. *The Review of English Studies, New Series*, Vol. 36, No. 142, pp. 180-198.

[30] Booth, M. (1978). Proportion and Value in Johnson's "Lives of the Poets". *South Atlantic Bulletin*, Vol. 43, No. 1, pp. 49-57.

[31] Chapman, R. (1937). Johnson's Letters. *The Review of English Studies.* Vol. 13, No. 50, pp. 139-176.

[32] Redford, B. (1992). The Letters of Samuel Johnson 1731-1772. Princeton, New Jersey. Princeton University Press.

[33] Anderson, H., Daghlian, P., Ehrenpreis, I. (1966). The Familiar Letter in the Eighteenth Century. Lawrence, Kansas. The University Press of Kansas.

Chapter 3

[1] Boswell, J. (2006). *Life of Johnson.* Retrieved from http://www.gutenberg.org/files/1564/1564-h/1564-h.htm. Aug. 2, 2012.

[2] Ward, J. (1972). Johnson's Conversation. *Studies in English Literature, 1500-1900*, Vol. 12, No. 3, Restoration and Eighteenth Century, pp. 519-533.

[3] Greene, D. (1979). Do We Need a Biography of Johnson's "Boswell" Years? *Modern Language Studies*, Vol. 9, No. 3, *Eighteenth-Century Literature*, pp. 128-136.

[4] Macaulay, T. (1895). Macaulay's and Carlyle's Essays on Samuel Johnson. New York, New York. Henry Holt and Company.

Chapter 4

[1] Adams, H. ed. (1992). Critical Theory Since Plato. Fort Worth, TX. Harcourt Brace Jovanovich College Publishers.

[2] Greene, D. (1984). Samuel Johnson Major Works including Rasselas. Oxford, U.K. Oxford University Press.

[3] Bronson, B. (1953). The Pre-Romantic or Post-Augustan Mode. *Journal of English Literary History.* John Hopkins University Press. 20 (1), 15-28.

[4] Boyd, D. (1972). Vanity and Vacuity: A Reading of Johnson's Verse Satires. *Journal of English Literary History.* Vol. 39, No. 3, pp. 387-403.

[5] Eliot, T. (1930). London: a Poem, and the Vanity of Human Wishes, by Samuel Johnson, With an Introductory Essay by T.S. Eliot. London, UK. Frederick Etchells & Hugh Macdonald.

[6] O'Flaherty, P. (1967). Johnson as Satirist: A New Look at the Vanity of Human Wishes. *Journal of English Literary History.* Vol. 34, No. 1, pp. 78-91.

[7] Goldstein, L. (1977). Ruins and Empire: The Evolution of a Theme in Augustan and Romantic Literature. Pittsburgh, PA. University of Pittsburgh Press.

Chapter 5

[1] Bucholz, R. (2006*).* Foundations of Western Civilization II; A History of the Modern Western World. Chantilly, Virginia. The Teaching Company.

[2] Ford, B. (1957). From Blake to Byron. Baltimore, MD. Penguin Books Ltd.

[3] Barker, J. (2000). Wordsworth: a Life. New York, NY. Harper Collins Publishers.

[4] Fogle, R. (1951). John Keats: Selected Poetry and Letters. New York, NY. Rineholt & Company.

[5] Greene, D. (1984). Samuel Johnson Major Works including Rasselas. Oxford, U.K. Oxford University Press.

[6] Sutherland, J. (2008). Classics of British Literature. Chantilly, VA. The Teaching Company.

[7] Lacey, R. (2006). Great Tales from English History. New York, New York. Little, Brown & Company.

[8] Geller, J. (2001). Johnson Re-Visioned: Looking Before and After. Cranbury, NJ. Associated University Presses.

[9] Godwin, W. (2005). Memoirs of the Author of a Vindication of the Rights of Women. Retrieved from http://www.gutenberg.org/files/16199/16199-h/16199-h.htm June 2012.

[10] Basker, J. (2011). Tradition in Transition: Women Writers, Marginal Texts, and the Eighteenth-Century Canon. Oxford Scholarship Online. Retrieved from http://www.oxfordscholarship.com/view/10.1093/acprof:oso/9780198182887.001.0001/acprof-9780198182887-chapter-3.

[11] Wollstonecraft, M. (2002). A Vindication of the Rights of Women. Retrieved from http://www.gutenberg.org/cache/epub/3420/pg3420.html.

[12] Pope, A. (2007). An Essay on Man: Moral Essays and Satires. Retrieved from http://www.gutenberg.org/files/2428/2428-h/2428-h.htm.

[13] Greene, D. (1984). Samuel Johnson Major Works including Rasselas. Oxford, U.K. Oxford University Press.

[14] Quiller-Couch, A. (1900). The Oxford Book of English Verse. New York, NY. Oxford University Press.

[15] Austen-Leigh, J. (2006). A Memoir of Jane Austen. London. Retrieved from http://www.gutenberg.org/files/17797/17797-h/17797-h.htm.

[16] Austen-Leigh, W., Austen Leigh, R. (1913). Jane Austen Her Life And Letters A Family Record. New York, NY. E. P. Dutton & Company.

[17] Austen, J. (2006). Jane Austen – Seven Novels. New York, NY. Barnes & Noble Inc.

[18] Boswell, J. (1952). The Life of Samuel Johnson LL.D. Chicago, IL. The University of Chicago.

[19] Bronson, B. (1952). Samuel Johnson: Rasselas, Poems and Selected Prose. New York, New York. Holt, Rinehart and Winston, Inc.

[20] Elze, K. (1872). Lord Byron, a Biography, with a Critical Essay on his Place in Literature. London, UK. John Murray.

[21] Marchand, L. ed. (1973). Byron's Letters and Journals, Volume 1. Cambridge, MA. The Belknap Press of Harvard University Press.

[22] Brougham, H. (2011). Lord Byron's Poems. Harvard College Library. Retrieved from http://hcl.harvard.edu/libraries/houghton/exhibits/byron/critics/2_3.cfm.

[23] Marchand, L. ed. (1974). Byron's Letters and Journals, Volume 2. Cambridge, MA. The Belknap Press of Harvard University Press.

[24] Marchand, L. ed. (1974). Byron's Letters and Journals, Volume 3. Cambridge, MA. The Belknap Press of Harvard University Press.

[25] Marchand, L. ed. (1975). Byron's Letters and Journals, Volume 4. Cambridge, MA. The Belknap Press of Harvard University Press.

[26] Radcliffe, D. (n.d.). Spencer and the Tradition: English Poetry 1579-1830. Department of English, Virginia Tech. Retrieved from http://spenserians.cath.vt.edu/Welcome.php.

[27] Marchand, L. ed. (1976). Byron's Letters and Journals, Volume 6. Cambridge, MA. The Belknap Press of Harvard University Press.

[28] Marchand, L. ed. (1977). Byron's Letters and Journals, Volume 7. Cambridge, MA. The Belknap Press of Harvard University Press.

[29] Pratt, L. (n.d.). The Collected Letters of Robert Southey, part 1: 1791-1797. University of Maryland. Retrieved from http://www.rc.umd.edu/editions/southey_letters/Part_One/HTML/letterEEd.26.41.html.

[30] Sadler, T. ed. (1808). Diary, Reminiscences, and Correspondence of Henry Crabb Robinson. Boston, MA. Houghton, Mifflin and Company. Retrieved from http://archive.org/stream/diaryreminiscen01robigoog#page/n6/mode/2up.

[31] Wordsworth, W. (1967). The Prose Works of William Wordsworth, in three volumes, volume two. New York, NY. AMS Press, Inc.

[32] Byron, G., Coleridge, E., ed. (2005). The Works of Lord Byron. Retrieved from http://www.gutenberg.org/cache/epub/8861/pg8861.html.

[33] Byron, G. (2007). Don Juan in Sixteen Cantos with Notes. Halifax, UK. Milner & Sowerby. Retrieved from http://www.gutenberg.org/files/21700/21700-h/21700-h.htm#2H_4_0001.

[34] Griggs, E. (1930). Coleridge and the Wedgwood Annuity. *The Review of English Studies*, Vol. 6, No. 21, pp. 63-72.

Chapter 6

[1] Mitchell, S. (1996). Daily Life in Victorian England. Westport, Connecticut. Greenwood Press.

[2] Morris, P. (1999). Heroes and Hero-Worship in Charlotte Bronte's Shirley. *Nineteenth Century Literature*. Vol. 54, No. 3, pp. 285-307.

[3] Bucholz, R. (2006). Foundations of Western Civilization II; A History of the Modern Western World. Chantilly, Virginia. The Teaching Company.

[4] Bucholz, R. (2009). London a short history of the greatest city in the Western World. Chantilly, Virginia. The Teaching Company.

[5] Picard, L. (2005). Victorian London: The Tale of a City, 1840-1870. New York, New York. St. Martin's Press.

[6] Mitchell, S. (1996). Daily Life in Victorian England. Westport, Connecticut. Greenwood Press.

[7] Hilton, B. (2008). New Oxford History of England, 1783-1846: A Mad, Bad and Dangerous People? Oxford, U.K. Oxford University Press.

[8] Allitt, P. (2002). *Victorian Britain.* Chantilly, Virginia. The Teaching Company.

[9] Carlyle, T. (1966). *On Heroes, Hero-Worship, and the Heroic in History.* Lincoln, Nebraska. University of Nebraska Press.

[10] Bruce, J. (1907). *Disraeli as a Novelist.* The Sewanee Review. Vol. 11, No. 3, pp.353-369.

[11] Cline, C. (1943). *Disraeli and Thackeray.* The Review of English Studies. Vol. 19, No. 76, pp. 404-408.

[12] Bryce. (1921). *The Life of Disraeli*, V., VI. The American Historical Review. Vol. 26, No.4, pp. 672-682.

[13] Disraeli, B. (2006). Henrietta Temple. Retrieved from http://www.gutenberg.org /files/19771/19771-h/19771-h.htm.

[14] The National Gallery. (2012). "Sir Joshua Reynolds." Retrieved from http://www.nationalgallery.org.uk /artists/sir-joshua-reynolds.

[15] Baker, G. (1891). *George William Frederick Howard, seventh Earl of Carlisle (1802-1864).* Retrieved from http://historyhome.co.uk/people/morpeth.htm.

[16] Bate, W. (1975). *Samuel Johnson.* New York, NY. Harcourt Brace Jovanovich.

[17] Disraeli, B. (2006). The Young Duke. Retrieved from http://www.gutenberg.org /files/20008/20008-h/20008-h.htm.

[18] Fears, J. (2001). Famous Romans. Chantilly, Virginia. The Teaching Company.

[19] Breslow, J. (1977). *The Narrator in Sketches by Boz.* Journal of English Literary History. Vol. 44, No. 1, pp. 127-149.

[20] Dickens, C. (1950). *The Life and Adventures of Nicholas Nickleby.* Oxford, U.K. Oxford University Press.

[21] Watson, J. (1861). The Life of Richard Porson, M.A. London, U.K. Longman, Greene, Longman and Roberts.

[22] Dickens, C. (1997*). David Copperfield.* Oxford, U.K. Oxford University Press.

[23] Bruce, J. (1903). *An Estimate of Thackeray.* The Sewanee Review. Vol. 11, No.1, pp. 21-35.

[24] Thackeray, W. (1898). The Memoirs of Barry Lyndon, Esq. New York, New York. Harper & Brothers Publishers.

[25] Thackeray, W. (2001*).* Vanity Fair: A Novel Without a Hero. Hertfordshire, U.K. Wordsworth Editions Limited.

[26] Hays, D., McKenna, A. (2004). New Standard Encyclopedia, vol. 15. Chicago, Illinois. Standard Education Corporation.

[27] Chapone, H. (1814). *Memoirs of Mrs. Chapone.* The Belfast Monthly Magazine. Vol. 12, No. 70, pp. 382-386.

[28] Dooley, D. (1971). Thackeray's Use of Vanity Fair. *Studies in English Literature 1500-1900,* Vol. 11, No. 4, pp. 701-713.

[29] Bailey, J. (1913). Dr. Johnson and His Circle. Retrieved from http://www.gutenberg.org/ cache/epub/24066/pg24066.html. April 2012.

[30] Macaulay, T. (1896). Macaulay's Life of Samuel Johnson along with his essay on Johnson. New York, NY. Longmans, Green, and Co. Retrieved from

https://archive.org/stream/macaulayslifesa01beuhgoog#page/n12/mode/2up.

[31] Humphreys, A. (1954). The Augustan World: Society, Thought, Letters in Eighteenth Century England. New York, NY. Harper Torchbooks.

[32] Thackeray, W. M. (2009). The History of Pendennis. Retrieved from http://www.gutenberg.org /files/7265/7265-h/7265-h.htm.

[33] Bentley, G. E. (1945). Shakespeare and Jonson: Their Reputations in the Seventeenth Century Compared. Chicago Illinois. University of Chicago Press.

[34] Addison, J. (1853). *Joseph Addison.* The Illustrated Magazine of Art. Vol. 1, No, 5, pp. 305-308.

[35] Damrosch, D. (1999). *British Literature: the Victorian Age.* New York, New York. Longman.

[36] Gaskell, E. C. (1995). Cranford. Retrieved from http://www.gutenberg.org /dirs/etext96/crnfd10h.htm.

[37] Breslow, J. (1977). *The Narrator in Sketches by Boz.* Journal of English Literary History. Vol. 44, No. 1, pp. 127-149.

[38] Patten, R. (1967). The Art of Pickwick's Interpolated Tales. Journal of English Literary History. Vol. 34, No. 3, pp. 349-366.

[39] Grubb, G. (1943). The Editorial Policies of Charles Dickens. Publications of the Modern Language Association. Vol. 58, No. 4, pp.1110-1124.

[40] McMaster, J. (1968). Theme and Form in the Newcomes. *Nineteenth-Century Fiction.* Vol. 23, No. 2, pp. 177-188.

[41] Boswell, J. (1904). *Life of Johnson.* Oxford, U.K. Oxford University Press.

Chapter 7

[1] Thackeray, W. M. (2006). The Rose and the Ring. Retrieved from http://www.gutenberg.org /files/897/897-h/897-h.htm.

[2] Mitch, D. (1992). The Rise of Popular Literacy in Victorian England: The Influemce of Private Choice and Public Policy. Philadelphia, Pennsylvania. University of Pennsylvania Press.

[3] UNESCO. (2012). Ragged Schools, Industrial Schools, and Reformatories. Retrieved from http://www.hiddenlives.org.uk/articles/raggedschool.html.

[4] Gaskell, E. (2005). Life of Charlotte Bronte. Retrieved from http://www.gutenberg.org /files/1827/1827-h/1827-h.htm.

[5] Fielding, K. (1958). Charles Dickens: a Critical Introduction. Boston, Massachusetts. Houghton Mifflin Company.

[6] Grubb, G. (1943). The Editorial Policies of Charles Dickens. *Publications of the Modern Language Association.* Vol. 58, No. 4, pp.1110-1124.

[7] Fielding, K. (1958). Charles Dickens: a Critical Introduction. Boston, Massachusetts. Houghton Mifflin Company.

[8] Bate, W. (1975). *Samuel Johnson.* New York, NY. Harcourt Brace Jovanovich.

[9] Dickens, C. (2008). Little Dorrit. Retrieved from http://www.gutenberg.org/files/963/963-h/963-h.htm.

[10] Adrian, A. (1952). Dickens on American Slavery. *Publications of the Modern Language Association.* Vol. 67, No. 4, pp. 315-329.

[11] Lacey, R. (2006). Great Tales from English History. New York, New York. Little, Brown & Company.

[12] Bailey, J. (1913). Dr. Johnson and His Circle. Retrieved from http://www.gutenberg.org/ cache/epub/24066/pg24066.html April 2012.

[13] Gaskell, E. (2008). Curious If True. Retrieved from http://www.gutenberg.org/files/ 24879/24879-h/24879-h.htm. July 2012.

[14] Lowe, C. (2007). The Everything Health Guide to OCD. Avon, MA. Adams Media.

[15] Boswell, J. (1952). The Life of Samuel Johnson LL.D. Chicago, IL. The University of Chicago.

[16] Carlyle, T. (1966). On Heroes, Hero-Worship, and the Heroic in History. Lincoln, Nebraska. University of Nebraska Press.

[17] Peacock, T. (2007). Gryll Grange. Retrieved from http://www.gutenberg.org/files/21514/21514-h/21514-h.htm.

[18] Butler, S. (2004). The Fair Haven. Retrieved from http://www.gutenberg.org/ dirs/etext04/fhvn10h.htm. Aug. 1, 2012.

[19] Hardy, T. (n.d.). Far From the Madding Crowd. Garden City, New York. Nelson Doubleday, Inc.

[20] Eyrecrow.com. (n.d.). A Scene at the Mitre: Dr Johnson, Boswell, Goldsmith (1857). Retrieved from http://eyrecrowe.com/pictures/1850s/a-scene-at-the-mitre/. March 2012.

[21] Piozzi, H. (2007). Anecdotes of the Late Samuel Johnson, LL.D. Retrieved from http://www.gutenberg.org/files/2423/2423-h/2423-h.htm March 2012.

[22] Gasson, A (2012). Wilkie Collins Information Pages: Little Novels. Retieved from http://www.wilkie-collins.info/index.htm.

[23] Collins, W. (2004). Mr. Lismore and the Widow. Retrieved from http://www.gutenberg.org /cache/epub/6039/pg6039.html. August 8, 2012.

[24] Eliot, G. (2009). The Essays of George Eliot. Retrieved from http://www.gutenberg.org /files/28289/28289-h/28289-h.htm. May 2012.

[25] Gissing, G. (2003). The Nether World. Retrieved from http://www.gutenberg.org /files/4301/4301-h/4301-h.htm. August 9, 2012.

[26] Lorraine, E. (1996). Attributions of Authorship in the Gentleman's Magazine, 1731-1868. Retrieved from http://etext.virginia.edu/bsuva/gm/gm-intro.html August 9, 2012.

[27] Hart, E. (1967). Portrait of a Grub, Samuel Boyse. *Studies in English Literature, 1500-1900.* Vol. 7, No. 3, pp. 415-425.

[28] Gissing, G. (2008). New Grub Street. Retrieved from http://www.gutenberg.org/files/1709/1709-h/1709-h.htm. August 10, 2012.

[29] Gissing, G. (2005). The Private Papers of Henry Ryecroft. Retrieved from http://www.gutenberg.org/files/1463/1463-h/1463-h.htm. August 9, 2012.

Chapter 8

[1] Bailey, J. (1913). Dr. Johnson and His Circle. Retrieved from http://www.gutenberg.org/ cache/epub/24066/pg24066.html April 2012.

[2] Bronson, B. (1952). Samuel Johnson: Rasselas, Poems and Selected Prose. New York, New York. Holt, Rinehart and Winston, Inc.

[3] Alkon, P. (1966). Robert South, William Low, and Samuel Johnson. *Studies in English Literature, 1500-1900.* Vol. 6, No. 3, pp. 499-528.

[4] O'Flaherty, P. (1967). Johnson as Satirist: A New Look at the Vanity of Human Wishes. *Journal of English Literary History.* Vol. 34, No. 1, pp. 78-91.

[5] Whelan, R. (2010). The poetry anthology: The Augustan poets. West Long Branch, NJ. Kultur.

[6] Goldstein, L. (1977). Ruins and Empire: The Evolution of a Theme in Augustan and Romantic Literature. Pittsburgh, PA. University of Pittsburgh Press.

[7] Miles, D., Pooley, R., Greenlaw, E. (1935). Literature and Life: Volume 4, English Literature. Chicago IL. Scott, Foresman and Company.

[8] Anderson, H., Daghlian, P., Ehrenpreis, I. (1966). The Familiar Letter in the Eighteenth Century. Lawrence, Kansas. The University Press of Kansas.

[9] Bate, W. (1975). Samuel Johnson. New York, NY. Harcourt Brace Jovanovich.

www.ingramcontent.com/pod-product-compliance
Lightning Source LLC
LaVergne TN
LVHW051729080426
835511LV00018B/2958